CLAY ALLISON

CLAY ALLISON
Facsimile of the Original 1956 Edition

by
F. Stanley

New Foreword
by
Marc Simmons

SANTA FE

New Material © 2008 by Sunstone Press. All Rights Reserved.

No part of this book may be reproduced in any form or by any electronic or mechanical means including information storage and retrieval systems without permission in writing from the publisher, except by a reviewer who may quote brief passages in a review.

Sunstone books may be purchased for educational, business, or sales promotional use. For information please write:
Special Markets Department, Sunstone Press,
P.O. Box 2321, Santa Fe, New Mexico 87504-2321.

Library of Congress Cataloging-in-Publication Data

Stanley, F. (Francis), 1908-
  Clay Allison / new foreword by Marc Simmons ; by F. Stanley.
    p. cm. -- (Southwest heritage series)
  Originally published: Denver : World Press, 1956.
  "Facsimile of the original 1956 edition."
  Includes bibliographical references and index.
  ISBN 978-0-86534-685-7 (softcover : alk. paper)
  1. Allison, Clay, 1840 or 41-1887. 2. Outlaws--West (U.S.)--Biography. 3. Frontier and pioneer life--West (U.S.) 4. West (U.S.)--Biography. I. Title.
  F594.A46S73 2009
  978'.02092--dc22
  [B]
                                         2008022957

WWW.SUNSTONEPRESS.COM
SUNSTONE PRESS / POST OFFICE BOX 2321 / SANTA FE, NM 87504-2321 /USA
(505) 988-4418 / ORDERS ONLY (800) 243-5644 / FAX (505) 988-1025

The Southwest Heritage Series is dedicated to Jody Ellis and Marcia Muth Miller, the founders of Sunstone Press, whose original purpose and vision continues to inspire and motivate our publications.

CONTENTS

THE SOUTHWEST HERITAGE SERIES / I

FOREWORD TO THIS EDITION / II
The Controversial F. Stanley
by
Marc Simmons

A MAN'S REACH / III
from
The F. Stanley Story
by
Mary Jo Walker

TRIBUTE TO F. STANLEY / IV
by
Jack D. Rittenhouse

CLAY ALLISON'S CIMARRON / V
by
Norman Cleaveland

FACSIMILE OF THE ORIGINAL 1956 EDITION / VI

I

THE SOUTHWEST HERITAGE SERIES

The history of the United States is written in hundreds of regional histories and literary works. Those letters, essays, memoirs, biographies and even collections of fiction are often first-hand accounts by people who wanted to memorialize an event, a person or simply record for posterity the concerns and issues of the times. Many of these accounts have been lost, destroyed or overlooked. Some are in private or public collections but deemed to be in too fragile condition to permit handling by contemporary readers and researchers.

However, now with the application of twenty-first century technology, nineteenth and twentieth century material can be reprinted and made accessible to the general public. These early writings are the DNA of our history and culture and are essential to understanding the present in terms of the past.

The Southwest Heritage Series is a form of literary preservation. Heritage by definition implies legacy and these early works are our legacy from those who have gone before us. To properly present and preserve that legacy, no changes in style or contents have been made. The material reprinted stands on its own as it first appeared. The point of view is that of the author and the era in which he or she lived. We would not expect photographs of people from the past to be re-imaged with modern clothes, hair styles and backgrounds. We should not, therefore, expect their ideas and personal philosophies to reflect our modern concepts.

Remember, reading their words and sharing their thoughts is a passport back into understanding how the past was shaped and how it influenced today's world.

Our hope is that new access to these older books will provide readers with a challenging and exciting experience.

II

FOREWORD TO THIS EDITION

The Controversial F. Stanley
by
Marc Simmons

As a professional historian, I've often been asked my opinion of the author who wrote under the pen name, F. Stanley. According to his 1996 obituary, he published 190 books and booklets on New Mexico history, quite a record by any standard. The problem is, F. Stanley has been almost universally condemned for the innumerable flaws that litter his writings. However, behind the man and the work lurks a curious story.

He was born Louis Crocchiola in New York's Greenwich Village on October 31, 1908 to Italian immigrant parents. After receiving a Bachelor's degree in English at Catholic University in Washington, DC, Louis entered the priesthood in 1938. On that occasion, as was allowed, he formally added the new names Stanley and Francis to his birth name, Louis Crocchiola. Thereafter, he was called simply Father Stanley.

Shortly after his ordination, the young priest was diagnosed with the beginnings of tuberculosis. Following medical advice of the day, the Church sent Father Stanley to Hereford, Texas in the Panhandle, hoping the arid climate might cure him. It did! Something else occurred at the same time. Father Stanley fell under the spell of the Southwest, leading him to become one of the most prolific historical writers of his day.

In 1940 he applied for pastoral work in New Mexico, since he was fluent in Spanish and thought he could be most useful there. The Archbishop of Santa Fe accepted him, assigning Father Stanley first to the Guadalupe church in Taos and then to the San Miguel church at Socorro.

During the 1940s, he served six or so different parishes in northern or eastern New Mexico, thereby becoming familiar with rural and small town life. It was while stationed at Taos, though, that Father Stanley caught the writing bug through mingling with local authors. But later as he was transferred by the Archbishop from one parish to another, he would begin looking into the history of his temporary residence and compiling a file of notes.

His first book, *Raton Chronicle*, appeared in 1948. Then in rapid succession F. Stanley published full-length histories on Cimarron, Socorro, Las Vegas, and the Maxwell land grant. Soon to his line of books, F. Stanley added an on-going series dedicated to a single small town or fort that other writers had ignored. These little booklets remain easily recognizable with their canary yellow covers and crimson red lettering, plus the New Mexico state emblem, the Zia sun symbol. Eventually, these small works alone numbered 123 titles.

One of the earliest treatments of the historic and controversial Maxwell Land Grant was published by F. Stanley in 1952, titled *The Grant That Maxwell Bought*. Although other books on the subject have appeared since, serious readers still need to go back and examine what Father Stanley had to say. Otherwise, small nuggets buried in his pages, and nowhere else, may be missed.

Remarkably, F. Stanley personally financed all of his publications, often going deeply into debt. The several printers he used were generally tolerant of the delay in paying his bills.

Even more stressful for Father Stanley was the harsh criticism his writings received from historians and book reviewers. They unmercifully picked apart his unedited and untidy prose, pointed out frequent mistakes, and condemned the neglect of standards in the composition or format of his books.

For one example, a serious slip occurred in the naming of F. Stanley's longest work, a history of the New Mexico state capital in three volumes, titled *Ciudad Santa Fe*. Under the old Spanish system, Santa Fe in reality never achieved the rank of a *ciudad* (chartered city), but retained the status of a town (*villa*). The author had missed that pivotal fact and thus launched his three volume set with a conspicuous error on the covers.

In 1985 Mary Jo Walker, a librarian at Eastern New Mexico University, Portales, published a sympathetic biography, *The F. Stanley Story*. The book contains quotes from interviews given by Father Stanley in which he defends himself and his methods.

His main plea was: "Pardon the mistakes, but say a kind word for my effort." Painfully aware of his failings, he claimed that his intent was merely to assemble fugitive information from obscure courthouse records, old newspaper files, and archives so that others more able could pick up the thread where he left off and carry on.

After publication of Walker's biography, some historians, myself included, began to look more charitably toward Father Stanley Crocchiola. The fact is, despite his deficiencies, he managed to make in his own quirky way a not insignificant contribution to our regional history.

Today, F. Stanley books and booklets are worth collecting. I'm always happy when I can add another one of his to my personal library. I just wish he was still around so that I could tell him that.

Sunstone Press in choosing to include F. Stanley books in its honored Southwest Heritage Series is wisely making this book available again to the reading public.

III

A MAN'S REACH
"Take him for what he is worth"
from
The F. Stanley Story
by
Mary Jo Walker

It is difficult to say to what extent negative criticism and neglect may have personally affected Father Stanley. Some of his works in the 1970s showed considerable care in preparation, but no more so than his major efforts in earlier decades. He knew his own limitations as well as any of his critics did, but he believed quite sincerely that the flaws in his work were largely literary in nature and therefore of little overall significance; or alternatively that they represented realities over which he had little control, such as his limited time or the cost of typesetting footnotes. His first reactions may be surmised from comments in the foreword to *Dave Rudabaugh*.

> *I used to apologize for my mistakes. Come to think of it, why should I? I tried; that's more than my critics did. I investigated to the best of my ability, often going sleepless and hungry in order to attain the facts. No patron has come along the way. I had to rough it alone.... The book may not be literary, but it is factual. In the long run, truth survives.*

Two years later, in *The Duke City*, he confessed from a somewhat different perspective:

> *I am grateful for all criticism—constructive or otherwise.*

And in *Satanta and the Kiowas*, 1968, he pled:

> *Let my mistakes be my Calvary, and let my readers be my confessors from whom we hope to obtain pardon and forgiveness.*

Simply and with a kind of humble determination, he persevered for many years, his principal resources being his formidable drive and his eagerness to help preserve the history of the region he loved so well. No doubt he attempted too much; probably, as with so many of us, his reach exceeded his grasp. His hope, which he stated over and over again, was that his books would provide guidance for others and "prove a...contribution to Western Americana." That purpose and his dedication to it do not serve to be lightly dismissed.

Taken as a whole, with all its human flaws, F. Stanley's work stands as a unique contribution, as much a part of the written record "as Coronado's visit." Even Ramon Adams acknowledged that "he deserves a full measure of credit for supplying hitherto unpublished information," for putting something into print about obscure places and people, for adding to the body of recorded knowledge about the Southwest. Whatever the final evaluation may be, however, it is certain that F. Stanley has earned a place in southwestern history in his own right.

F. Stanley

IV

TRIBUTE TO F. STANLEY
by
Jack D. Rittenhouse
from
The F. Stanley Story
by
Mary Jo Walker
Albuquerque, New Mexico / March, 1984

Some historians write because they hope their writing will bring them money or promotion or tenure. Some write to espouse a cause. A few write because they must, because it is the only way they can quench an inner thirst or scratch an itch of curiosity. The last class is the happiest, and F. Stanley is in this group.

The term historian has many shadings. Among academic people, a historian is a certified scholar whose commission of rank is a degree of Doctor of Philosophy in history, and whose income results from full-time teaching or writing history. Some of these go on to glory and excellence in their work; some gain renown as researchers or as teachers, become a historian's historian, but find writing a difficult task. Many bank their inner fire when they don their doctoral robes and are content to plod along as routine teachers, living as comfortably as a toad in a puddle of buttermilk, looking upon their diploma as a union card.

The grass roots historian is another type, curious about people and places around them. Their writings are their only certification. Some become antiquarians, with a dilettante interest in ancient things and more curious about precision in minutiae than in the social significance of their subject. The term antiquarian has a different meaning among historians than among bookmen.

Still another type of historian is the buff, an individual who is an enthusiast or devotee of a specific subject. When it comes to sheer bulk of knowledge about a subject, or even to accuracy on a point of information, I have seen many buffs who outclassed Ph.D's. I personally know only three individuals who have their own microfilm readers at home, and all three are buffs. They travel great distances to look at a gravestone or a courthouse record, which is not to say that professional historians and grassroots historians also do not do this, of course.

We owe much to the grassroots historian and the buff. They are the prospectors who discover new lodes. They are curious about people and places and customs, combining the interests of the folklorist and the historian, and if they are good at what they do, they find their work accepted and even honored.

F. Stanley is one whose curiosity and inner fire has drawn him to the study of people and places and events that had gone unnoticed until he saw them. He advanced knowledge in many directions, lit many candles to dispel darkness.

His works are only beginnings, and he knows this. In a sense, history writes itself merely by occurring, and thus there is the axiom that history is not written but rewritten. Another New Mexico local historian, Fray Angélico Chávez, once spoke to El Corral de Santa Fe Westerners and said that history is not a static, pure thing that can be discovered once, written down, and preserved intact forever. Instead, he said, history is a living, growing body that must be nurtured...and which occasionally requires surgery.

F. Stanley has wandered across the Southwest like a Johnny Appleseed of history, planting seedlings in the form of booklets and leaving their later nurturing to others. Later historians will convert these seedlings into trees, by pruning, fertilizing and grafting. The work will require more research, more verification, correction and amplification. But F. Stanley planted the first seed.

The historian who uses only *one* source for his work is a fool, but the historian who refuses to review any source is an idiot. Any source may have errors caused by lack of information, or poor proofreading, or hasty writing. But some questionable bit of old-timer's lore may raise the possibility of truth; it is then up to the later historian to prove or disprove the fact. Once, when I was gathering information about the New Mexico ghost town of Cabezón, I read an old-timer's memoir that mentioned a stage line running through the town. Nowhere else did I find any mention of this, and I sought to verify the story. A usually reliable professional historian scoffed at the notion that the town had ever been on a commercial stage line. Then a museum curator found a printed timetable of the Star Stage Line, listing the route and showing Cabezón as a stop. Although many dissertations do not list F. Stanley works as sources, the padre's booklets have nonetheless been studied for similar possible clues. Given the time and resources, F. Stanley himself would have gone farther; he leaves that to others.

His severest critics often have been people who never wrote a recognized book, or whose books themselves are not without the flaws of typesetters and human errors, or whose dyspeptic nature made them discard a sculpture because of a chip.

The body of work produced by F. Stanley will become part of the vast lore about the Southwest. It will remain as long as libraries stand and will be consulted and used by generations as part of the grassroots literature. Future writers will correct its errors, just as their mistakes will be corrected by still later scholars. But someone had to start it, and F. Stanley was the man.

V

CLAY ALLISON'S CIMARRON
by
Norman Cleaveland
from
New Mexico Magazine
March/April 1974

For one whose name would make Western history, Robert Andrew "Clay" Allison began life inauspiciously.

Allison was born on a Tennessee farm in 1840. He served as a Confederate artilleryman for three months, then was discharged for a mental condition caused, his papers say, by a blow to the skull received years before. What's more, a crippled foot caused him to limp. Despite these deficiencies, he was allowed to enlist again in September 1862. War's end found him in a Union prison camp.

Clay joined the ranks of restless adventurers heading west. He first saw New Mexico while driving cattle up the storied Loving-Goodnight Trail as a wrangler for the renowned Texas cattlemen after which it was named. After trail-bossing a herd for other employers, he used his payment of 300 cattle to buy a ranch north of Cimarron in 1870.

Clay's reputation as a gunfighter dates from January 1874, when he outdrew a trouble-making desperado, Chunk Colbert, over a dining table at the Clifton House near Raton.

Herewith is an account of Allison's exploits during the ensuing Colfax County War.

Clay Allison earned his greatest fame as a corpse-maker in Cimarron, then the county seat of Colfax County in northeastern New Mexico. In the 1870s, Allison became a legend in his own time.

Legends about Clay emanated both from devoted friends and implacable enemies. They were gradually embellished by narrators of those tall tales that were a major source of frontier entertainment. It's only natural that Clay's true character remains shrouded in the mists of controversy.

One thing seems certain: a historical judgment of Allison based on the true character of his most powerful foes makes him a hero in New Mexico.

My grandfather, William Raymond Morley, was an executive of the Maxwell Land Grant and Railway Company, with headquarters in Cimarron. For a time, Clay considered Morley to be an enemy because:

- Morley had marched with General Sherman of the Union Army of the Tennessee, while Allison had ridden with General Nathan Bedford Forrest of the Confederate Army of the Tennessee.
- The Maxwell Land Grant was illegal and unjust. Though its owners put it at almost two million acres, there were legal arguments that it was only about 97,000 acres. The Maxwell company sought to collect rents from ranchers and miners whom it considered squatters.
- The Maxwell company and local officials were manipulated by the Santa Fe Ring, a clique that had dominated New Mexico's political and economic life from about 1868.

The life expectancy of enemies of either Allison or the Ring was short. When Morley was on the hate lists of both, it is little short of a miracle that he survived.

A common foe—the Ring—eventually caused Allison to forgive Morley's Civil War role and become an ally ... which almost certainly prolonged Morley's life.

Grandfather Morley, born in Massachusetts in 1846, had been orphaned early and raised by an uncle in Iowa. After the Civil War, he studied two years at Iowa State University, then went to work as a civil engineer on westward-expanding railroads. In 1871, he joined the Maxwell company, the next year becoming its executive vice president.

In 1872, Morley persuaded Frank Springer, a brilliant classmate, to come to New Mexico. Springer was a lawyer. Morley needed legal talent to cope with the complexities of managing the Maxwell company, with its British and Dutch fiscal entanglements. In time, Morley also needed Springer's expertise to cope with the abundance of legal talent in the Santa Fe Ring.

The next year, Morley married and brought to Cimarron 21-year-old Ada McPherson, his golden-haired childhood sweetheart. As a fringe benefit of his job, they occupied part of a luxurious 40-room adobe mansion built by Lucien Bonaparte Maxwell, former owner of the grant. My grandmother Ada, an accomplished pianist, played for many a Cimarron social event.

Allison's admirers maintain he never killed anyone who didn't need killing. It should be emphasized that Clay was primarily a rancher, a particularly competent one. He was just as competent with six-shooter and bowie knife. This competence he was willing to demonstrate even when justice for himself was not involved.

As rancher George Coe put it, "When Allison butted in, business started to pick up." (Coe was to become a figure in the Lincoln County War that boosted the young Billy the Kid to fame.) The late Southwestern literateur J. Frank Dobie described Clay as "Don Quixote of the Six-Shooter." Perhaps "Ombudsman With a Six-Shooter" would be even more appropriate.

In his ably researched *The Gunfighters*, Dale T. Schoenberger concludes that Allison "suffered from manic-depressive psychosis." Many another crusader—John Brown, Johnny Appleseed, Billy Mitchell—has been called mad.

Addiction to liquor increased Clay's mental instability. When in his cups, he would bring Cimarron business to a full stop, all doors locked, all streets deserted. Drunk or sober, though, he commanded respect.

While not a regular churchgoer, Clay himself had much respect for religion. And, drunk or sober, he was inclined to the robust singing of hymns. There's an apparently valid story that, summoning a reluctant clergyman, he interrupted roistering one Christmas Eve in a Cimarron saloon with a demand for a full church service. With Clay's six-shooter much in evidence, all present reverently took part.

Next to liquor, dancing was Allison's favorite hobby. He was addicted to the fandango, a lively Spanish dance. His presence enlivened many a Cimarron social gathering.

With women present, Clay's manners accorded with the best tradition of Southern gallantry. This appeal was augmented by a lithe six-foot-two figure, wavy brown hair, handsome features and striking blue eyes that were ever so slightly cocked. A sparkling sense of humor added to his popularity among the women ... all of them, that is, except mothers of marriageable daughters.

Among the latter was Scotland-born Mrs. Robina Crawford Bishop, yesterday's "hostess with the mostest" along the Santa Fe Trail. When her family emigrated to Wisconsin, she married Bishop, who worked his way west in railroad construction. Meantime, she bore "the three prettiest girls on the frontier," in the opinion of future Territorial Governor Miguel A. Otero.

The vivacious but diminutive Mrs. Bishop tried to teach the lanky Clay the Highland fling—which in itself must have been an eyeful—but Clay's eyes were on her second daughter Josephine.

Clay was not what Mrs. Bishop had in mind for a son-in-law. When Clay came a-courtin' Josephine one evening, Mrs. Bishop took up a broom and chased him out of the house.

Clay feigned great indignation. Common decency, he proclaimed far and wide, demanded that nothing less imposing than a shotgun should have been used to get rid of a man of his reputation ... particularly when the aggressor was a woman and not quite five feet tall.

At his ranch some 10 miles north of Cimarron, Clay saw to it that at least one cowhand could play the fiddle. At his ranch house and around campfires, there often would be dancing. If his wearied hands proved reluctant, Clay would dance solo.

Dancing stopped abruptly when injustice demanded attention. In Clay's eyes, as well as those of many others, injustice was becoming rampant in Colfax County. Blamed were both the Maxwell company and the Santa Fe Ring.

The Ring's key figure was Stephen B. (Smooth Steve) Elkins, who in 1873 became New Mexico's territorial delegate to Congress. Close to Elkins was Thomas B. Catron, the U.S. attorney. Both Elkins and Catron were lawyers from Missouri.

Elkins proved to be one of the most accomplished politicians in Washington, eventually becoming a secretary of war and a senator from West Virginia. Elkins teamed with one of the nation's most potent lobbyists, Collins P. Huntington of the Southern Pacific Railroad. Huntington sought a monopoly in New Mexico to match the railroad's in California. Samuel B. Axtell, who was appointed New Mexico's governor in 1875, had come from California, where he served Huntington well. Thus, the Ring was firmly entrenched in Washington as well as in Santa Fe.

The Ring's political control extended from successive territorial governors down to town constables. *Pistoleros* were handy when bought officials and corrupted courts needed support.

A neat arrangement of New Mexico's courts simplified matters for the Ring. Justices of the State Supreme Court also served as judges of the district courts. They handled appeals against their own decisions. Thus, one Joseph G. Palen not only sat as chief justice but also was district judge for the Colfax area.

The Ring's judges adopted a common means of harassing uncooperative persons living some distance from the seat of a court. This was to have a summons served on such a person for some frivolous reason. Upon the accused's appearance, the judge repeatedly would delay a hearing. This caused much expense and inconvenience.

Among Colfax County ranchers so inconvenienced were George Coe—whom you've already met—and several Coe relatives. The Coes had settled in the Sugarite Valley, some 50 miles northeast of Cimarron. They were charged with trespassing by a cattleman who had leased the Sugarite from the Maxwell company.

After their hearing before Judge Palen in Cimarron had been postponed one week for a third time, Allison "butted in," to use George Coe's term. Clay let it be known that the situation was "graveling" him. This was a clear indication, again to cite Coe, that business was about to pick up.

Allison told the plaintiff to move on, the farther the better. Then Clay called on Judge Palen with word that he was now acting as the Coes' special attorney. He "urged" that there be no further delays to a hearing.

Allison made no apology for neglecting to remove his six-shooter before entering Palen's chambers. An indignant Palen said he had a good notice to charge Clay with contempt of court. For whatever reason, he didn't.

At a hearing next day, the plaintiff failed to appear. The charges against the Coes were dismissed.

Such a bold challenge to legal authority added many hardy ranchers to Clay's devoted backers. With such support, he became an ever sharper thorn to the Santa Fe Ring.

Morley clearly comprehended the Ring's land policy: "... to divide the people by getting some to lease all the ranges at a nominal price and try to drive others off by ... [getting] up a feud ..." As for his own policy toward "squatters," he was "claiming that they [the Maxwell company] are entitled to rent but making no fuss about it on account of the question of unsettled title."

From Morley's arrival in Cimarron, he had operated a weekly paper for the Maxwell company. In late 1874, he and Frank Springer bought what became the Cimarron *News and Press* and hired one Will Dawson as an editor-printer. "It promises to be disconnected with the [Maxwell] corporation and independent in politics," they pledged. Within 14 months the *News and Press* could boast a circulation "second to none in the Territory," largely because it was one of the few papers not dominated by the Santa Fe Ring.

In June 1875, Francisco (Pancho) Griego, a deputy sheriff and foreman of the Colfax County grand jury, was dealing monte, a gambling card game, at his usual stand in the St. James Hotel's saloon. Three soldiers from Fort Union, some 50 miles south, were on hand. Griego got into a row with them. They ran from the saloon. Griego shot at all three, killing two and wounding one. It turned out that all three soldiers had been unarmed.

Reported the *News and Press*:

... the military now assert that he [Griego] has killed two or three soldiers before in gambling rows. He is well known throughout the county, and it seems hardly probable but that sooner or later he will be ... tried before a legal tribunal for his part in the bloody affair.

All this probably lost Griego his job as deputy sheriff and grand jury foreman, but Pancho retained sufficient political influence in Santa Fe to obtain an amnesty. Of equal importance to the Ring probably was Griego's reputation as a pistolero, one perhaps surpassed only by Clay Allison's in Colfax County.

That same spring of 1875, Mrs. Morley's mother, Mary Tibbles McPherson, came from Iowa to visit the family and see for the first time the Morley's daughter Agnes, born the year before.

Mrs. McPherson's late attorney-husband Marcus had been an Iowa politico who crusaded for women's property rights. A brother Thomas was a Methodist minister and Nebraska editor; he and his wife Bright Eyes, daughter of a Ponca chief, crusaded for Indian rights. With such a background, it was instinctive for Mrs. McPherson to react to the skullduggery seen all about her in New Mexico ... and to do some crusading herself.

Mrs. McPherson wrote a scathing letter to Washington, probably either to the secretary of the interior or to the attorney general. She dropped it into an uncovered wooden receiving box at the post office.

Daughter Ada learned of this. She felt the Morleys were having troubles enough without her mother's getting into the act. In full view of Mrs. Bishop and others, she retrieved the letter from the box. (One of Mrs. Bishop's daughters had married John McCullough, who was the Cimarron postmaster. Mrs. Bishop helped her son-in-law.)

The story of the letter's retrieval quickly made the Cimarron rounds. Two Santa Fe Ring henchmen, Dr. R. H. Longwill, the probate judge, and Melvin W. Mills, a member of the Territorial Legislature, heard it. Postmaster McCullough had no recourse but to report the incident. This brought U.S. Attorney Catron into the matter. The Ring was alert for any chance to strike at the increasingly antagonistic Morley.

In July 1875, Ada made a buckboard round trip of some 300 miles to Santa Fe with plaintiff McCullough and witness Mrs. Bishop. She was indicted by a federal grand jury for robbing the mails. Later, a warrant was issued for her arrest.

Though Clay Allison still considered Morley an enemy, he found it intolerable that a woman, even a Yankee woman, be prosecuted—persecuted, that is—to harass her husband. Clay again butted in. He issued an edict, probably in a crowded Cimarron saloon, that "if Mrs. Morley is ever brought to trial, not a man will leave the courtroom alive."

The arrest warrant was never served.

Therein lies another story. Both of the Morleys actually seemed eager to have a trial proceed. In fact, grandfather eventually wrote U.S. Attorney General Alphonso Taft (whose son would become President) to that effect. But Catron was having second thoughts. It is presumed he feared the letter's becoming part of the public record. It would have provided much unwelcome evidence against the Santa Fe Ring.

Living in Cimarron was the Rev. T. J. Tolby, a Methodist circuit rider. Tolby was crusading to have the bulk of the Maxwell Land Grant bought by the U.S. government and turned over to the Utes and Apaches, as Kit Carson had advocated earlier. Tolby also shared the mounting indignation over the Santa Fe Ring. And he was publicly appalled by the amnesty granted Griego.

Both Mrs. Morley and her mother, devout Methodists, admired Tolby. Morley himself, while not a Methodist, cooperated with Tolby in *News and Press* attacks on the Ring. What's more, they were jointly credited, perhaps erroneously, with writing a series of letters to the New York *Sun* about conditions in New Mexico. Publication of these displeased Elkins, Catron and other Ring members.

In September 1875, Tolby was met on a Cimarron street by Chief Justice Palen. In the presence of bystanders, Palen denounced the minister for remarks he had made about his court. Tolby defiantly replied, Springer was to depose later, that he would "write up the judge so that 200,000 readers should see the record."

On September 14, Tolby conducted services at Elizabethtown, some 35 miles west. Two days later, his body was found, a bullet in the back, in Cimarron Canyon. There was no evidence of robbery.

This caused an uproar in Colfax County, including the Allison contingent. Clay's respect for religion extended to its clerics, especially to the crusading Tolby.

Clay limited his initial concern to Tolby's widow and two small daughters. He promptly raised enough money to send them back to Indiana. Clay was an ingenious fund-raiser for causes he considered worthy, as was soon to become evident.

The duly-constituted authorities seemed reluctant to question even the most obvious aspects. For instance, Pancho Griego's nephew Cruz Vega had been in the vicinity of the murder site during a one-day stint as a substitute mail carrier. Fresh in the minds of Tolby's friends was Griego's own immunity to the law. Had his nephew also acquired a license to kill?

And certainly the threats of New Mexico's chief justice supported a grave suspicion that the Santa Fe Ring was involved.

Allison's patience became exhausted after six full weeks of inaction. He butted in, leading a mob that not only questioned Vega, who implicated one Manuel Cardenas, but finally lynched him.

At Vega's funeral, Griego publicly vowed to kill Allison on sight. News of Pancho's challenge brought Clay on a brisk trot from his ranch. He knew he would find Griego at the St. James saloon. Of many versions as to what ensued, the late Fred Lambert, son of the hotel's French-born proprietor Henri, told me his father had witnessed the following:

Arriving after dark, Clay met Griego at the door and said, "I understand you're looking for me."

"Yes," replied Griego.

"What do you want?"

"I want to kill you."

"Let's have a drink first."

Griego agreed. They did so. Glasses replaced on the bar, both went for their guns. Allison's first shot hit Griego in the forehead. As Griego fell, Clay put two more bullets into him. Then he shot out the barroom lights.

The Colfax County War was on!

Griego's body was not removed until morning. Allison came in for some criticism because Griego's horse remained saddled and tied to the hitching rack all night—not good enough for a cowboy and particularly not worthy of a former cavalryman.

On the other hand, ex-Confederate Allison had unwittingly

avenged the murders of several federal troopers. This probably earned him much respect at Fort Union.

Cardenas, the man fingered by Vega, told a justice of the peace in Elizabethtown that Vega had killed Tolby. Cardenas did add that Longwill and Mills had offered him $500 to do the job.

When word of this reached Cimarron, Longwill took off for Fort Union with Allison in hot pursuit. Longwill got there just in time. He came under military protection at the dictates of the Ring's Governor Axtell. Later, he went on to Santa Fe and out of the scene.

Mills, arriving at Cimarron by stage from a business trip to Colorado, faced a lynch mob, but cooler heads prevailed. A detachment ordered from Fort Union by the governor took Mills into custody.

At a justice of the peace trial in mid-November 1875, Mills was dismissed for lack of evidence, while Cardenas was found guilty as an accessory. Led back to jail, Cardenas was killed by a shot in the night. His assassin was never identified.

In a desperate effort to restore its control in Colfax County, the Ring now, in January 1876, had a submissive Territorial Legislature attach Colfax to Taos County for judicial purposes. The Tolby investigation would be further stymied. The aroused Colfax citizenry would be bypassed for jury duty. As Morley later put it, the Ring was taking this means "to punish Colfax County for presuming to interfere in such matters."

The Ring's leadership was determined to indict Clay Allison and destroy his leadership of the Colfax County cattlemen and townspeople. This was a Ring retaliation for the killing of Vega, Griego and Cardenas and the effort to involve Longwill and Mills in the Tolby murder.

With the outbreak of the Colfax County War, the Maxwell company's affairs became so involved that Morley and Springer sought to cut their workload by turning over editorial duties entirely to Dawson. Dawson, apparently unable to resist the Ring's blandishments, promptly reversed *News and Press* policy. Becoming ever bolder, Dawson referred unkindly to Clay Allison.

On January 19, 1876, Clay and some of his cohorts registered their displeasure by blowing up the weekly's press (black gunpowder being readily at hand) and throwing its remnants into the close-by Cimarron River.

In his cups, Clay then picked up an armful of a partially printed edition and made the rounds of Cimarron selling the issues as "the Clay Allison Extra." He charged whatever he thought a customer could afford. None dared haggle or refuse to buy. Bishop was one of many indignant citizens who paid $1.

Morley had long maintained a reliable early-warning service of Clay's rampages. He was not to be found that night.

Next morning, Clay met grandmother standing at the scene of destruction. She raked him over the coals, for the loss of the press was a financial blow.

For once set back on his heels, Clay apologized profusely and handed Ada Morley a roll of greenbacks (variously reported from $200 to $600), probably proceeds from sale of "the Clay Allison Extra." "I don't fight women," he said abashedly. "Go buy yourself another press."

(Actually, the Morleys took parts from an older press in the shop and cannibalized some from the smashed press to get back into publication promptly.)

Of even more significance in the Clay-Ada confrontation, Allison assured Mrs. Morley that henceforth the Morleys would receive his wholehearted support. This was a major shift in the Colfax County power structure.

As for editor Dawson, he speedily disappeared from the scene.

Morley family financial woes that grandmother had professed to Clay were real indeed. Maxwell had sold the grant for $750,000. British and Dutch stockholders put up $5 million to take it over. Ring policies were milking the investment. Catron was on the verge of acquiring the grant for $20,000 in delinquent taxes. Only a last-minute effort by grandfather, including a personal payment of some $1,500, had saved the grant for the stockholders and from Catron and the Ring.

In February 1876, Springer, at the request of Morley and other prominent Cimarron citizens, went to Santa Fe to ask Governor Axtell to annul—as he legally could—the court site bill. Axtell was "very bitter in his allusions to the people of Colfax county," Springer deposed later, "and especially in his allusions to one R. C. [Clay] Allison, whom he denounced as a murderer ... and declared he was going to have him indicted and punished and compel him to leave the country."

Returning to Cimarron, the group drafted a formal invitation to the governor to come there to discuss the courts and other troublesome matters. Signers included Allison. In a subsequent affidavit, Springer explained he had prevailed on Clay to sign because this would guarantee the governor the utmost courtesy and hospitality, "since Allison was a stickler about such things."

About mid-March, word was received that the governor would indeed visit Cimarron. He wanted to be met only by a small "welcoming committee" that specifically included Morley, Springer and Allison.

At the same time, Ben Stevens of Albuquerque was sent to Cimarron to act as district attorney of Colfax County. Stevens would have at his orders a cavalry troop to be sent from Fort Union, under Captain Francis Moore, as the governor's escort.

Stevens received a secret "Dear Ben" letter from Axtell: "... Have your men placed to arrest him [Allison] and to kill all the men who resist you or stand with those who do resist you [Morley and Springer].... do not hesitate at extreme measures...."

While Stevens owed his job to the Santa Fe Ring, assassination was too much. Stevens was on cordial terms with Morley. Thus Morley "became aware" of Axtell's letter, as he said later in an affidavit. He promptly warned Springer and Allison.

The governor was not on the designated stage. There was no one in Cimarron for the cavalry troop to escort nor was there anyone readily at hand to arrest or shoot.

It is highly probable that Captain Moore also "became aware" of the governor's instructions. He merely went through the gestures of compliance. The troop rode out to Allison's ranch. Moore's offer to escort Allison back to Cimarron apparently was readily accepted. After a couple of hours in Moore's Cimarron headquarters, Allison returned to his ranch—not having been disarmed, much less arrested. As between a corrupt politician and a first-class fighting ex-cavalryman, there can be little doubt where the captain's sympathies lay.

Henry L. Waldo, an Elkins-Catron law partner also from Missouri, became chief justice when Palen died in December. Shortly,

Waldo called a grand jury into being in Taos.

In a charge to it, Waldo said: "Since the beginning of the year 1875, at least 16 or 18 men have come to their deaths in brawls or by assassination, to say nothing of numerous shootings and woundings." Such had been the ferocity of the Colfax County war!

About the Tolby murder, Waldo said, "The matter should be sifted to the bottom and the guilty planners and perpetrators of this diabolic crime be brought to the bar of justice."

The jury called some 50 witnesses from Colfax County. One way, this was a trip of 55 miles over 9,102-foot Palo Flechado Pass. Besides the time and expense this meant for witnesses, the pass often was deep in snow.

In a most curious legal procedure, Attorney General William Breeden, another Ring leader, sat with the jury to "assist" in its investigation. To no one's surprise, the jury found that it "was unable to discover the least evidence" against Longwill and Mills.

Sometime during this period, Governor Axtell arranged to meet Allison aboard a stage at Vermejo, just north of Cimarron. Axtell and Allison spent the entire day together en route to Trinidad, Colorado.

Shortly, Clay was in Taos to face indictments for first-degree murder in the deaths of Chunk Colbert, a gunman he had outdrawn in 1874, Charles Cooper, a friend of Colbert who had mysteriously disappeared, and Francisco Griego. Clay was defended by Frank Springer.

The prosecutor could produce no witnesses to the Colbert killing. He couldn't produce evidence that Cooper was dead, much less that Allison had killed him. Luis Griego, Francisco's son, testified that Clay had shot his father in the back during their saloon showdown.

The jury refused to return any indictments.

What agreement had Axtell and Allison come to in that stagecoach? History gives us no answer. Clay continued to battle the Santa Fe Ring.

In October 1876, Springer married Josephine Bishop, whose hand Allison had sought. By now, the Colfax County War had made Springer and Allison firm friends, with great mutual respect. Previous bitterness over the Maxwell company and destruction of the printing press was disregarded. And the dollar that Clay had extracted from Josephine's father for "the Clay Allison Extra" apparently was considered adequate compensation for her mother's unmannerly use of a broom instead of a shotgun when chasing Clay out of her house.

The Morley-Springer-Allison Axis soon had the Santa Fe Ring in deep trouble because of Morley's mother-in-law. Mrs. McPherson became an unrelenting fury after her daughter's indictment for postoffice robbery. In Washington, she undertook a year-long, one-woman crusade against the Ring, to the embarrassment of Elkins and Huntington.

Finally, the big break came. In February 1878, John Henry Tunstall, an English merchant-rancher, was gunned down by a Ring-instigated posse in Lincoln County of south-central New Mexico. This signaled the outbreak of the Lincoln County War. It also brought the British Embassy into the picture, raising awkward questions about the propriety of duly-constituted American authorities murdering an unresisting British subject and leaving his body where it fell.

Finally, Frank Springer's father, Judge Francis Springer of Iowa, exploited potent political connections in Washington—including a talk with President Hayes.

From all this pressure, Secretary of the Interior Carl Schurz in July 1878 sent Frank Warner Angel of New York, a perceptive and energetic investigator, to dig into Tunstall's murder and other violence in New Mexico.

The Ring was rude and balky, but Springer produced many affidavits for Angel testifying to its corruption. Springer also wrote one himself testifying to Clay's character: "... a man of Southern birth and education, of sensitive feelings and strong passions, quick to resent any indignities and a man of well-known personal courage and determination."

Angel's report was devastating. The "Dear Ben" letter was quoted in full with Angel's comment: "... was there ever a cooler devised plot with a Governor as sponsor?"

As for the Ring: "It is seldom that history states more corruption, fraud, mismanagement, plots and murders than New Mexico has been the theater of under the administration of Governor Axtell."

President Hayes promptly replaced Axtell with the distinguished General Lew Wallace, who had been sponsored by Judge Springer. (Wallace was to finish writing *Ben-Hur* while in Santa Fe.)

Breeden, the attorney general, resigned, as did U.S. Attorney Catron.

The Colfax County War was over.

Headlined the Cimarron *News and Press*: AXTELL'S HEAD FALLS AT LAST ... FIFTY GUNS FIRED IN HONOR OF EVENT. Upon hearing the news in Tucson, Arizona, Grandfather Morley, who had left the Maxwell company to return to railroading, wrote Ada: "I just wanted to go out in the street and throw up my hat and howl, but being a stranger it would not look well. . . . Darling, we are completely vindicated, and when I say we, I mean all who have so long struggled against this terrible ring."

Morley was to die of accidental gunshot at 36 while surveying a rail line in Mexico. What irony after having survived the Civil War and years among pistoleros!

Grandmother took her family, which had grown to three children, to west-central New Mexico and what was to become—another irony—Catron County. She became a successful rancher. Daughter Agnes was to become my mother and a New Mexico literary figure for her *No Life for a Lady* and *Satan's Paradise*.

Springer eventually abandoned law and, through much research and writing in scholarly publications, became a world-famous paleontologist.

As for another of those who "so long struggled" against the Ring, one who was a boy in Cimarron at the time provides an epitaph. In December 1935, George Crocker wrote George Fitzpatrick, former *New Mexico* editor, that "Colfax County should erect a monument in honor of Clay Allison for hunting down the Tolby murderers."

In 1876, Allison shot and killed a deputy sheriff at Las Animas, Colorado, but was released when no witnesses would testify against him. There are stories that Clay, in Dodge City, Kansas, in 1878, tangled with Sheriff W. B. (Bat) Masterson and Marshal Wyatt Earp; a more reliable report is that it was a friendly get-together of gunmen. By 1879,

Clay had sold his New Mexico ranch; in 1880, he was ranching anew in West Texas. There he was known as the "Wild Wolf of the Washita [River]."

That same year, Clay married Dora McCullough, a niece of John McCullough, the Cimarron postmaster. They had two daughters.

In 1886, Clay was ranching in the Seven Rivers country of New Mexico's huge southwestern Lincoln County. That June he drove a herd to Wyoming Territory. While at Cheyenne, he went to a dentist for a toothache. The dentist drilled a sound tooth. Clay had it repaired by another dentist, then returned to the first dentist and extracted one of his teeth with forceps.

In 1887, Clay fell under a wagon while returning from a supply trip to Pecos, Texas. A wheel rolled over his neck and killed him.

VI

FACSIMILE OF THE ORIGINAL 1956 EDITION

CLAY ALLISON

CLAY ALLISON

by

F. STANLEY

COPYRIGHT 1956
by
F. STANLEY

This book is copyrighted at the Office of Registrars in the Library of Congress, Washington, D. C. Beyond use in quote or book reviews no part of this book may be used without permission of the author.

Printed in the United States of America.

WORLD PRESS, INC.
Denver, Colorado

DEDICATION
to the memory of
THE LATE EARL VANDALE
of Amarillo, Texas
*who had hoped to live long enough
to write the story of Clay Allison*

CLAY ALLISON

Table of Contents

FOREWORD
CHAPTER ONE   TENNESSEE
CHAPTER TWO   CIVIL WAR DAYS
                    SECTION ONE—
                             GENERAL FORREST
                    SECTION TWO—ALLISON
CHAPTER THREE   THE BRAZOS COUNTRY
CHAPTER FOUR   NEW MEXICO
CHAPTER FIVE   VIGILANTES
CHAPTER SIX   COLORADO
CHAPTER SEVEN   THE TEXAS PANHANDLE
CHAPTER EIGHT   THE PECOS COUNTRY

BIBLIOGRAPHY
    Appendix A   PRIMARY SOURCES
    Appendix B   SECONDARY SOURCES
    Appendix C   NEWSPAPERS
    Appendix D   MAGAZINE ARTICLES

Foreword
CLAY ALLISON

They were two men in a darkened room. Enemies. Armed with daggers, it was understood that they were to fight to the death. Ben Thompson killed his opponent and fled New Orleans for Houston where he began his career as one of the border breed. Thus the story makes the rounds. Said to come from the very lips of the gambler himself. No bother about searching the dockets, sheriff's files, newspapers. Allison's career had the same beginning. Only he fought a man named Johnson in a grave; the winner to bury his victim. Men like Thompson, Allison, Longley, Bass, Rudabaugh, Hardin, found that the only thing faster than a six-shooter was what is known today as the "bull-shooter." Stories out of nowhere that smack of reality. So, Otero, Mills and others print them. The test of time makes them gospel, like a custom automatically becoming a law. But—find one newspaper, courthouse record, diary in the country that makes mention of the incident. After all, a man was killed. Some mention would be made of it, if only by the dead man's relatives or friends. As always, such stories break into print after the hero is dead; whenever someone who knew him slightly or intimately has the urge to write memoirs and decides the book will sell better if he tells how he knew Billy the Kid, Clay Allison, Masterson, Garrett, Stoudenmire and frontiersmen. At least Allison's victim had a name. Johnson. One might have said Smith or Jones. Thompson's victim is nameless. But the score is evened. Thompson's story takes place in New Orleans—Allison's somewhere in Texas. And when you mention Texas you cover a lot of ground. The fact of the matter is that none has bothered to investigate. It makes good reading. The origin being obscure, repetition makes it a fact. Allison pulled a dentist's tooth in more places than the poor man had teeth to subject to the mercy of the cattleman. For Allison was essentially this—a cattleman, out to give Charles Goodnight, Loving and others a run for their money. Many authorities refused to give Allison billing in their books, because (still quoting others) they accepted his deeds—or misdeeds—as the antics of a man under the influence of intoxicating drinks. Some of the events related here would win the admiration of Jim Courtright, John Slaughter, King Fisher, Butch Cassidy, Pat Garrett, Red River Tom and the ice-nerved group of individuals whose names always come up when the history of the West makes up the conversation. Just the incident of detaining the Governor of the Territory of New Mexico outclasses all the heroics of Buffalo Bill, Pawnee Bill and Wild Bill. And not under the influence of liquor.

We are neither pro nor con—for we do not wish to be stamped with that class of writers like the one who gave Wyatt Earp to the world—Allison was human and had his faults. In reading Earp I didn't think he had any until I delved into courthouse records and periodical rooms of libraries in New Mexico, Arizona, Kansas, Texas and Colorado. I was startled to find out he was a human being. The same goes for Bat Masterson and his brothers. Whether it be Jim Gillett, John Hughes, Pat Garrett or Hickok, there is yet to be a frontier marshall with all the qualifications for canonization.

But let us leave the legends regarding Allison to others. For the past fourteen years we have lived with the man in Waynesboro, along the Brazos, in Cimarron, Trinidad, Dodge, Hays, Seven Rivers, Lincoln, Mobeetie, Las Animas, Sedalia. Wherever Allison was known to have spent any length of time, even to the Civil War scenes—with but few exceptions. If Clay Allison set a foot anywhere not covered in this book it is because the author did not have a lead to follow. Many of the leads proved false. This the author deeply regrets for because of such information, from people who should have known better, he wrote several articles about Clay Allison which he now retracts, and which he regrets. Let this book atone for the mistakes of the past. It is lamentable that Wayne county officials burned many of the more informative records before the Federals marched into town during the Civil War. Our search took us to New York, Tennessee, Wyoming, Colorado, New Mexico, Texas, Kansas, California, Illinois, Missouri, Alabama, Washington. We are grateful to Henry J. Dubester of the Congressional Library, Mrs. Bourne of Raton, Mary Lail of Cimarron, Frank Alpers of Cimarron, the county clerks in Raton, Pecos, Wheeler, Sedalia, and other courthouses. We are particularly grateful to Helen Harding Bretnor of the Bancroft Library, Vivian Hedgecoke of Highlands University Library, Gertrude Hill of the Museum Library in Santa Fe, as well as to the librarians in the university libraries visited; the librarians of the State Historical libraries; the members of the War Department; J. E. Haley, Viola Webster, Mary Abreu, Frank Gumm, Frank Peiffer, James Barber, Mrs. Moorehead, Mrs. T. Smith, E. Vandale, E. Carr, J. Wood, E. P. Lamborn, Jesse Tipps, who grew up in Tennessee and had the "twang" of its expressions. Many of these have since passed on. They are not forgotten. Especially the old timers who helped me re-live the days when Clay Allison roamed the earth. To the last few intimates—relatives and friends—who loved him, let me say that only pulp magazines make him sensational. He was above all, normal. If Clay Allison looked like what the artist in the Otero book painted him to be, then the artist must have had in mind either an oriental or Fagin in Oliver Twist. There is only one picture of Clay Allison that has ever been put in books. It is in the possession of M. Lail of Cimarron. The others are all copies, whether in the Rose Collection or a private collection.

To the hundreds who helped, thanks . . .

F. STANLEY.

CHAPTER ONE

TENNESSEE

It was a halcyon, unruffled day. Off in a distance the farmhouse lay soaked in a honey fragrance of a too cursory Southern warmth that beguiled the uninitiated. Tomorrow the gales would blow across the shivering fields and rattle the farmhouse windows; there would be more wood to cut for the fires. But today the sun lay its warm hand on house and field alike. Peace and stillness pervaded the atmosphere, iridescent in the haze of shadow and sun-shot chimney smoke. March days, like any other part of the United States in those days, as in ours, were as uncertain as Rip Van Winkle's return from the Catskills. Spring had come early this year, with warm quick rains and sudden frothing of pink peach blossoms and dogwood sappling with white stars the backdrop about the farm and off into the hills.

Already the little plowing that was to be done was nearly finished and the sun baked into the fresh-cut furrows of the rich Tennessee soil as if measuring out life. The tramp of many feet would flatten out these furrows. Tomorrow. Today there was talk of jollification which the old folk somehow always managed to deaden with their doldrum looks and even more lugubrious talk of States Rights and Civil War.

Life was hard enough for the Allisons now that they laid away father in the knoll above the creek. He was so full of such talk that it made your head swim. Father, who found his life's vocation in the ministry very uncompensating, with so many mouths to feed, the pay being little enough at best. At times a buyer in the sheep and cattle markets; also a farmer when not preaching the word of the Lord, the gossip he heard deepened the crease in his brow and he foresaw ruination for them all. But he tried. His progeny agreed to that. It was all this strange talk about North and South, mutterings about conflict and disastrous ends, that seemingly alienated him. He was helpful and gay enough on opossum and coon hunts when he often laughed and always smiled and when he smiled the corners of his mouth spread until they were within an unimportant distance of his ears, causing his eyes to appear as mere chinks surrounded by diverging little wrinkles, giving a glow to the rotund countenance that always reminded them of the rising sun come to life. But one day after a rain he coughed and coughed. Then they laid him to rest. This was but a few short years ago but it seemed as if ages had elapsed. Time does not seem like yesterday to a boy of eleven. Last week is last year and there is more resentment than ache at the loss of the head of the family. True, there were older brothers and sisters to help Mother Allison keep the wolf from the door and a lad of eleven was not considered a boy anymore; he was a man with a man's job to do. He knew that he would never be a farmer. The plough he detested with all the aversion some lads showed for school. He was happiest with a rifle on his shoulder worrying squirrels, chasing rabbits, throwing sticks into the air and trying to hit them. He had a knife which his uncle had given him for his tenth birthday. He loved to stick it into fence posts, throwing it from a distance of thirty feet. Munroe was more of a companion because he was more his age. John was just a baby, only five years old and of little help in games and hunting. He was glad to be out of the house today. His mother was baking because a lot of people were coming for some kind of celebration. He enjoyed these days because everybody became so occupied that nobody paid much attention to him and he was able to go off wandering. This often annoyed Mother Allison, who had heard stories about men who roamed about to no good purpose. They never settled down and often died in the brakes with just wolves present at their passing. Ever since Robert Clay could walk his feet itched for other places. The small plot they farmed held little appeal. He hungered for the far away places. Farming is not in his blood, she would tell the other children; don't try to put it there. He'll come by what he wants when he's older.

Mother Allison bent over the fire, the smoke smarting her eyes as she labored to stir the big iron pot steaming away before her. Beads of perspiration, caught by the play of the open flame, glistened like so many tiny glass beads bunched up at the corners of her upper lip. She turned to watch old lady Lindsey contributing her feeble efforts at helping the other women clear the long room of all mobile effects to create the proper atmosphere needed for a successful quilting party. The men had piled the heavier furniture outside. She had a fleeting thought of how they would cackle if one of those sudden thunder storms should make a swift descent. And to think that she permitted them to talk her into rolling up her feather mattress, the one the boys bought her in Waynesboro, and putting it outside the cabin for all the neighbor children to jump on. She called this the farmhouse but actually it was a long room of squared logs hauled from the plateau. This would be her first quilting party since they gave poor Mr. Allison his place in the earth. There had been no times for tears. He left too many mouths to feed. The neighbors were gracious enough to buy eggs, milk and cheese. She would harness the horse to the shay and take needlework to Waynesboro close by. "No need ter fear fur the wida Allison," the neighbors would say. "She would care fer her young uns a mite better than her man did." It was high time the widow has a "jollification time," as the neighbors called it, and she agreed. "Jollification" came at the drop of a hat. A house raising, corn-shuckling, bean stringing, apple peeling, 'lasses stir-offs, clearings, log-rollings—all called for a celebration. Folks gathered from along Shoal creek, Second creek, Forty-eight creek and Moccasin creek to add to the festivity and give the Allison place near the Green river a holiday look.

Outside between the water mill and the tannery several boys set dogs on a coon track. They spied the coon up in the tree but it was too dark for the real fun. All they could do was let the hounds howl, and dare each other to climb the tree for the spoils. The little animal had sharp teeth, as many were aware from past experience. They would get a sound whacking instead of sympathy if they ran into the cabin with a show of blood. Discretion was the better part of valor. There were other days and this wasn't the last coon in the world.

"Let's catch old man Biffle for one of his yarns," said one boy named Kellough. " 'Tain't fittin' to stir up dogs at evening tide." The others agreed to this, so they went in search of the story-teller, the dogs following dejectedly behind, now and then stealing a glance towards the tree. They found the old man sitting against a poplar near the bank of the stream, fortifying himself from a jug of home-distilled brew. At their approach he glanced up, scrutinizing each face.

"Ain't never seed you before," he addressed the light-haired one, on whom his glance seemed to linger longer than the rest. "I don't rightly recollect."

But Grandpa Biffle always said that. It was an introduction ritual. "He be Robert Clay Allison, Mother Allison's boy," spoke up one.

The old man appeared to ignore this. Watching the play of water bugs as they skimmed over the water he reached for the jug beside him, uncorked it, made gurgling noises, recapped it, restoring it it to its former place.

"Sure as death, he be."

"Mr. Biffle, give us a story," pleaded Kellough. They took their places about him, never doubting he would refuse or object. Without another invitation he launched into his tale.

"One cold day one of my neighbors and myself, we took our old ram-rod guns and footed up the river a spell in search of an old bear stealing sheep. Well, lads, we walked three miles and couldn't see nary a trace of the old bugger. The old gun I had with me would hold only one load and my partner was a-carrying all the shells. We went on up the bank of the river where the bear used to come and git himself a drink. The place was smooth and you could still see the bear's tracks in the mud..."

Robert Clay Allison was hypnotized by the jug. The longer the old man talked the more he thought he would have no peace until he tested what was in that jug. Slowly he reached out, hoping that Grandpa Biffle was so immersed in the story that he would have no need for fortification for a while to come. Without seeming to break his flow of words, the old man said: "I wouldn't touch it, if I were you. It would not be to Mother Allison's liking." Startled, the boy jerked his hand back, a look of awe stealing over his features as if he had just encountered someone with supernatural powers. "Never, in all my borned days," he told his sister Mary later, "did I see the likes of it. The old man can see all around him."

"There was a large rock," Biffle continued, as if there had been no interruption, "out about middle way in the river. I told my partner that I'd wade out a mite ter see if'n I could discover the old bear. When I was on the rock, first thing I see'd was the big bear a-comin' down the mountain. I was about to shoot him when I see'd a large flock of geese, and down the river a piece was a drove of ducks. Now there I be with one load game a-plenty...."

He reached for the jug and turned a bit as if to tell Robert Clay that he had noticed his shift of position from the circle to a place just behind a tree. Tarnation take the lad; he seemed determined to share the contents with the old man. He caressed the jug as if fearing it would dissolve from lack of attention.

". . . I didn't know which way to shoot. I finally decided to git the bear. I took aim, pulled the trigger. The bullets went up and kilt the bear while at the same time they split the barrel in two pieces. One piece of the barrel went up the river and kilt the geese; the other went down the river and kilt the ducks, and the gun kicked so hard it knocked me off backward into the river. My partner gathered up my meat and I started for the bank, half frozen. When I got to the bank I found that my boots were full of fish. I started to reload my gun and accidently stepped into a mud-hole and walked ten miles to git a pick to dig myself out."

Even Grandpa Biffle joined in the guffaws that followed. This reminded him of the liquid cheer. He reached for the cork—the jug was gone.

"Thunder and tarnation. Drat that boy." The boys had never seen him more nimble. "Call Mary Allison and tell her snatch that brother of hers and whack him good. Bring back my jug."

Mary knew her brother. Accompanied by Munroe and several others she made for the river. She knew all his hiding places. "Don't know what's got into him," she kept saying. There was a spot of dense foliage with a hollow center like a den. Clay, as she called him, would be there. Clay and the jug were just getting acquainted when she found him. She picked up a stout limb and gave the jug a whack. The contents spilled all over Clay, who suddenly lunged for her. Knowing his moods, she ducked and caught him off balance and pushed him into the river. It was a very quiet and humbled boy who went to the fireplace to dry out his clothes.

"Sump'n tol' me that if I didn't move purty quick I'd purt'nigh drowned, and so I moved fast in the water but the poke o' water jist missed me. And Mary was a-standin' there laifin' at me. I wisht she was in torment."

"Hush yer words," warned the mother. "Next time behave yerself. Go tell Mr. Biffle yer sorry."

Over in the far corner of the room the fiddler, striking a chord, began singing:

> "Who will play the tune fer dancing?
> Who will play the fiddle sweet?
> All the girls are slyly waiting,
> Waiting with their itching feet.
> Fiddler, fiddler, come you soon
> And play us all a merry tune.
> Now before I make ye music
> Ye must pay the fiddler's fee.
> Oh, we've neither pence nor farthing,
> Poor and humble folk are we.
> Naught care I for what ye say;
> If ye must dance, then I will play."

The couples assembled for a promenade; the caller rang out the turns as the fiddler played, thumping his right foot against the floor to keep the beat; the stentorian voice of the caller drowned out the cricket in the fiddle as the dancers whirled and whirled like weather-vanes, darting in and out of the light from the fireplace.

> "Gents, hands in pockets, your backs to the wall,
> Swing your partners one and all.
> Take a chew of tobacco and balance all.
> Swing that lady in the checkered shawl;
> Swing your partners one and all.

Quit that beggin, ain't you 'shamed?
Promenade, oh promenade.
Chicken in the bread tray, pecking up dough,
Granny, will your dog bite? No, child, no.
Promenade, oh, promenade.
If it hadn't been for cotton-eyed Joe
I'd-a been married a year ago.
Promenade, oh, promenade.
Walk and talk;
Partners swing.
Chicken in the bread tray, pecking up dough,
Sally, will your dog bite? No, child, no.
Dance the Ocean Wave;
Swing your partners.
Ladies, bow,
And gents know how.
All run away.''

Clay watched the dancers, as most children did, by looking in the windows or crowding the doorway. He watched every move, fixing them in his mind against the day he would lead out his own partner to show the others how it was done. The commotion behind him informed him of the arrival of more guests. Those about the doorway opened a path to let them through.

"Howdy, Jack, how air ye?"

"Oh, jist so-so. Hain't feelin' so good this evenin' fer some reason."

"I'm jist tolable myself. Where ye been?"

"Over Gipson county ter pick up my little niece, the McCullough girl."

"I theink tomorrow I'll go to the doctor in Waynesboro. I theink I got a felon on my faingger."

"That's bad. How's yore wife?"

"She's purty porelt too. Her rheumatiz is a botherin' her considerable."

"She be dancin' well enough," laughed the other.

"That she be. That she be," he agreed.

Clay looked to see if he could spot the "little niece."

"Did she ever try what I told yer to tell 'er?" asked Grandpa Biffle, who had listened in on this exchange of words. "Did her try to makin' a poultice outa slippery ellum, and new lettin' hit set out in the sun fer a coupla days, an' thin tryin' hit on the knee?"

"No, she hain't. Her din't bin able ter find no slippery ellum yit."

"They's some on my place. Come over and git hit. Yer welcome to hit."

"Thankee, Tom, I'll do thet. Come over an' see me." Glancing at the group clinging to the entrance, he noted the intensity with which Clay's eyes followed the dancers, as if absorbed and carried away.

"Young fella, it strikes me as if yer mite dance a bit. Here be jist the gal. You be Mother Allison's boy, aren't yer? Yer don' look like yore gran' pap. He was a lootle short man, but he shore was stout. I've see'd him take a prize pole an' roll over a rock that they ain't no other two men in the valley coulda moved. An' I see'd 'im throw a steer oncet en' tie 'm up withouten any help. He done hit on a bet. Yep, boy, yer gran' pap sure was a man. Where in tarnation the girl go?"

He was back in a minute with the girl in tow. She was ten years of age, thin, spindle-legged, blond hair done up in pigtails, blue, startled eyes, pinafore checkered dress, black stockings covering the emaciated looking legs. They gathered into knobs above the knees, she having outgrown the dress and the parents not quite ready to buy a new one.

"This be my niece. Mind yer manners and dance."

He pushed the pair toward the dance floor amidst the cheers and jeers of the other boys, who thought this both funny and fatuous. Clay sought to duck out the door but the boys closed this avenue of escape. More late arrivals sought entrance.

"Come on in, come right in," said one of the men near the door. "Yer welcome 'nytime. I knowed yore brother. I knowed him well. They wa'n't no finer man thin yore brother, I said ter my woman when Bib Sittwell up an' shot 'im. 'Woman,' I says, 'this valley's done lost one o' hits most upstandin'est men.' Come right in."

Clay and Ella remained standing where they landed when they were pushed.

"Sure as death an' taxes, I'd like to be out of this," said Clay.

"If'en yer do'n fancy dancing wid me I don' mind," remarked the red-faced girl, as embarrassed as the boy. She had a sweet, soft voice, but it irritated him.

"I'd rather fin' old man Biffle ter see if'en he have another jug."

"Drinkin' be evil. Sure as death." The girl was horrified.

"Hit be evil fer girls, not fer boys." This only made the girl angry. She stamped her foot, stammering out between clenched teeth: " 'Tain't fittin' I dance wid yer, fer yer likes ter take to the jug. Drinkin' be evil fer all."

She left him abruptly, pushing her way through the boys, who knew better than try to stop her. Clay took his place with the others, the incident now closed. Yet here was a name that was to abide. He knew it during the Civil War; he was to know it in the Ponil and Cimarron country of New Mexico in the years to come, when he met Dora, associating her in his mind with this fighter of evil. He was to meet her at a dance, too, and he was to lose his heart. But that was years away; a war and the wanderlust was in between.

Several old women huddled in a corner, ignoring the dancers; for they knew that soon age would be in bed, while the young moved and whispered in the shadows. For they were old now and understood that the world had slipped away even though they did not expect death for some time to come. Their sense of values seemed so empty and false now that age made it too late for them to do anything about it. Still they wondered about all this talk of States Rights and slaves and secession. They dared not discuss such talk; it was for the men and the people at Washington. Theirs was more home talk. At the moment they were expostulating the remedies learned from a slave named Lydia. It was rumored she was in league with the devil, which they waved aside in favor of her miracles among the sick restored to health through her services. Now at the quilting, as they stitched, they compared notes.

"To stop a nose bleed," said Maria Fulton, "let the nose bleed on a knife blade; then stick the blade in the ground."

"And," chimed in Janet Barrett, "to cure an earache blow tobacco smoke in the aching ear. To cure chicken pox have the afflicted one lie down on the ground and run some chickens over him."

"There is a cure for shingles," ventured Mrs. Debrell. "All you do is rub the tail of a black cat over the body. It must be all black, mind you."

Mother Allison came by with a dish of meat from which they sliced choice, piping hot bits, placing them on the plates near them, then ignoring both talk and quilt patches for a time they made ruminating noises that plainly gratified the lady of the house, for such ambrosia put the seal of approval on her gastronomic efforts. She felt amply rewarded.

"Look," pointed Mrs. Fulton, "here comes Mrs. McCowan with that big, beautiful baby of hers. I should tell her of Lydia's cure for a baby cutting teeth. She should tie a mole's foot around the baby's neck and the little child will have her teeth without pain. Provided, of course, she did not let the baby look into a mirror before it was a month old." Mrs. McCowan merely smiled. She wondered what would happen if she told the old lady that she would have none of her superstitions. Poor souls, they were so credulous. Lydia probably laughed behind their backs. These people were supposed to be her superiors. As if to curtain her thoughts, she said:

"A woman over in Gibson county told me that if a baby is allowed to look into a mirror before a year passes, he will have the colic. A baby will become a thief if you trim his fingernails before he is a year old. If you rock an empty cradle the baby will have the colic. If a girl spills flour while she is baking, her husband will be a drunkard."

"Some day schools will teach different," remarked Mother Allison, who happened in on this last bit of information, "I keep my children from such fairy tales. Robert Clay, Munroe, John, and the others, will get schooling, mark my words, if I have to slave to the bone; most know how to read and write, for this their father did remarkably well. He had schooling. My boys will all be gentlemen. Just you wait and see. Come the winter and I will send Clay off to Waynesboro to learn his letters."

The others had nothing to say to this, merely glancing with knowing looks as if to say that Mother Allison was at it again with her pipe dreams and her grand airs that her children were better than the rest because their father was educated. From the way they noticed Clay gadding about chasing rainbows, fishing, throwing the knife constantly, shooting off his gun at sticks and old cans, they smiled to think that he would ever make a gentleman. He would get over his wild ways, grow up, marry, and settle down in his cabin along the river like the others. There were a good many years ahead of Mother Allison. She, too, would learn, after some of her brood broke her heart. Her three youngest boys might not grow up to be anything more than cannon fodder from the way the men talked.

Outside the boys built a fire, for the air had chilled, and they were too bored at watching the dancers. They would eat after all the grown-ups were served. Stretching his hands close to the flames, Clay said:

"I wish I were an Indian chief. I would dance around the fire all night and have my slaves bring me all the food I want."

"Aw," said one, "who wants to be an Indian and get scalped. Let's play the guessing game."

So, for a time, they occupied themselves with the game as they knew it in those days, and saw it played in Gibson and Wayne counties.

"House full, yard full, can't catch a spoon full, what is it?" asked Clay. The answer being "smoke," the boy who made the correct guess got to ask one. "It goes all over the hills and plains but when it comes to the river it breaks its neck, what is it?" Clay couldn't guess, and immediately tired of the game, getting up to see if he could find a half-used discarded cheroot. When they got together like this, one boy usually provided. He told the others what he was about, so they broke camp to go down by the river, where they usually hid when passing the cheroot around. They watched the play of the moon on the water, now silvery; now black, as the ripples seemed to break away in an effort to touch the bank. The crickets and the katy-dids made a music all their own as the glow at the end of the cheroot danced from place to place like a glow-worm or fire-fly, when inhaled. This was life. Far from the madding crowd that told you what to do and what not to. Here was peace as Clay wanted and loved it, even though short-lived. These were moments of blessedness that made his soul free. No grown-ups jumping down your throat, only the smooth, heavy smoke that you blew out to the moon, the stars, the vast world beyond where the fulfillment of your dreams lay.

"Some day we're goin' ter fight the Yankees, pa

says." Kellough always liked to make big talk like a grown-up.

"Let 'em," said Clay. "Me, I'm going to Texas. Davy Crockett and lots of folks from Gibson county went to Texas."

"Yea. Davy got hisself kilt. Do yer aim to git yerself kilt?"

"I kin take care of myself."

Suddenly everybody was talking at once about letters received from relatives living in the Republic of Texas. It was a new country, a whole new world. Lots of cattle, lots of Indians to shoot, horses to ride, captives to do your bidding. It was the country to live in, everybody knew that. Besides, the Mexican government gave you a lot of money for Indian scalps. Why, a fellow could get rich just killing Indians. Must be a good country or else why would Davy tell everybody to go to hell—yes, he did—told everybody to go to hell, and he went off to Texas. And he was a big man in Washington. The country gave his widow lots of land but she did not know whether she wanted to leave Gibson county to go where she might be "kilt" by the Indians for all the land in Texas. Old man Biffle said she would go all right for there were many mouths to feed and with all that space she ought to find enough food for them all. Clay remembered the things his father told him about Texas. About Sam Houston, Jones, Austin, Crockett, the Alamo. And he conjured up dreams of a mighty mansion, stately by the river bank, with thousands of slaves to pick his cotton, groom his horses, till, work, even cut wood. Pa said it was a land flowing with milk and honey but ma disagreed, telling him that it was a place too poor to remain a republic and some were talking even now of joining up with the United States. If this land was as poor as she said, how come so many were leaving Tennessee to live there? She had no answer except to tell him that some day he would find out for himself. She was swathy, Mother Allison was, and neighbors often whispered out of hearing that they thought she had Indian blood. Of course she didn't but those were gossipy days and people judged by appearances. Years later when he would be on trial for murder the prosecuting attorney would seek to stigmatize him as a half-breed. The people of Wayne county knew better. The Allisons didn't marry Indians. They hated them.

Texas seemed to be a warlike country. Clay heard but a few days ago that they were saying that the United States cheated and took more land than came by right of conquest in the year of Manifest Destiny. Texas aimed to get that land back if it meant war with the United States.

Nobody in Tennessee thought New Mexico was worth fighting for, but it was a President from Tennessee who preached the idea of a coast-to-coast America, which included New Mexico, and they believed in loyalty. California, now, that was the place. The abandoned farms about the river told the story of the great transcontinental exodus, for it was easier to dig for gold than for potatoes. Many returned empty handed. Some thought that perhaps New Mexico would vomit more gold than California so they would be patient and wait until the soldiers killed a few more Indians before they ventured forth. Mother Allison used to say when asked if she would go West: "I know what I have in Tennessee, I don't know what I'd find in Californy." Hildago Treaty, Gasden Purchase, were words bandied about but beyond the comprehension of young Clay. What he did understand was that the Governor of Texas was appealing to the youth of Tennessee to enlist in the Texas Army to fight President Taylor's troops collecting about Santa Fe. The distant drums were always beating for Robert Clay Allison. He had an idea that he would run away from home to join the Texas Army in some capacity or other. Fighting might be fun.

But President Taylor disappointed him. He gave a Fourth of July address in the boiling sun, then went home and ate some cherries and drank iced liquids. He was dead before he could declare a state of war existed between the Republic of the United States and the State of Texas. Fillmore knew how to smoothe things over and the catastrophe was averted, although Daniel Webster had ordered troops in readiness should the Governor of Texas prove recalcitrant. The Republic of Texas had been the State of Texas for several years now but it acted as if it never lost its sovereignty. Clay, who had first heard of it as an independent nation, was surprised to learn it was a state and, never once gave up the idea that it would one day be his home.

What the President of Texas hoped to accomplish through the Texas-Santa Fe Expedition, in an effort to divert Santa Fe trade, and the Governor hoped to accomplish wistfully thinking of gold, was happily settled for a sum of money. So, Clay's dreams of becoming a drummer boy at another Alamo were severely shattered. All these events were often discussed at table but mostly he went apart to his favorite hiding place by the river to think these things out alone. Talk of Yankees was rampant. Political uneasiness tempered the anodyne of rising business and profitable farming. Gold, imports and exports were making the Yankees increasingly bold and Southern gentlemen resented infringement on States Rights. Railroads were beginning to point in all directions, which alarmed Clay to no small degree, for he heard that this would replace the horse and he had centered his dreams around horse races. All his life he treated horses with about as much respect as you would show a lady. Yankees. This was the sound. The Panic of 1857 would help bring on the fury which was to lay low the land. Then he was able to fight for he was a grown man. The damn Yankees were sure up to something laying cables, building railroads, buying up cotton, opening more factories than you could ever hope to visit in a lifetime. This talk of war made him practice with knife and rifle; the game was no longer rabbits, coons, ducks.

Restlessness stamped him from birth. Another age might call him a problem child. Actually his dreams were too fast for his motion. Also he was wholehearted. If the Yankees were to be hated, it was to be done without reservation. He fought the Civil War in his own mind years before the irrepressible conflict. Among his playmates he never openly sought a fight nor did he ever flinch from one. He preferred to be called Clay because the name of the great statesman was on everyone's lips and it gave him a sense of kinship, a feeling of responsibility, a name to live up to, a sense of duty, a feeling of security, a bulwark on which to pile his dreams. Mother Allison would tell him much about the family as she worked yams over the fire. This was a dish! Piping hot and dripping molasses. The family tree was a heritage. It began in America with Patrick Allison, who crossed the ocean from Donegal. His restless blood coursed through Clay's body. The others seemed content enough but he would meander through Tennessee, Aabama, Indian Territory, Texas, Missouri, Kansas, New Mexico, before his bones would be deposited in the good earth of the Pecos Valley of Texas. The Father Founder eventually came to rest in the Mecklenburg country of North Carolina. A son migrated to Gibson county in Tennessee. He was a member of the Presbyterian faith, many of his descendants taking their places in communities as elders and clergymen, for the Allisons were always religious. Clay was never to lose sight of religion, even in the day when he was to be sought out and marked for death by gunfighters. Often when riding from Dodge to Mobeetie on the Sweetwater in the Panhandle of Texas he was to ride the stage with Father Wolfe, who attended the spiritual wants of the soldiers at Fort Elliott, and religion was always the main topic under discussion.

John Allison, born at Sugar Creek, North Carolina, December 8, 1801, studied for the ministry. After service at Shelbyville, Clarksville, Princeton, Clarksville, Nashville and Smyrna, he settled in Wayne county where he died on March 7, 1845. Among the children he left were Jane Anne Elizabeth, Mary Elvira, Sarah Anne, Margaret Rebecca, Munroe, Elijah Edward, Robert Clay, John Edmund. The mother was Nancy McCullough Lemmond (1798-1864). Jane Anne was the oldest of the girls; Robert the third boy. It must have been hard for the family to be constantly moving, which accounts for John's settling down as a farmer and a cattle and sheep buyer. Then, too, clergymen were as underpaid then as now.

Wayne county is composed of hills which surround a plaeau that shelters Waynesboro, the county seat. Beyond these hills steep ravines radiate in every direction except eastward. These are criss-crossed by other ravines. The traveler may still note here, as he wends his way along the banks of the numerous streams, abandoned water mills, tanneries, sharecroppers' cabins—links with the past and favorite haunts that helped wile away days of youth. Clay was a likable lad and always made welcome.

Perry Davis was the first pioneer to settle on Mill creek in 1799. Here he built a log house, hunted and traded with the Indians. Mark Edwards, Lavic Rasburg, Craig W. Pope, Rich Churchwell and John Choat did not settle the Buffalo river country until 1815. David Carter, who received his land grant in 1809, the first within the limits of Wayne county, induced others to follow his example. His place was known to Clay as the Frank Walker farm. His settlement extended from Allen's creek to Opossum creek. The settlers stirred up talk of a new county, and the Legislature acted on November 24, 1817. Wayne county, named for a Revolutionary War hero, was created from parts of Hickman and Humphries counties. This act, however, was not engrossed and approved, consequently it had to be re-passed during the 1819 session, the year Anderson Stonewall and Malachi Wimberley opened the first country store at the Ashland settlement.

The first meeting for the organization of the county court was held at the home of Benjamin Hardin on the Factor's Fork of Shoal creek at the crossing of the Natchez Trace. The second meeting was held at William Barnett's on the Old Town Branch where Barnett had constructed a log courthouse. The following magistrates were present at this meeting: Benjamin Hardin, Jesse Cypert, William B. Curtis, William Burns, Perley and David Gallaher, Ruben Kyle, John Meredith, C. W. Pope, William B. Poss, Henry Rayburn and William B. Walker. These names are relatively unimportant but they are the fathers of the boys who were to serve with Clay during the Civil War and many were to be with him as cowboys in Texas and New Mexico, after the conflict. These are names he was to repeat from 1860 to 1877. The county officials elected were William Barnett, county court clerk; Benjamin Hardin, sheriff; John M. Barnett, circuit court clerk; John McClure, register; John Meredith, trustee; John Hill, ranger; W. B. Payne, coroner. Court sessions were held at this place until 1823 when the county seat was moved to Waynesboro, founded by William Burris in 1821. The Commissioners appointed to locate this county seat were Nathan Biffle (also appears as Biffer), Charles Burnes, James Hollis and John Mill. The land, forty acres, was divided into lots which were sold for the proceeds to be used to defray the expenses in the erection of a courthouse. Clay Allison was almost seven when Judge Terry H. Cahal presided over the first chancery court at Waynesboro in 1847. His mother took him to town that day for the dedication services. On this day he also saw Ashland School, which was to be a familiar sight as he made progress with his letters.

One custom in Wayne county annoyed him. The poor you have always with you. Wayne county was no exception. From the earliest days, the county fathers inaugurated the custom of farming out the poor to the highest bidder. The first farm beyond the townsite limits was thirteen miles below Waynesboro. This was a small place fast running to ruin from lack of attention. In 1849, Washington Morris bought out the owner for one hundred dollars. He applied for farm labor, and since none was forthcoming, put in his bid and the county sent its poor to this place. They reminded Clay of driven cattle. This would never happen to him; this he resolved. He would rather die than find himself working on a farm at the expense of the county. Thus his dreams began, stretching over the far horizons.

It is difficult to fill in the pre-Civil War years for all the Wayne county records were destroyed by the Confederates, who feared they would fall into the hands of the Federals. After 1851, one must rely mostly on the works of Wayne county historians, and old timers who remember what their fathers told them, of these years. The county was by no means entirely for the South. During the war as many enlisted for the North as for the South. When asked to vote for Secession, nine hundred and five cast their ballots for the Union; four hundred and nine voted for Secession. One can imagine Clay, an ardent Secessionist, constantly on his guard, and, no doubt, in many a scrape, for he looked upon the South as an underdog in need of a champion. All his life he was to be that way sticking up for one he thought to be in the right tread upon by might. Wherever there was a Secession meeting he rallied to the cause. Even here he had his dreams. The rank and file was not for him. In the event of war he would lead his own men. So he thought. He was to act independently of troops and troop movements but as a scout. The thirty men he was to lead at the close of the war were not guerillas in the sense of wanton destruction but the beginning of a resurrected army that was to push the detested Northerner out of Tennessee. It failed to materialize simply because Southerners themselves were tired of fighting, and branded him an upstart. But this was still years away. There was still that education Mother Allison promised.

The imitators of Horace Mann and other liberal educators did not infiltrate Tennessee until 1830, when the popularity of some system of state education forced the hand of the Legislature. Many of the most talented politicians of the State labored earnestly to secure an efficient system but so deep-rooted was the free school idea that they were powerless to effect any reforms. People believed that free schools were established primarily for the benefit of the indigent. Decades were to pass before they thought otherwise. If a farm boy showed lack of propensity for work he was singled out as the one to represent the family in book learning, and, since the school was free, it was the more reason to pack him off. The idea of a system of schools as a measure of economy, for the benefit of the rich as well as the poor, would never broaden under the then existing state of society. A State fund was at the disposal of schools since 1827. Counties were divided into school districts of convenient size, in each of which five trustees were elected whose duty it was to meet at the courthouse on the first Saturday of June of each year for the purpose of electing not less than five, nor more than seven, discreet and intelligent citizens as Common School Commissioners. The trustees were given full power to employ and dismiss teachers and to judge their qualifications, capacity and character. They controlled the money for school use. They divided the county into five districts each, over each of which one Commissioner was to exercise general supervision. The interest arising from the school fund was to be distributed among the school districts in proportion to the number of children in each, between the ages of five and fifteen, but before any district was entitled to its share it was compelled to provide a comfortable schoolhouse. All children under the age of fifteen were induced to attend school, a practice followed in towns but not in country settlements. The average pay per month for each teacher never reached above seventeen dollars. Some counties reported twenty-five percent of its children as pupils; others less.

Not all the children were in school because the parents classified them as indigent. Many were sent in the hopes of making Commissioners of them. A person unable to read nor write would hardly qualify for a position involving arithmetic and letter writing. Too, anyone who was schooled was treated with respect by the community and usually called upon for speeches, civic representation, politics. There were many poor farmers too proud to send their children to the free schools because they thought it another way for the high and the mighty to show their contempt by way of condescending to the destitute. Bitter resentment developed on both sides. It was not until 1855 that the first public grade school was established in Knoxville.

Meantime Mother Allison worked out a plan to send Clay to school. He had some tutoring when he was six, and learned his A-B-C's in the little school close by. Also the late Mr. Allison left some books but these were heavy reading for a boy not yet in his teens. She sent Clay to the Ashland school in Waynesboro, where he boarded with some people who once lived near the river. He was ever grateful to his mother for her interest in his education. Later on he was to use the medium of letter-writing to editors to defend himself against their verbal assaults and to give biographical data concerning himself which otherwise would have perished. He was by no means a brilliant student, nor was he at the foot of the class. Had he applied himself he might have excelled. He was friendly and the people of Waynesboro looked upon him as a lad of promise. He often referred editors to the people of Waynesboro for reference as to his integrity and ability. He made no distinction; any one they cared to write to would do. This speaks well for his popularity since many years were to elapse which could easily have erased his memory.

Henry Clay and the Clay Compromise was still the talk of the town. School boys, in imitation of their elders, weighed the pros and cons. As with the nation, so at the school. There were two factions. Those who argued for the Union; those who stood steadfast for Secession. Clay was readily acknowledged the leader of his own age group, that would stone to death any Yankee in sight. The situation was a ticklish one for the school officials, no more so than in any other school, but a problem nevertheless. Neutrality was their password. They would declare well enough when the issue came to a head and war was a fact. Allison exhibited a loyalty for Clay, Calhoun and others that was almost savage. He would take the defensive upon the least provocation so that the school was often the scene of a civil war, boys pummeling and thumping each other in defense of their side. The Wilmot Provisio, or the Compromise was enough to set them off, and the teachers found that they were more useful as policemen restoring law and order than instructors preparing youths for a place in the sun.

The Wilmot Proviso, introduced in the House during the Mexican War period, asked that slavery be prohibited in any territory acquired by right of conquest. While the Proviso was never passed by Congress it blossomed into a major political issue, being the subject around which was built the Southern Convention at Nashville on June 3, 1850. The aim at the nine-day session was to determine the best means of securing constitutional rights for the South while still preserving the Union. Henry Clay made the proposal that California be admitted into the Union as a Free State and the remainder of the territory gleaned from Mexico be considered slave. John Bell, also of Tennessee, proposed a plan for compromise. Congress ignored the proposals, passing what history calls the Clay Compromise.

Nothing the North did was right to the pro-Secession element at Ashland. Tennessee was still agog at the action of seventy delegates representing ten States meeting at Nashville and fighting tooth and nail for the acceptance of the Compromise. They argued that it was unjust, but would be willing to accept it as a proof of their sincere affection for the Union. They were not warmongers, as some in the North said. They were willing to make sacrifices to stave off this constant talk of conflict. Their resolution was rejected whereupon some retaliated that the North was doing everything in its power to hasten Secession. Tennessee itself was uncertain. Men like Andrew Jackson abhorred any talk of Secession, and since his death in 1845 his adherants sought to follow through. Andrew Jackson on his great charger surmounting the hill at the State House in Nashville; had he lived he might have influenced Clay's way of thinking. The dead have no voice. But William G. Brownlow did, and he was very much alive. Of caustic tongue, he was bitterly pro-slavery, anti-Yankee even though pro-Union. His sentiments were part and parcel of the passing scene. Turmoil and confusion beat down the doors of the school. East Tennessee alone accounted for nearly one-fifth of all anti-slavery societies in the United States, and nearly one-sixth of the total national membership. Churches in Tennessee were not immune from the taint as Christian denominations split over the slavery issue. How could the growing Clay Allison be other than partisan getting it like food or clothing. It helps explain the enigma that made up the man. A product of his time, the winds of rumor, wild talk, hate, war, carried like shifting sands, burying the original cause of the differences so that

States Rights no longer entered the picture as the wedge that split the nation.

Above and beyond all this there was the fact of stern reality. Clay would not remain in school forever and until the advent of war there was work to be done at home. He was interested in the agricultural outlook for Tennessee, reading everything he could get his hands on dealing with the subject. It pleased him to know that as far away as London his State received recognition, paying a special compliment by way of a booth during the Great Exhibition. Clay's mother would often stoop down, scoop up a handful of earth and say that a man's wealth was in the soil. "Hold on to some property. Till the earth. As long as a man has this he is the proud possessor of something no one can take from him. If you work for another, it is not yours. When something is your own, you have some explanation for what you did with your life."

So he gave his attention to the soil, horses and cattle. He attended the first Biennial State Fair at Nashville, eager to learn the latest methods in farming. He never lost sight of the vision of the future. War might devastate the land and crush his interest in farming but it never erased the hope that one day he would be the lord of many acres, own race horses, graze countless herds of cattle. A product of his environment he hoped he would soon be able to buy slaves to commence him on the road to power and riches. Numerous newspapers and periodicals fed the flame of his ambition. They also saturated his hate for all things Yankee. Thus the days passed on the farm after leaving school. There were drills, too, so certain were the youth of war. When it did come it was no surprise. They were keyed up for it.

CHAPTER TWO

CIVIL WAR DAYS

Section 1

GENERAL FORREST

The Confederate sympathizers in Tennessee furnished 115,000 soldiers to help the cause. These took part in two hundred and ninety-six battles, combats and skirmishes. Of these enlisted men sixty-four were Allisons. Five wrote out their names as Robert Allison. Thirteen simply signed R. A. Possibly because of this confusion, Robert Clay Allison emerged from the war as Clay Allison. The Allison that was with General Forrest as an escort from July 1, 1864, to February 28, 1865, was in Captain J. C. Jackson's company and official papers sign him as J. D. Allison. Either this is a mistake on the part of the enlisting officer or there was more than one Allison with Forrest. After the fight in St. Louis, Allison made it clear that he served as a scout for General Forrest. He was proud of his part in the Civil War, the only boasting he did in his life. Clay spoke of Forrest in awe and reverence. As Allison enlisted from the very beginning of the conflict, it is hard to be precise and definite as to how many of the almost three hundred engagements he took part in. We can only trace his war days through his commanding officers, the more prominent being Biffle, McCollough and Forrest. In order to adequately gauge these years in the life of the lad from

Waynesboro it is best to review the commanding general's part in the conflict to fit the parts of the puzzle.

General Nathan B. Forrest rendered conspicuous service at Donelson and Shiloh. While at Tupelo in Mississippi, in June, 1862, he was ordered by General Beauregard to proceed to north Alabama and middle Tennessee to take over the command of the cavalry under Colonel Scott, Colonel Wharton and Colonel Adams. He proceeded to Chattanooga where he was informed that he had been promoted to the rank of brigadier general.

He left Chattanooga on July 9th at the head of 1,400 troops. These included his own regiment under Major Smith; the 8th Texas under Col. John A. Wharton; the 2nd Georgia under Col. Lawton and two companies of Kentuckians under Captains Taylor and Waltham. Staging forward marches the command reached Murfreesboro at 4:30 a.m. of July 13. The town at the time was in the hands of the 9th Michigan and 3rd Minnesota regiments of Infantry; two hundred Pennsylvania cavalry; one hundred 8th Kentucky Cavalry; Hewets's Battery of four guns. Fourteen hundred men commanded by Brigadier General Thomas Crittenden. Following an attack and a four-hour battle the entire Federal force was surrendered as prisoners of war. Forrest lost twenty-five killed, sixty wounded. The Union forces lost seventy-five killed, one hundred and twenty-five wounded. Forrest was richer by sixty wagons and teams, cavalry horses, arms, ammunition, equipments of the garrison, quartermaster and commissary stores and the four-gun battery complete. Forrest marched on to McMinnville. Meantime a great hue and cry was raised. All loyal men were called to defend Nashville against possible invasion. Federal troops were sent to Readyville, Statesville, Wilton, and to a point on the old Franklin road as well as toward Lebanon in an effort to cut Forrest off.

The general rested a few days at McMinnville, leaving on the 18th with seven hundred effective troops to

March on Lebanon, Tennessee. He took undisputed possession and on the 21st moved on towards Nashville. On the way he destroyed the railroad bridges across Mill creek, skirmished with the garrison at Antioch, where he captured ninety-seven prisoners, frightened the garrison at Nashville and retired in good order. His next campaign was an expedition to the western part of Tennessee. He crossed the Tennessee river ten days before Christmas and on the 18th attacked the Federals at Lexington, Tennessee. This force consisted of eight hundred cavalry and artillery under Col. R. J. Ingersoll, who was to champion another cause after the war. He lived for a time at Dorsey, New Mexico, and several canyons, creeks and mountains in the area are named for him. But that was yet to come. Clay Allison met him a few times in the early Eighties but he never said one way or the other whether Ingersoll impressed him. The colonel was not very successful against Forrest. His command retreated to Jackson, Tennessee. Ingersoll himself was among the one hundred and forty-eight prisoners taken. He commanded the Eleventh Illinois Cavalry. Forrest dispatched Col. G. G. Bibbell to pursue the retreating Federals and at Carroll Station one hundred and one more prisoners were taken. After burning the railroad station Bibbell rejoined Forrest at Spring Creek, Tennessee.

Forrest again took up the march to Jackson leading two companies commanded by Colonel T. G. Woodward, Kentucky Cavalry, and Colonel J. B. Biffle's Nineteenth Tennessee Cavalry, with a section of Freeman's Battery. Satisfied that the Federals vastly outnumbered him at Jackson, the Confederate general divided his forces, sending Colonel J. W. Starnes of the Fourth Tennessee Cavalry against Humboldt, where he took one hundred prisoners and destroyed the stockade and railroad bridge. Colonel Biffle was sent to the rear of Trenton (Tenn.) while Forrest himself took Major N. N. Cox's Second Battalion, Tennessee Cavalry, his escort company and

Freeman's Tennessee Battery and made a bold dash at Trenton, which he captured after a brief engagement. He took seven hundred prisoners. The garrison was composed of the Second Tennessee Federal Regiment, commanded by Col. Isaac R. Hawkins. Forrest lost two men killed and seven wounded. Hawkins escaped Forrest at Lexington.

Colonel A. A. Russell, Fourth Alabama Cavalry, who was guarding Forrest's rear pending these operations, skirmished for parts of two days with a column of Federals, who retreated across Spring Creek. On December 21st, Forrest moved north to Rutherford Station, where he captured two companies of the enemy. From there he went on to Union City where he took over a hundred prisoners. On the last day of the year he moved from Flake's Store, sixteen miles north of Lexington, and engaged in a battle at Parker's Crossroads, where he fought Col. C. L. Dunham's Brigade. General Sullivan came up to help Dunham, forcing Forest to retreat. The Confederate leader lost sixty men in killed and wounded and one hundred and twenty-two prisoners.

Forrest was in the attack on Fort Donelson, February 3, 1863. On March 27, 1863, General Bragg telegraphed Richmond: "Forrest made a successful attack on Brentwood with his division; burned the bridge; destroyed and took all property and arms; captured eight hundred prisoners, including thirty-five officers." The leader of the opposition in this engagement was Lt. Col. Bloodgood, 22nd Wisconsin Cavalry. Forrest next went to Franklin, where Union forces were guarding the railroad bridge. They surrendered two hundred and thirty prisoners to him.

April 9—Forrest and General Stanley of the U. S. 4th Cavalry had a skirmish which seems to have ended in a draw. In this engagement, Forrest lost Col. Freeman, his best artillerist.

May 3—After five days and nights of fighting and marching, Forrest captured Col. A. D. Streight's (51st Indiana Volunteers) entire command.

December 4, 1863—Forrest entered Western Tennessee and camped at Bolivar.

December 5th—Etablished headquarters at Jackson, where he raised new troops, re-shuffled his commmand, left western Tennessee with three thousand new troops. (Could this be the time that Clay Allison joined Forrest as a scout?)

General Hurlbut, with 20,000 Federals, was assigned the task of capturing Forrest. Engagements took place at Jack's creek, Estanaula, Somerville, Lafayette, Colliersville. General Sherman next sent Brig. Gen. W. S. Smith, Commander of the Union Cavalry Forces of Tennessee, to stop Forrest. Forrest reported that his Brigade, commanded by Colonel Jeffery Forrest, successfully disputed Smith's crossing of the Sakatonchee creek, forced him to retire toward West Point, drove him from that place to within ten miles of Pontotoc in two days. Forrest pursued the retiring enemy with his escort—a section of Morton's Battery, a detachment of Faulkner's Regiment, a Regiment from McCullogh's Brigade. As Allison definitely stated he fought with McCullogh we assume that he joined Forrest in the shake-up at Jackson. Forrest himself spelt the name—McCulloch. Allison spelt it McCullogh, possibly because of the way his friends in Wayne county spelt it, or because Dora, his wife, used this spelling. At Okolona Forrest charged the enemy with Bell's Brigade under Col. Barteau. Five miles out of Okolona General Smith reformed his ranks to await the second Confederate attack. This was made by McCullogh, Forrest and Hoole. Smith seems to have had the upper hand. Forrest lost one hundred and forty-four men, among them Col. Jeff E. Forrest, who was succeeded by Col. Duckwater.

The next attack was on Yazoo City under Brig. Gen. R. V. Richardson of the Forrest Command. He accomplished but little.

March 4, 1864—Forrest advanced into western Tennessee with a new command under Brig. Gen. A. Buford.

March 22—Forrest at Trenton. Accomplished nothing.

March 23—Forrest ordered an attack on Union City. Accomplished nothing.

March 26—Captured the city of Paducah.

April 11—At Fort Pillow (more about this later).

McCullogh's Brigade was definitely in the attack on Fort Pillow, which means that Allison had a part in the action there.

After the Fort Pillow affair Forrest proceeded to Mississippi, where he fought at Tishomingo creek. Here he suffered his greatest loss, nearly five hundred in killed and wounded. McCullogh's men were also engaged in the battle of Tupelo and Harrisburg. Forrest attacked Memphis on August 21, 1864, taking four hundred prisoners. Next we find him in Athens, Alabama. Col. Jesse Forrest fell in this engagement. At Sulphur Springs, Forrest received the surrender of Lt. Col. Minnis. Other engagements in Alabama were at Elk river, Richland creek, Pulaski, Columbia. On October 16th he moved for the fourth time to Western Tennessee. His troops were in the engagements at Fort Herman and Paris Landing. This was a new kind of fighting to his men, for both battles were gunboat affairs. It has been estimated that Forrest did a million dollars worth of damage along the Tennessee river.

January 27, 1865—Forrest was assigned to command the Confederate Department of the District of Missisipi and Louisiana. He marched to Selma, Alabama, and was in Alabama when the war ended.

Section Two

ALLISON

Robert Clay Allison was ten when W. L. Morris came to Waynesboro to edit the *Family Visitor,* the first newspaper in Wayne county. The completion of the Central Turnpike determined his course but not his policy. He was a staid, dyspeptic individual who lamented the changing world and took the middle ground in his editorials, being neither belligerent nor rebellious. Seeking to be fair, he presented both sides of the political situation, leaving it to the reader to decide for himself which party to follow. The surge of industry during those years before the war made Waynesboro a beehive of activity. Before long the *Family Visitor* had a competitor. The *Waynesboro Times* left no question in the minds of its readers on its course of action. If you subscribed to this paper you were known as a Secessionist. This was the paper Clay Allison read. He aired his views in the barbershop, the market place, on the farm, in the home.

Over in Baxter county another Allison, kin to the Wayne county clan, was terrorizing the countryside and a movement was afoot to outlaw him from society. He had adherents, mostly because his raids were against confirmed Northern sympathizers. Clay knew of him and thrilled at each new exploit, hoping some day to join his cousin, if only to satisfy his thirst for adventure, wild and furious riding, care-free plunges into danger and defiance hurled at those who refused to recognize that the South had a cause. It is not known whether Allison ever rode with his Baxter kin but the accusations to arise against him after the war lead one to suspect the possibility. After a time the Baxter Allison refused to discriminate. He raided everybody and anybody. Both North and South were to war against him and his guerrillas.

This Baxter Allison was said to have been the son of a Cherokee woman. Years later when Clay was on trial for murder, the prosecuting attorney called him a halfbreed and brought into play all that was known about the Baxter Allison. Clearly a case of mistaken identity. Clay repeatedly mentioned the names of the men he served under during the conflict; the Baxter Allison served only himself. Tension was everywhere. State after State decided to bring matters to a head by way of the polls. Wayne county voted on June 24, 1861. The final count registered 361 in favor of the Union; 409 decidedly Secessionist. The county was certainly a house divided.

During the Civil War, Wayne county was divided into districts in an effort to reach out to all able-bodied men interested in military duty. These districts comprised Beach creek, Eagle creek, Hardin creek, Indian creek, Cyprus creek, Buffalo river, Forty-Eight creek, and Rich creek. Each of these had a company headed by Captains William Gambrul, G. H. Tucker, Isaac Roberson, H. J. R. A. Morris, Thomas Reeves, John Rayburn, Frank Mayberg, J. Sherrill, T. T. Thompson and J. Aydlotte. Confederates were highly successful in recruiting at Ashland, Flatwood and Waynesboro, enlisting these troops in the North Tennessee Cavalry of the Confederacy. Company A was commanded by Captain J. T. Biffle and Lt. J. M. Binham. The captain for Company B was James M. Reynold and the leader of Company C was Captain John A. Johnson. Allison, now in his twenty-first year, enlisted under Johnson. Many have written the War Department for Allison's record. It does not exist simply because the Confederates of Waynesboro burned all records when the Federals marched into town, rather than have them fall into enemy hands, for fear of reprisals. Allison's record is to be gleaned from his own testimony and the word of friends and relatives of those years.

Allison was not the only one to come to the realization that war was something more than marching towards the enemy with a gun. Months of inactivity around camp was convincing proof that everything was a matter of orders and counter-orders. Like so many others, Clay thought that it was all just a matter of marching to the Yankee front, whipping them and returning home to the new and independent nation of the Confederate States of America. It was only later on when he became a scout that he felt happy with army life. During the months of waiting he transferred to Company A under Captain Biffle. The Ninth Tennessee Cavalry of the Confederacy was not called into action until August 12, 1862. Even then the boys murmured, for instead of combat their job was to guard the railroad at Summerton, Hohenwald, Centerville, Lawrenceburg, Pleasant Point. Sentry duty was also in order along rivers and at bridges. Discipline was lax during those early days of the war, the boys taking leave at will. It was argued at the campfire that guarding bridges, rivers and railroads was for old men and half grown boys. The enlisted men sought action. Allison, like many of the others, often went home until such time as he felt that he would be led into active combat. It was their opinion that they signed up to fight. From the looks of things, war, in that area at least, was rather remote; a man could do better attending his farm until such time as needed. Again Allison transferred. This time to Company F. But inactivity around Waynesboro did not mean that other parts of Tennessee were not helping the reality of war.

In southeastern Tennessee, between Savanah and Red Sulphur Springs, on the Tennessee river, is the little hamlet of Pittsburg Landing. South was Corinth and Mississippi. West of Pittsburg Landing, on the Corinth Road, was the solitary Shiloh church soon to number with the immortals because of the battle to be fought there. General Johnston had toyed with the idea of taking his weary troops to Corinth in order to feed them. Instead, he lined up Hardy, Bragg and Polk near the Landing. Hardee covered the area from Owl creek to Lick creek. Johnston thought it time to address his troops:

"I have put you in motion to offer battle to the invaders of our country. With the resolution and disciplined valor becoming men fighting, as you are, for all worth living for and dying for, you can but march to a decisive victory over agrarian mercenaries, sent to subjugate and despoil you of your liberties, property, honor. . . . The eyes and hopes of eight million people rest on you. . . . With such incentives to brave deeds and with the trust that God is with us, your generals will lead you confidently to the combat, assured of success."

Sunday, April 6, 1862, Major James E. Powell was out on a reconnaissance at a time when most people were abed—3:00 A. M. B, H, and E Companies preferred to drop where they were instead of the alternative of meandering through the woods that made a dark, moonless night seemingly darker. With little enough rest they were ordered on past the fields of farmers Rhea and Seay, across the soft flowing Shiloh creek, on to the branch of the Corinth road that led beyond the unpretentious little chapel in the wilderness. Suddenly, before the first streak of dawn, the cavalry vedettes fired three shots, wheeled, and back-tracked at a fast gallop. Powell sprang forward and was within ninety yards of the Confederate infantry pickets before they opened on him, then retreated. The Battle of Shiloh was on. Hardee had four brigades in line; Bragg, five; Polk, four in column; Breckenridge followed Polk with three brigades in column. And among all those men somewhere in the fighting was Clay Allison. So said some old timers who knew him in Tennessee. He was tired of waiting for action around Waynesboro, so, on one of his trips home, re-enlisted where he thought there might be some action. There are twenty-three R. Allisons enlisted in the Army of the Tennessee (Confederate). Any number of these might be Robert Clay re-enlisting where he thought there might be action, a practice not uncommon in the early years of the conflict.

The important figure to emerge from the battle—General Grant—was as yet unaware of the encounter. He was busily stacking away his breakfast when Private E. N. Trembly reported firing up the river. That was one breakfast the general never finished. He was not expected to attack until Monday or Tuesday. Hardee had four hundred and twelve officers in the Infantry; five thousand five hundred and thirty-seven men. In the Artillery he counted nineteen officers, three hundred and ninety-five men. The Cavalry boasted fifty-two officers and five hundred and forty-four men. It was with this latter group that Allison was said to have taken part in the Battle of Shiloh.

Hardee's Corps (Third), consisting of three brigades, formed the first line of battle just behind Wood's field and cotton press. Since the three brigades did not fill out all the space desired, Gladden's Brigade from Bragg's Corps was added to the right and placed under orders. The Corps in line of battle had its center on, and perpendicular to, the Pittsburg road, its left near Owl creek, its right across the Bark road in the following order of brigades from left to right: Cleburn's Second Brigade, Wood's Third Brigade, Shaver's First Brigade, and Gladden's Brigade. General T. C. Hindman was entrusted with the command of his own and Wood's Brigade, for this reason he is often referred to as commanding a division. He remained with his own brigade and does not appear to have given orders to Wood. He was disabled about 11:00 a. m. on the 6th, near the northeast corner of the Review field. As it advanced, the Third Corps had a skirmish on Friday in which a few prisoners were taken on both sides. There was another engagement with a picket post near Howell's on Saturday and on Sunday morning the picket of this corps under Major

Hardcastle, stationed at the corner of Fraley's and Wood's fields, was attacked at 4:55 a. m. by a reconnoitering party sent out by General Prentiss. The pickets on both sides exchanged fire for considerably over an hour, the corps meantime forming lines and advancing to drive back the reconnoitering party and following it to the first line of camps where the engagement became general. Hardee moved with the right of his line where General Johnson directed the progress of the battle. Passing the first camps he consulted with Johnston, went to the left, taking general direction on the left flank of the army the remainder of the day. On Monday he was in command of the extreme right of the line. His corps remained intact until about 9 a. m. of the 6th, when his troops intermingled with other troops. With the possible exception of two or three regiments of Cleburne's Brigade, none of his corps were under his command on Sunday after he had moved to the left. Neither of his brigade organizations were under his command on Monday. Hardee commenced the withdrawal of his troops at 1 p. m. that day following orders from General Beauregard.

When the chalking up came at the end of the war, Shiloh proved to be one of the bloodiest battles. It also marked the final resting place of Albert Sidney Johnston, who might have risen to even greater heights for the Confederacy had he lived. Hardee was wounded, as were eight thousand other Confederates; nine hundred and fifty-nine were reported missing. One of these was supposed to have been Robert Clay Allison. Hardee's recruits were mostly from Tennessee. William J. Hardee had been a brilliant military figure for more than twenty years. He had served as a United States representative in Europe in the study of cavalry methods. Once he commanded West Point and was the author of the official textbook on infantry drill and tactics used by both Federal and Confederate Armies. The boys from Tennessee had great confidence in him.

As far as Robert Clay Allison was concerned, Shiloh had little meaning for him. As he rode along the thicket that edged Fraley's field, his horse stumbled, throwing him. Before he could recover either his mount or composure several Yankee soldiers rushed from the thicket to number him among their prisoners. While relations between captors and captured were strained, as would be expected in war time, Allison seemed to fare better than most under the circumstances, and it is known that his guards found him to be a very likable fellow. He joked and told tall tales. He did what he could to cheer up his fellow prisoners. While he won the admiration of the Yankees, prison life did nothing to increase his esteem. He hated Yankees almost to the day of his death and those he didn't hate he tolerated. Parson Tolby, Charles Springer and possibly Oliver P. McMains were to be the few exceptions.

He was conducted along with others to Camp Chase near Columbus, Ohio. Daily rations were scant. There were times when he was assigned to K.P. duty to help ready the fare for his comrades. Camp Chase was not equipped to accommodate the prisoners from Shiloh. This was soon evidenced by riots, bikerings and threats. Allison was among the ring leaders clamoring for better table fare, bedding, less cramped quarters. The officer in charge pleaded in vain that this was a prisoner of war camp not a hotel. Feeling ran high. The rioters refused to acclimatize themselves, if prisoners could do such a thing, and daily it looked as if the camp would become another battle ground, with or without weapons. Finally the commanding officer decided to send a number of the prisoners to Johnson's Island. Here they were less cramped and even pernitted to swim in Sandusky Bay. Ropes marked off the limits for this exercise. After all, the commander reasoned, the men in the compound were Americans—mixed-up Americans—and sought to treat them as such. He permitted fishing in the lakes, walks, and greater liberties than normally found under such circumstances.

Johnson's Island was not much over three acres in length and was entirely occupied by the prison. Escape seemed almost an impossibility, although Allison was to prove it not improbable. The wall surrounding the prison was sixteen feet in height and equipped with sixteen sentinel boxes. A platform ran along the top and outer side of this wall, and on this the sentinels kept their beats, meeting half way between the boxes. On the inside of the enclosure, eight feet from the wall, a chain marked the deadline. At night it was earmarked by lanterns placed upon the supports. The rooms occupied by the prisoners were about twelve feet square, with two tiers of bunks around the walls. Taps were sounded at nine when the sentinel called: "Lights out." All lights were extinguished immediately. Anyone failing to obey this injunction was punished. The prisoners eagerly picked up bits of wood and saved bone from meat, gathered metal and buttons and usually carved some keepsake over and over again, all for the sake of something to do and to keep their minds off their loved ones. Sometimes a card game was started and the keepsakes would change hands often.

Allison made it a point to be seen by the sentries every time he went swimming. Now and then he would duck under water, then bob up again to show the guards that he was still around. Each day he stayed under longer and longer until the sentries became accustomed to his antics. One day he was able to divert the attention of the guard nearest him, and in that split second was able to throw pants, shirt and shoes, which he had bundled together, into the water, diving in after them to hide them with his body. By the time that the sentries awakened to the fact that he had escaped he was already resting in the shrubbery on the opposite shore, again getting into the water and hiding under some water-logged limbs until nightfall when he was certain that the search for him was abandoned. For the next few weeks he traveled by night and hid away during the day. He did the best he could with what he found in fields and on berry bushes. He usually contrived to sleep in hay stacks, in the woods or wherever there was less danger of being discovered. Again he was in Tennessee, among his own.

About thirty miles southeast of Nashville, to the east of present Highway 70, flows Stones river. Here one may see the Stones River National Military Park where the Battle of Murfreesboro was fought. General W. S. Rosecrans, leading the Army of the Cumberland, was in pursuit of Confederate General Bragg. It was General Wheeler who informed the commanding officer on the morning of December 26, 1862, that Rosecrans was on the march. Hardee's Corps was ordered in from Triune and Wheeler was instructed to protect its flank, hinder the Federal advance, and, if hard pressed, to fall back upon the main body of the Confederates hoping to strike in front of Murfreesboro. Hardee's Corps, consisting of the Breckinridge and Cleburne Divisions, with Jackson's Brigade in reserve, composed Bragg's right wing. The right of this wing rested on the Lebanon pike to the north of Murfreesboro; the left on the Nashville road; Polk's men were on Hardee's left. On the night of December 30, Hardee's men were east of Stones river. Wheeler opened the engagement by attacking Starkweather's Brigade. He made a complete circuit of the rear of Rosecrans' men; took and paroled over a thousand prisoners, destroyed over a million dollars worth of stores and left miles of road strewn with burning wagons.

General Bragg had definite plans about ensnaring the Federals. He sought to turn Rosecrans' right by leaving Breckinridge's division to hold the right against Rosencrans' left. Hardee was ordered to march Cleburne's division from the right to the left, take command of that and McCown's division and open the battle at daybreak by an attack upon McCook's right. Hardee's attack was to be followed up by Polk's divisions in succession to the right. On the night of the 30th Hardee led Cleburne's division to the left and placed it to the rear of McCown. At daybreak McCown advanced and fell upon the right of R. W. Johnson's division just as the men were about to sit down to breakfast. The battle raged until January 3rd when a cold and heavy rain storm caused Rosecrans to call a halt because of the rising river. Allison seems to have been in this battle. His was a charmed life. Not a bullet scratched him. Indeed the only wound he was to receive in life came from his own hands.

The year 1863 found him a seasoned veteran. His superiors were pleased with his efforts although he received no promotions. Yet they agreed that he had the qualities of leadership. He said himself later on in life that he was liked by both Confederate and Federal officers whenever in contact with them. General Forrest was particularly fond of him and referred to him as his favorite scout. He does not explain why he never received a promotion, for his daring and courage entitled him for recommendation. It could not have been his drinking, for this was a vice found on both sides from the ranking general down to the menial buck private. It could not have been insubordination, for Forrest and McCullogh both trusted and respected him as a soldier and a gentleman.

One factor may have been his failure to take army life and the war more seriously. He was forever playing pranks on his buddies, refusing to believe that war could change a man into anything other than what he was. Also he was restless. This was looked upon as instability. Army discipline irked him and he sought leaves on the least pretext, or none at all. He was an independent spirit —too independent for his own good. Drilling, forming ranks, keeping horses abreast, saluting, seemed a sham to him. It may have been none of these reasons, but rather his weird reaction under stimulants. Invariably when intoxicated he pulled off his clothes, gave himself an Indian name and insisted that he was an Indian chief. No one could reason with him, and he was ready to fight with knife, gun or fist anyone who would challenge or question his tribal dance, his views on the war, or just merely comment on his antics. It is a mistaken notion to think that Clay Allison was a man of measure only under the influence of liquor. He was to prove later on in New Mexico and Texas the fallacy of this way of thinking.

Next we find him serving under Robert McCullogh of the Chalmer Division of General Forrest's command. As this brigade was not organized until January of 1864 we must accept Allison's word that he served the year before as scout and messenger for General Forrest. No doubt names confused Allison. In a letter to a St. Louis paper, Clay said that he served the last two years of the war as scout under Ben McCullogh and Forrest.

Living in Texas at the time, he could have identified the popular hero with the colonel of the First Brigade without realizing that Ben had been killed by a Yankee sharpshooter on March 7, 1862, long before he scouted for Col. Robert. Besides, he had very little contact with the commanding officer. His immediate superiors were Captain J. J. Guyton and First Lieutenant T. M. Turner. Allison was scout for Captain John T. Chandler in the engagement at West Point, Mississippi, in February, 1864, and under Captain W. J. Vankirk in the encounter at Tom creek on July 14 of that same year. When Allison claimed that he was a friend of Ben McCullough (more popularly spelled McCullogh), almost twenty years had passed since Fort Sumpter, which could help account for the mistake. Bob and Ben could easily have been confused by the editor who printed Allison's letter. Also Allison may merely have written McCullogh (to use the widely accepted spelling) and the editor, acquainted with

the exploits of the more popular Ben, inserted the name.
It is strange that for as close as Allison claimed to have
been to General Forrest, the officer never once mentioned
him in his writings after the war. War records do yield
the name Allison as scout for General Forrest.

Nathan Bedford Forrest of Bedford county, Tennessee, was one of the more popular Confederate generals to emerge from the war a legend. He was forty when the war began. Although a wealthy planter, circumstances compelled him to neglect his own education in order to provide for his brothers and sisters. He enlisted in the cause of the South on June 14, 1861, raising his own regiment shortly afterwards. He served with distinction at Fort Donelson and Shiloh. He received the rank of brigadier general on July 21, 1862. When he captured McMinnville, southeast of Murfreesboro, his force numbered less than a thousand men. At this latter place, he surprised a garrison of two thousand Federals, taking prisoner all the survivors, including General Crittenden. Chickamauga disappointed him to the extent that he tendered his resignation, which was refused. He was promoted to the rank of major general and assigned the command of all the cavalry in West Tennessee and North Mississippi. It was when he decided to march through west Tennessee that he received reinforcements numbering several thousand hardy volunteers. Clay Allison no doubt was among this number. This is not the place to recount the general's exploits, but it does seem likely that Allison was his scout at the time of the so-called Fort Pillow Massacre. The records are not explicit enough for fitting together the complete story.

Forrest was not satisfied with several of his subordinates and appealed to his superior officer (March 4, 1864) for the services of Col. Robert McCullogh and Col. Bell. Forrest had great admiration for the hero of Starkville (Miss., Feb. 23), who refused to go to the rear even though wounded. Col. Jeff E. Forrest, brother to the general, recommended McCullogh for promotion. Allison seems to have been with McCullogh at the time. He had fought in the battle above Senatobia and Okolona. While McCullogh was victorious there was little celebration in camp for Col. Forrest had been killed.

Whether Forrest was aware that Allison was with McCullogh, or was simply looking for any scout to carry a message to Fort Pillow, he was found leaning against a tree singing a song written by A. E. Blackmore of New Orleans. It was written in the first year of the war and gained widespread popularity. Perhaps the victory made him think of it, or even the death of Col. Forrest, who was well known to him.

> Sons of South, awake to glory,
> A thousand voices bid you rise,
> Your children, wives and grandsires hoary,
> Gaze on you now with trusty eyes;
> Your country ev'ry strong arm calling,
> To meet the hireling Northern band
> That comes to desolate the land
> With fire and blood and scene appalling;
> To arms, to arms, ye brave;
> Th' avenging sword unsheath!
> March on! March on!
> All hearts resolved on victory or death.

Whatever the orderly thought as he listened he kept to himself. He informed Allison that General Forrest wished to see him. There were no formalities. They were old friends.

"I want you to carry a message to the commander of Fort Pillow. You will take two other men along with you, and a flag of truce. Keep your eyes open."

Allison was surprised to see so many Negro troops at the post. He had heard that the North was making use of the freed slaves, and that even General Lee recommended the enlistment of Negroes. He was to see such troops for the rest of his life in Kansas, New Mexico and on the Sweetwater at Mobeetie in Texas. Major Booth opened the message:

"I have force sufficient to take your works by assault. I therefore demand an unconditional surrender of all your forces. Your heroic defense will entitle you to be treated as prisoners of war, but the surrender must be unconditional. I await your answer."

The major rubbed his chin a moment, glanced into space, picked up his pen and wrote: "Your demand for the surrender of United States forces under my command is received. I ask for one hour for consultation with my officers and the commander of Gunboat No. 7 at this place."

Forrest was mad, raving mad. Allison thought the clenched fist would be used on him and wondered if he would strike back even if it meant court martial. These temperamental generals and their wars! He threw over a chair, uttered an oath, called the Yankee major a fool, thumped into a seat, and wrote:

"I do not demand the surrender of Gunboat No. 7. I only ask the surrender of Fort Pillow, with men and munitions of war. You have twenty minutes for consideration; at the expiration of that time if you do not capitulate, I will assault your works."

"Get this back to Major Booth immediately."

The major looked at Allison, his only comment being, "What, you again."

Again he sat down to pen an answer: "Your second demand for the surrender of my forces received. The demand will not be complied with. I will not surrender."

Forrest crumbled the answer, throwing it on the floor. He thanked Allison and dismissed him. This Robert Clay Allison must not be confused with J. D. Allison who served as escort to Forrest from July 1, 1864, to February 28, 1865. There was no time for rest. The march for the capture of the fort was begun before he had time to report to his immediate officer. McCullogh's Brigade occupied the left extending from the center, to the river. Bill's Brigade occupied the right. McCullogh's Brigade commanded the advance, surprised the enemy picket, capturing four of them. The Confederates then marched down the Fulton road to Gaines' farm, thence north to the post on a road running parallel with the Mississippi; then moved up the left. This is what Forrest said in his official report:

"Arrived on the morning of the 12th and attacked the place with a portion of McCullogh's and Bell's Brigades numbering about 1,500 men and after a sharp contest captured the garrison and its stores. A demand was made for the surrender, which was refused. The victory was complete and the loss of the enemy will never be known from the fact that large numbers ran into the river and were shot and drowned. The force was composed of about five hundred negroes and two hundred white soldiers (Tennessee Tories). The river was dyed with blood of the slaughtered for two hundred yards. There was in the fort a large number of citizens who had fled there to escape the conscript law. Most of these ran into the river and were drowned. The approximate loss was upward of five hundred killed, but few of the officers escaping. It is hoped that these facts will demonstrate to the Northern people that the negro soldiers cannot cope with the Southerners. We still hold the fort."

When news of the encounter at Fort Pillow reached the Northern press, the editors vied with each other in calling Forrest a butcher, savage, blood-thirsty pirate, and the like. Even the South was alarmed. The Confederate Senate demanded an investigation. The Federal officers testified that they thought they were accorded gentlemanly treatment under the circumstances. The investigation on the part of the South ended with a vote of thanks to Forrest and his men for their work in the

Mississippi, west Tennessee and Kentucky campaign. President Jefferson Davis wrote General L. Polk, asking him to call in Forrest or to get from him exactly what took place. Forrest wrote from Jackson, Tennessee, April 15:

"I attacked Fort Pillow on the morning of the 12th, inst. with a part of Bell's and McCullogh's Brigades, numbering 1,500, under Brig. Gen. James R. Chalmers. After a short fight, drove the enemy, seven hundred strong, into the fort under the cover of their gun-boats. Demanded a surrender, which was declined by Major L. F. Booth, commanding United States forces. I stormed the fort and after a contest of thirty minutes captured the entire garrison, killing five hundred and taking two hundred horses and a large amount of quartermaster's stores. The officers in the fort were killed, including Major Booth. I sustained a loss of twenty killed and sixty wounded. Among the wounded is the gallant Lt. Col. Wiley M. Reed, while leading the 5th Mississippi. Over one hundred citizens who had fled the fort to escape conscription ran to the river and were drowned. The Confederate flag now waves over the fort. N. B. Forrest —Major General."

Whenever an article on Clay Allison is written the story makes the rounds of a daring deed. Nobody knows where it originated; no one quotes the source. Actually, Allison told it to Howard, Curtis and other cowboys working for him in New Mexico. Mrs. Coleman, Clay's sister, may have been the one passing it on to Hunt and Clark. Once, when on an important mission for General Forrest, he found it expedient to don a Federal uniform. Slipping by the outposts he mingled with the Union soldiers. His Tennessee twang would hardly betray him since there were about as many soldiers from that State fighting for the North as for the South. Nobody questioned him. A question here, a mental note there, he was ready to return to Forrest with the information. Boldly he walked to the picket. Challenged for the password, he realized it was the one important thing he overlooked. The guard, suspicious of a soldier attempting to leave camp at night, and suspecting Clay sought to desert, arrested him. Searched, papers and maps were found in his shoes. He was court martialed and condemned as a spy. The sentence: death. The firing squad would be ready at dawn of the morrow.

Perhaps there were other spies in the ranks. He killed the guard, broke jail and made his escape. All this could hardly have been accomplished without accomplices. Nor could the man he killed have been shot. The sound would have aroused the camp. Allison was an expert with the knife. One could have easily been slipped to him. Later on, a prosecuting attorney is to bring before the attention of the court Allison's deadly accuracy with a bowie knife. Had Allison been confined in a jail rather than consigned to a guard his story would have ended at dawn before the firing squad. He continued as a scout for the duration. General Forrest disbanded his men at Gainesville, Alabama, May 9, 1865. He addressed the assembled troops:

"Soldiers: By an agreement made between Lt. Gen. Taylor, commanding the Department of Alabama, Mississippi and East Louisiana, and Major General Canby (known to New Mexicans for his part in the Battle of Valverde), commanding the United States forces, the troops of this Department have been surrendered. I do not think it proper or necessary at this time to refer to the causes which have reduced us to this extremity; nor is it a matter of material consequence to us how such results were brought about. That we are beaten is a self-evident fact, and any further resistance on our part would be justy regarded as the very height of folly and rashness. The armies of Generals Lee and Johnston having surrendered, you are the last of all the troops of the Confederate States Army east of the Mississippi river to lay down your arms. The cause for which you have so long and so manfully struggled and for which you have braved dangers, endured privations and sufferings and have made so many sacrifices, is today hopeless. The government which we sought to establish and perpetuate, is at an end. Reason dictates, and humanity demands, that no more blood be shed. Fully realizing and feeling that such is the case it is your duty and mine to lay down our arms—submit to the powers that be and aid in restoring peace and order throughout the land. The terms upon which you were surrendered are favorable, and should be satisfactory and acceptable to all. When you return home, a manly straightforward course of conduct will secure the respect of even your enemies . . .''

Everybody was aware of the inference. Lincoln was no longer the man of the hour. Johnson, forever brooding over his humble origin, was President. Stanton still believed that the entire South, not Booth, was responsible for that eventful night of April 14, at the Ford Theatre in Washington. Here at camp talk was of Paine, Herold, Atzerodt, Mrs. Surratt, Dr. Mudd, O'Laughlin, Arnold, Spangler, and others evidently in the pay of the Confederacy. Allison couldn't believe that the North would hang a woman. When Mrs. Surratt met her end on the gallows, it did nothing to increase his respect for the Bluecoats. Rancor was rampant.

Again Clay Allison was in Wayne county, Tennessee. Was he the Allison who turned guerrilla to make night raids on Yankee sympathizers? Was he the Allison sought by both North and South alike? He was accused of being the one but the accusation has never been substantiated. Relatives are of the opinion that it was the Baxter Allison rather than Clay. More of this later.

Hemmed in by the serried battalions of the Blues; stymied by the blockade, a number of officials at Richmond were quick to grasp the meaning of the handwriting on the wall. Enthusiasm and confidence failed to change the facts. Men and a cause were not the only things lost in the South. It was estimated that the advance of the Union Army caused two and a half million bales of cotton to be put to the torch. Many planters abandoned cotton in favor of foodstuffs, causing many to advance the argument that large amounts of grain and corn served to encourage the use of alcoholic beverages and the price of whisky rose to five times that of 1861. During the war the Confederate Congress insisted that soldiers in the field be issued whisky only in cases of battle fatigue and exposure. General Johnson did not hold with Congress. He ordered a regular issue for the Army of Tennessee despite the opposition of many who disagreed with him.

Allison seemed to be well supplied, usually winning another's share as the result of a game of cards, or a wrestling match. The discussion regarding this commodity became so heated that the Southern army and navy set up their own distilleries to avoid haggling with the civilian. Before Lee's surrender whisky was selling for one hundred dollars a gallon and four dollars a shot in many places in Tennessee. Many saloons did business as cafes and grocery stores. When blockade runners failed willing merchants in the North stood ready to ship to the enemy at a price.

People refused to live on their farms, swelling the already overburdened cities. Somehow, Mrs. Allison managed to survive these tragic years without apparent difficulties. She was able to manage a little garden each year, the younger children now grown enough to take on the chores. It is possible that John, Munroe and the other boys saw some service before the war was over. But the girls were there to help. It was suggested that Mrs. Allison's parlor was a classroom for the neighboring children during those years. It was also a place where women contributed money, jewelry, prepared bandages, carded lint, aided in relief work. Peace societies held secret ritualistic meetings almost within sight of the

Allison home because members believed that peace was the answer to starvation. There was even talk that the high and the mighty around Waynesboro and other towns were no better than they were for all were born equal. The day of the squire, country gentleman, rich planter was doomed.

When, on March 13, 1865, the Confederacy authorized the employment in military service of three hundred thousand former slaves, many shook their heads and agreed that it was now just a question of time. Southerners also realized that they had still to assume their proportionate share of the Federal war debt, which eventually proved three times the amount of the North.

Allison was not alone when he mourned that righteousness had fallen before strength. He noticed the ravished fields as he made his way home—smoking homes, ruined towns. Then there was the carpet-bagger who never lost an opportunity to remind one who had won the war. It would be long before the South would lift its head above the ruins. Poverty was rampant. Slaves were no longer property. Insurance companies were as dead as slavery. Men like Clay Allison saw little prospect for the future. Violence and terrorism continued because they argued that the war was over and there was no need for the Federals to remain. Many moved westward for a new lease on life but mostly to get away from the hated Northerners who showed no signs of leaving the Volunteer State and doubled their impudence since the assassination of Lincoln. Union soldiers supported the negro, supplying rations in an effort to start him on his new career of citizen farmer. Carpet-baggers did little to help. They painted rosy pictures for the former slaves, many of whom mistook freedom for license. While the Emancipation Proclamation was pronounced in 1863 it was not until February 25, 1865, that Tennessee enacted an amendment to the State Constitution freeing slaves, which did little to alleviate the state of confusion. Clay

Allison came back to a changing world. Unable to adjust himself there was the escape into the wilderness to new horizons, practically untouched by the war. Compared to Tennessee, Virginia, Pennsylvania and Maryland, Texas, Colorado, New Mexico and Arizona got off very lightly. Here the cattle industry and the advance of the railroad were to help many a Southerner on the road back to peace and prosperity; to dim the scenes of poverty, hate and slaughter.

Fatigued, bitter, irritable, undernourished, the sight of the detested Union uniform riding the length and breadth of Wayne county ostensibly for the protection of the freed slaves and carpet-baggers but actually bent on plunder, debauchery and suppression. No wonder Wayne county officials tossed records into the fire. Also men return from wars with itchy feet. A glance at statistics following World War I and World War II make this clear. Nerves on edge, they feel out of adjustment and want to be on the move. Any mother is willing to agree that the son who returned is hardly the son who left.

There is a story told that Clay Allison killed one of these plunderers who broke Mother Allison's best pitcher despite her pleas. To escape capture he went to Indian Territory (present Oklahoma) and then to Texas. The killing may have taken place, an occurrence not unusual after Tennessee established the Freedman's Bureau, but it hardly would have precipitated Allison's flight. The incident had to take place some time before 1864, the year of Mrs. Allison's death. He was rather the type to lie in hiding to make sure no member of his family suffered in retaliation. He left Tennessee simply because that is what most young men of his age were doing. The West beckoned. There a man could take a new lease on life. Clay had decided long before the war that his future was off in the direction of the setting sun. This was the time to make the move.

Chapter Three

THE BRAZOS COUNTRY

The Brazos is a storied river from its extreme source high up in northern New Mexico to its meandering down course through the plains country of Texas. There the ancient Caddoan tribe knew it as Toko-no-ho-no; LaSalle, the Frenchman, gave it the undignified name of Maligne; Domingo Ramon, with the piety becoming his race, called it Santisima Trinidad; equally pious Spaniards insisted that it was Los Brazos de Dios; realistic, mono-tongued Americans referred to the stream as the Brazos. The river could tell you things. Here the story of the Republic of Texas begins. Wealthy cotton and sugar planters built stately mansions that looked like picture cards and people paddled their canoes up and down the stream just to see these beautiful plantations. Up in the northern part, where there were plains, forts, soldiers, Indians and traders—this was the real Brazos country as the cowboy was to know it. Here rancheros were to surplant the cotton and sugar ricos of the down stream settlements. Here cow men were beginning to operate large scale ranges known as spreads. This was the country Clay Allison heard so much about before the war. Here were his dreams of empire; here his visions of splendor under the high, wide, blue sky gave him the zest for life and took the sharp edge off a defeat he imagined could never be lived down. Also, it was like coming home. Every other man seemed to be from Tennessee. All the time these Tennessee pioneers were unconsciously moulding themselves into a breed apart—the American cowboy. Ever since the Spaniards first laid eyes on the Brazos country they recognized it as a paradise for cattle; this valley with its grass and moisture; its rich bottom lands; its flowing river. Branding irons rusted here long before the first settler from Tennessee ever heard the name. Authors vary in their explanations as to how cowboys came into being. Let us say they just evolved. Drawn to cattle like a moth to a flame, they contributed to the American scene like the Mountain Man, the Frontiersman, the Squatter.

Old Shap Ross was shrewd enough to recognize this. He bought five hundred head of cattle in the Brazos country, paying thirteen dollars a head for them, drove them to Missouri, where he sold them at a profit of seven thousand dollars. News like this needed no telegraph. All these Tennessee boys in the Brazos country wrote home. At dances, in hotel lobbies, at trading posts, on the farm, in the home, the talk was divided between further insults perpetrated by those "Damn Yankees" and the lush, profitable cattle country along the Brazos. Mind you, no fences to bother with; no one to ask where you were last night; no permissions to leave one spot for another. Here a man was as free as the flowing river. Yep, the Brazos country. That's where I'd go if'n I were free.

The ground was level. You just followed it to get away from the settlements. You gave Indians a wide berth whenever possible, and it was very possible in the Brazos country. Pasture the herd wherever the grass was shoulder high, ford rivers, keep the herd moving along a given trail, take all the time in the world, in the end you would find a market. Then you returned and started all over again. Fine. If you had no cattle to sell you still had your dreams.

This was cattle country time out of mind. In the days when the Mexican flag flew over Texas and border patrols survived in name rather than action, European breeds of cattle were driven to pasture where they mated with the rangy Mexican type to produce the romanticized, famous longhorn breed. Pioneers in this field were Joseph Abner and Robert Kuykendall, who brought their cattle in from along the Sabine to the Brazos in 1821. Then followed Dan Shipmar, Allen, Pool, Caulfield. Soon the Brazos country was dotted with dugouts, ranges, spreads. Mexican loyalists left many cattle to their fate following the engagement at San Jacinto, so that when the Lone Star replaced the Eagle, one hundred thousand cattle roamed the Brazos country. Brazos cowmen went on hunting expeditions rounding up these strays to augment their own herds, so that stock raising was an infant industry even before the Civil War.

During the war the cattle took care of themselves due to shortage of man power. The round-up boys were with Hood, Sibley, Baylor, Green, McCullogh and others stirring up events that would eventually open up this vast open range to industry. Henry Caulfield rounded up cattle, drove them overland to Louisiana, where he sold them "on the hoof" to the quartermaster of the Confederate Army. The boys in the ranks heard of this, storing it away in the corner reserved for after-the-war activity. They returned to their dilapidated huts, but the ranges were bursting at the seams. The boys were not as bad off as others. They would take up where they left off and drive the cattle to the Ohio and California markets. The gold fields were still operating on the West Coast. It would be a fair exchange—beef for gold. You see, the boys had come home to a million cattle.

Tennessee gave more than its quota of settlers to the Brazos country. The prospect of becoming ranchers appealed to Clay Allison, two brothers and brother-in-law Coleman. In the fall of 1865 Clay and Coleman left Tennessee, never to return. John and Munroe returned after the Washita-Gageby experiment in the Texas Panhandle.

They were farmers, not cattlemen. If Clay stopped to spend some time in the Nations Territory, where he was to have his fight with the ferryman, there is no record of it. It may have happened, but there is no reference made to it at anytime during Clay's lifetime.

One thing about a pioneer: by choice or circumstance he manages without the comforts of home. Mother Allison would have been horrified at what her boys called home. It was built of logs, the roof covered with brush and sod. The windows and doors were covered with stout timbers which could be barred from within when hostile Indians put in an appearance. Buffalo hides covered chair bottoms and table tops. The cabin was fourteen by fourteen. Cornbread, salt pork, molasses and dried fruits made up the diet. Flour bread or biscuits—these were luxuries reserved for Sunday, or guests. Molasses shipped from Louisiana was used to sweeten coffee. There were times when Mrs. Coleman used it to make cakes and pies but it was more often used to spread over bread and butter. If the men brought in rabbit, quail or fish this was skewered—stripped of skin, entrails, head and feet, washed clean, salted, then impaled on a sharpened stick, held over glowing coals until cooked on one side, which was picked and eaten. The raw side was then placed over the coals and the process repeated. Bread, when it was baked, was made in a Dutch oven. This was a flat-bottomed cast iron vessel whose lid had a rim around it to keep coals spread over its surface from falling off. Bread dough was treated with baking powder and left for fifteen minutes. Sometimes the meals varied —corn pone, turnip greens, buttermilk or a soup made of boiled turnip greens and salted pork. Shoes were made at home and known as brogans.

The roster of the original cowhands making the trip to Colorado with Charles Goodnight is lost. Howard, and several others who worked for Allison later on, were of the opinion that Clay was with Goodnight on that all-important cattle drive. As Goodnight sold some stock to L. B. Maxwell it is possible that Allison first saw the Cimarron country on this trip. He was not a stranger to this country when he came in with the Dalton herd and with his brother-in-law's herd. The fact that Allison knew practically all the boys who rode with Goodnight on that first trip would seem to indicate that he had worked with them. We will know for sure if, and when, the list of the cowboys who first signed up with Charles Goodnight is ever found. That same year of 1866 Allison came to New Mexico with another outfit. One of the cowmen to move from Tennessee to Texas was M. L. Dalton. He married a girl from Kentucky and started a ranch in Palo Duro county east of the Brazos. He was looking for cowboys to trail a herd of eight hundred longhorns to New Mexico. Clay, never idling the dream of one day becoming a cattleman in his own right, hired himself to Dalton. At Las Vegas he had his picture taken. This is the only known photograph of Allison in existence. The legend reads: Clay Allison—Age 26. Las Vegas, N. M. Allison gave it to Hunt in the Vermejo country. Hunt gave it to Whitman, who gave it to his daughter, Mrs. Mary Lail. Fred Lambert borrowed it for the Rose Collection, although it made its first appearance in any book in one entitled *One Half Mile from Heaven, the Cimarron Story*, several years before the Rose book made history.

Again, one of the buyers was Lucien B. Maxwell, interested in maintaining his beef contracts at Fort Sumner, Fort Union, Las Vegas, Albuquerque, and other military posts. Books have emphasized the Kansas markets but Loving, Goodnight, Dalton, Crawford, Curtis, Rivers, Lacy, Coleman and others trailed herds to New Mexico, Colorado, Utah, Nevada, Arizona, California, before railheads made Kansas the popular resort of the stockman. There were several reasons for moving herds into New Mexico. Maxwell's herds were not sufficient to meet the demand that resulted from peace treaties with the Navajos and Apaches, to supply the large reservation at the Bosque Redondo, to keep up with the hungry soldiers at the new posts General Carleton opened up, for in addition to Fort Union, Fort Lyons, Fort Craig, there was Fort Selden, Fort Bascom, Fort Cummings, and others spread into Arizona. While Goodnight, Loving, Dalton and others of lesser note were not interested in selling direct to the government because of the competition of bids, they did sell to Brown, Manzanares, Blanchard, Owens, Maxwell, Chisum, Sellar, Cuellar, McIntyre and others from El Paso to Trinidad, who were interested in obtaining the government beef contracts. Prospectors were beginning to take more than a casual interest in New Mexico. Gold camps were to be an added inducement for trailing herds up from the Brazos country. It has always been a source of wonder why none of the Allisons availed themselves of the opportunity for prospecting, especially when they lived in the mining region near the Red river. Gold in the ground had no attraction for Clay Allison. Gold on the hoof in the form of longhorns held greater appeal.

Santa Fe was the terminus of the old Santa Fe Trail, the Chihuahua Trail, the Los Angeles-Santa Fe Trail, the San Antonio-El Paso Trail, as well as all the trade from Taos, Fort Union, Denver and points north. Whatever Dodge, Abilene, Caldwell, Wichita were to become, Santa Fe was all that before and more. Fandangos, gambling, cantinas, brawls, shootings, fiestas, processions, colorful pageantry, the admixture of the Spanish culture with the lack of culture of the muleteer, the bushwhacker, the fur trapper, and the flow of humanity that followed the Santa Fe Trail to the ancient capital eliminated the need of a chamber of commerce to advertise the city. The cowboy spent his money here with as much zest and youthful fling as in Kansas a few years later. No matter how grimy and dirty he was along the trail, he spruced up for his entrada into Santa Fe, where he found the cyprian, the gambler, the cantina all happy to relieve him of his hard-earned wages. In the evening there was the fandango. And who could resist those dark-eyed, olive-complexioned, loosely dressed senoritas? The laughter of their eyes, the softness of their language, the gaiety of their constant chatter, the whirl of their dance. All this was a new experience for the cowboys. Even during off moments in the war they had never experienced the like. Many returned to marry and settle down to the manana way of life. These were happy moments for Clay. He danced, visited cantinas, and fought, too. Not with the natives over the way their muchachas lost their heads and hearts to the wild youths from Texas, but with the boys in blue from Fort Marcy and Fort Union. The least provocation brought the late war into focus again and the Grants and the Lees engaged in battle.

Allison was a jovial fellow. Pay in pocket, he resolved to keep it there. Some day he would trail his own herd of longhorns. After Dalton had paid off the men he was still richer by sixteen thousand dollars. Eight hundred head of steers were involved in the transaction. Here was more money than he had ever seen in his life. Coleman, his brother-in-law, was also aware of the wealth that passed hands at the end of the trail and resolved to enter partnership with Lacy for a spread on the Brazos. John Allison was also with Clay and Coleman on this trip. They entered the Exchange Hotel bar for a drink. After a few rounds some soldiers from Fort Marcy came in, checking their guns with the clerk according to the law. Clay stiffened as he watched the uniformed men line up at the bar. He asked them to leave. The men replied they had as much right to be there as he did. To which Clay retaliated that they were mistaken since they were Damn Yankees they were not permitted to drink at the same bar with Southerners. Other cowboys in the room lined up behind Clay. Now this was fun.

"John," whispered Coleman, "run out and find Dalton. We want no trouble with the Army right now."

One soldier, bolder than the rest, stepped up to the bar and picked up his drink. Allison knocked the glass from his hand.

"I said Damn Yankees and Southerners do not drink together in the same room."

The soldier looked at Allison a moment, turned to the bartender and said in a quiet, polite tone:

"Fill up another glass, please."

The bartender hesitated.

"We want no trouble. Why not go to Burro Alley. Plenty of drinks and fights there. Bad for business here." He sounded as if his talk was useless but he was giving it a try.

Just then John and Dalton entered the room. The stockman spoke to Clay. He enjoyed a good fight as well as the next, but the Exchange was not the place. He regretted that Fort Macy would stand behind the boys in uniform, so that the handful of cowboys did not stand a chance. Some other time, perhaps, the odds would be more even. For the present they would continue their drinks elsewhere. The cowboys were disappointed but recognized the wisdom of his words. There would always be another time. The bartender sighed his relief.

The first time Clay Allison saw the Rayado and Cimarron country he liked it. Lucien B. Maxwell and Kit Carson impressed him. Maxwell more so because he was a land baron. As Allison could not decide whether he was a Northerner or Southerner, he gave him the benefit of the doubt, especially because everything about him marked him for a Southern gentleman. This was the country for him. Some day his cattle would roam these ranges and his home would be as spacious and pretentious as Maxwell's. But by the time Allison saw the fruitification of his dream the panorama changed. The bed of Willow creek contained gold. The influx of the prospector sent Maxwell searching for a buyer and the great land baron made a fresh start at Fort Sumner. Soldiers at Fort Union, spurred on by General Carleton who sought to eliminate discontent in the ranks, never gave up hope that the surrounding hills were all hidden gold mines. Whenever they were not on duty they were out prospecting. Even when building the road to the Raton Pass they kept their eyes glued on every upturned stone. Maxwell's protests availed nothing. While the discovery of gold annoyed Maxwell to the extent that he sold out, but did aid the cowman for it opened up new markets—Baldy, Willow Creek, Virginia City, Prairieville, Elizabethtown—and a host of other camps whose names are barely recalled. These roaring, lawless camps beside which Dodge, Caldwell and Wichita were to be tame, made life possible for men like Chisum, who recognized the advantage of moving into New Mexico, to raise cattle because pounds counted when it came time for the sale. Each steer lost pounds of good beef along the trail. With a ready market practically in the back yard the additional pounds meant additional income.

All the time the railroad was moving closer and closer to New Mexico. The cowmen from the Brazos country watched its progress. Not to be outdone, Kansas put in its bid for some of the coin exchanging hands by opening stockyards at the railheads. This was an opportunity for the stockman. Rather than trail herd up to Colorado, New Mexico and other points he merely hit for the nearest railhead, found a buyer, and was on his way back to prepare the next herd. Nevertheless, the life of a cowman in the Brazos country in those early days was not as easy and soft as merely rounding up steers for the market. The war years had left the cattle very much on their own. Herds increased. Unbranded cattle swelled the ranches, causing womenfolk some anxiety, for herds had to be grazed in new pastures, mavericks had to be branded.

The dust of the pre-war round-ups had long since settled on the land. Many of the honorable men gave the best years of their lives to the Confederacy. To many of the unhonorable in the wake of the mavericks—collecting, branding, or changing brands, running off stock to Fort Sumner, Fort Bascom, Fort Union, where unscrupulous "cattle buyers" paid a price, no questions asked. Often Comancheros were the "go-betweens." Easy money. Also dirty money. Not the kind a man like Clay Allison could, or would, stomach. Rustlers were a breed apart. There are those who claim that in those days when he called the Brazos country his home he was not above taking steers, mules and horses that were not his own to be sold in parts unknown, wherever he could command a good price. Out of battles with pursuing posses grew his reputation as a gun fighter. No recognized authority classifies Clay Allison as a gun fighter. Actually, he became a stockman with the ability to kill, which is a little different than saying that he killed for the sake of killing.

What with mavericks running all over the country and rustlers on the prowl, men like Goodnight, Dalton, Loving and others were forced to take the law into their own hands. A stockman might gather, drive and sell his neighbor's stock with the understanding that the neighbor was to accept in payment strays found roaming his range. On a given day each year they met to balance the books. Rustlers were especially partial to this practice because it legalized a system which offered opportunity to impound strays, sell them to willing buyers, then make tracks before the victimized ranchers discovered the loss. Naturally, many without a steer to begin with swapped at a terrific profit. Because they were victimized, not a few of the cowmen stooped to this practice. Furthermore, cattlemen knowing they were disfranchized owing to the stand of the State during the late rebellion, were not surprised when carpet-baggers sought to control their affairs. Allison already at odds with them in Tennessee gave vent to his feelings in extra work and often in extra drink. He refused to recognize his as a lost cause laying all the blame for the trouble caused by the carpet-bagger at the door of the "Damn Yankees." Actually, simply because the opportunity presented itself they saw reason why they should not avail themselves of the profits derived from the Tallying Law. The millions of cattle in the Brazos country were not all on their own ranges when North and South came to terms at Appomattox. Animals also want attention. In quest of it they often strayed miles from the home range. The Tallying Law favored anyone who rode these ranges to round up the roving steers. Thus enriched the animals were headed to a Tallying center where an inspector (a carpet-bagger or a friend of his) would oblige by miscalling marks and brands in the expectation of a remuneration. He then took his tally to be recorded at the county courthouse. Sometimes the "pay off" party made it rough for him. He would move the cattle out of reach of both carpet-bagger and cowman, promise the county clerk that they would be paid for from the proceeds of the sale, then disappear. As the real owner would never show up to claim his stock, some people were amassing riches at the expense of the stockman. Nor were they above burning down courthouses in an effort to wipe out any trace of recorded tallies.

Coleman and Lacy would hardly have resorted to such practices as ranchers if they expected the Allisons to work for them. Honesty was a trait they carried with them to the grave. Possibly they got their start as so many did by maverick hunting. This was a legal way of starting a herd without resorting to rustling or tallying. Cowboys rounded up unbranded strays in the brakes, the timberland, the bosque where they made their homes much like wild horses. Indeed, many of the steers proved recalcitrant and dangerous. Their horns were often covered with moss so long were they away from the sight of man. Building up a ranch with this type of cattle was to a man's praise rather than denunciation.

If Indians proved a menace to the cowman before the war, they were doubly so after peace was declared. The conflict itself was beyond their comprehension. They hoped that the white man would fight to extinction so they could re-claim the country for themselves and live the lives they knew prior to the advent of the settlers. They looked upon the returned soldier as too weak to give him battle. Also, Comancheros told them that the Texans lost the war and were under subjugation. Comanches, Kiowas and Apaches raided and plundered as never before in frontier history. The Indians had no particuar use for cattle, especially since bison still roamed the range. But they were interested in firearms, ammunition, Taos lightning, lead, paint, beads, knives, axes, cloth, wines and bread. These could be obtained from Comancheros, wiley New Mexican traders who knew how to pack a burro or a carreta and to return with stolen cattle. These traders met on the Llano Stacado, giving over their supplies for the cattle. The Indians could have killed them, taken the goods without giving up the stolen steers but they would only cut off their supply line in so doing, for an Indian valued a gun, a jug of firewater and a knife.

Granted that the ranchers of the Brazos country missed numerous cattle because of the Comancheros, this did not rile them half as much as the raids on their remudas. The Comanches stole cattle for an ulterior purpose; the horses they took for themselves. It belittled an Indian in the tribe to have few horses. His standing and wealth was computed according to the number of horses he owned. Not simply any horse. The poorer animals were turned over in trade to the Comancheros. In the three years following the Civil War over one hundred thousand horses found ther way into New Mexico through the Comanchero trade. As careful as men like Coleman and Allison were to protect their stock from the Indians, the marauders always managed to pick the right moment for their raids.

This is about as good a place as any to fit in the legend of Clay's fight in the grave with a man by the name of Johnson. It was because he killed Johnson that he was supposed to have come to New Mexico. Some authors place the incident in the Texas Panhandle. How vividly they portray every grunt and groan, every twist and turn that passed between the two contestants. Granting the incident took place, the only witness was Allison and he never mentioned it. The prosecuting attorney, who did everything he could to blacken and smear Allison when he was on trial for murder following the deaths of Cardenas and Vega, never once made reference to the fight to the death in a grave. He was not the type to by-pass anything that contained a grain of truth, or a breath of rumor. This can only mean that either the attorney recognized it for what it was—a legend—or the story was not circulating at the time.

Allison was chagrined at a neighbor named Johnson, who over-stepped frontier courtesy by seeking to keep Clay from using a water hole which he claimed was on his property. Clay begged to differ. One thing led to another and the two decided to settle the matter once and for all by digging a grave. They were to enter the pit armed only with bowie knives. The winner buried the victim and kept the water hole. Allison buried Johnson. But he had to flee to New Mexico for fear of reprisals from Johnson's friends and relatives. Not because of the law, mind you, but because of others. Taken at its surface value it makes Allison to be a very stupid man indeed, to deliberately and carefully plan a rather unique way of settling an argument without weighing the consequences, also at a time when it was known that Allison had no property in the Brazos country. If the incident took place in the Texas Panhandle as some authors say,

Captain Arrington, always ready to clamp Allison behind bars, must have been asleep on the job.

Another incident about this time was the ferry-crossing fight also placed at various points according to the author you are reading. Some place it at Red river; others the Cimarron, and still others the Nations Territory. All are sure not to pin point the exact location. Two cautious writers get around it by saying—"History does not record the particular fork or the exact location . . ." The name of the ferryman was Frank Tolbert, a rather tough hombre, who resented Allison's haughty manner in demanding to be ferried across the stream. An argument ensued, during which the two resorted to bowie knives. Wiley, cagey, lithe Clay against chuky, broad-shouldered, bull-necked Tolbert. The fight was sharp and furious. Round and round the boat they stalked until grappling in an arm lock they fell into the river where Clay made fast work of his opponent. Then he is off to the Brazos country. An expert with the bowie as Allison was he took a long time to dispatch his enemy. Chunk Tolbert, a nephew, comes storming in later on when Clay is at the Clifton House in New Mexico to avenge his uncle.

Actually the name of the ferryman was Zach Colbert, nor was he killed by Allison. Perhaps the cool dip sobered their tempers. While the cattle industry is brought into focus because of the activities of Loving, Goodnight, Dalton and others in 1866, Brazos country cowmen were using other trails. The very year Goodnight started his drive, 260,000 head of cattle crossed the Red river into Nations Territory and while unprofitable it did prove that others were at work. It also brought about the development of four other cattle trails: The East Shawnee, West Shawnee, Chisholm and the Doan's Crossing. One and a half miles upstream from the present Denison bridge where it spans the Red river to connect Texas with Oklahoma, Colbert worked his ferry. Colbert is an old name in Okahoma, dating back several decades prior to the Civil War. This particular Colbert obtained authorization from the Chickasaw Nation to establish a ferry on the basis of a yearly fee. He was a trader who recognized profit as pouring into the post of Fort Preston, just east of where he was to put up his own trading post and ferry. (Preston, Texas, was submerged in 1940 when Lake Texoma was created, the rural delivery going to Pottsboro, a hamlet with a population of twenty). The village of Colbert (population 612) on the M.K.&T. Railroad was named for Colbert, who, like Chisholm, seems to have had some Cherokee blood. The fact that Colbert's Toll Bridge was built in 1874 proves that Clay Allison did not kill him, for the fight is said to have taken place sometime in 1866, possibly when Clay was on his way down to the Brazos country. The present Denison Bridge stands within sight of the old Colbert Crossing. Allison himself made no reference to the fight, but all authors from Otero down do. Since Otero was a personal friend of Allison's it is possible that the former governor of New Mexico got the story from his friend.

Whatever his exploits Clay's thin butternut jeans polished the saddle. When not riding herd for Goodnight, Loving, Dalton, Lacy or Coleman, there was always the round-up, branding, mavericks, the chase after Indians, rustlers, tally dodgers. All the while events were stirring that would have a direct bearing on his life.

Will Suggs drove a herd of cattle from the Brazos country to Illinois, selling them to Joseph McCoy of McCoy, McCord and Chandler. "Plenty more where these came from," suggested Suggs, who told McCoy to go to the Brazos country to see for himself. The cattle buyer looked up J. J. Meyes of Lockhart, Texas, at that time in the sorting yards near the McCoy firm in Illinois. Lockhart had been with Col. Fremont and knew the Kansas country. McCoy asked him whether it wouldn't be better to trail herds through this country to the railroad in order to keep poundage on steers than to drive them all the way to Illinois. He was a firebrand. He haunted every cattle buyer's office, looked up all stockmen he knew, visited every railroad yard from Illinois to Kansas, spoke to every mayor and official along the right of way. Salina and Solomon gave him the cold shoulder. Abilene, an out-of-the-way place of a half dozen log huts, listened. A thirty-five thousand dollar handshake and yards, pens, spurs, buildings crowded out the huts.

Suggs, wideyed at the daring plan, dashed back to the Brazos country. He was the Paul Revere of the cattle man. "Round them up, the railroads are coming." Old man Thompson was one jump ahead. He already had an inkling of what was going on and before the rumor was too widespread he had a herd on the road. Taking his course by the North Star at night he lay his wagon tongue on it and settled down for a hard day's drive. He met Smith, McCord and Chandler at the outskirts of Abilene. He holds the distinction of herding the first Texas steers through the streets of the city. Bewildered longhorns overran the place, sending people scuffling back into doorways, much to the amusement of the cowboys who were soon crowding the saloons to use their new pay in making up for the long dry spell of the trail. Thompson was a very happy man. His profit was greater than if he had driven to New Mexico or Nations Territory. Wilson & Hicks came up from the Brazos country with the next herd. Thirty-five thousand head. The race was on. Prosperity had come to Abilene.

Politicians and railroads intended to keep it that way. They monopolized the market in every available town of Southern Kansas. McCoy, the man who gave Kansas life, was brushed aside. The era of trail riding days had arrived. The Brazos country was prepared. During these early days the owner of the stock was trail boss. This was especially true of smaller outfits. When Allison became a rancher in his own right he was his own trail boss for several years. He was well qualified. He could ride, shoot, swim, doze in the saddle, eat as comfortably from horseback as from a table, throw a few cuss words at nervous animals or sing to soothe them, crack a bull whip so that its sound and fury carried loud and far, knew how to head off a stampede, when to bed down.

A trail boss risked his life in a midnight stampede. His men were intolerant of the least sign of fear. He was expected to expose himself to greater danger than they. He was to be as fearless in dealing with Indians as with scampering cattle. His word was law all the way. To keep the respect of his men he was often called upon to punch the fear of the Lord into some bullies, as hard to handle as cattle.

Despite the rise of the industry in Kansas, New Mexico continued to remain a good market. Henry Caulfield drove a herd from the Brazos country to New Mexico and returned with saddle bags ripping at the seams. In those days a man could travel with seventy-five thousand in hard cash without having to guard it against his cowboys. Small wonder then that this sudden surge renewed the taste for "cow hunting" in the thickets, the bottom lands, the bosque. Wild strays would soon be as extinct as buffalo. No doubt Lacy, Coleman and the Allison boys spent a good deal of their time on the hunt.

It was always a good policy with the trail boss to bed the cattle without water before crossing the Brazos, pushing them directly across in the morning. One reason for this was that too many herds were crowding the trails, mingling at river crossings and spoiling the grass for the late comer. The farther in front your herd was from another, the easier you handled your cattle and your cowboys. Convenience often made it expedient that the range boss joined his steers with another outfit, but they had to be divided—cut out—was the coyboy expression. Drives usually took place in March or April. Col. Potter related how he had diffculty because of bunching cattle. He was trailing a herd to Dodge. Before he could quite prevent it they were infiltrated with another. Anxious to avoid delay and hoping to beat his competitor to market he rode to the other camp just as the cowboys started the herd in motion. Sighting a rider hardly recognizable due to the grey-brown dust of the trail that covered him from head to foot, Potter shouted at him angrily:

"Where's the trail boss?"

"I'm the trail boss."

"What do you mean by running your herd with mine?"

"Nothing in particular."

"Well, you just stop the drive. I'm cutting out my cattle."

"Too late for that. When we get to Dodge your cattle will be cut out. You have my word."

"And who are you, Mr. High and Mighty?"

"Clay Allison is the name."

Relating the incident years later at Clayton, New Mexico, the colonel said that when he heard the name he froze in his saddle. His only thought was that momentarily he would be filled with lead. Talk had already made the rounds in the Kansas cow towns that of all the men driving herds to market Allison was the fastest on the draw. Prompt in cooling down, he told Allison that the arrangement suited him just fine. Both herds made it to Dodge without mishap. Allison kept his word. His cowboys cut out Potter's steers, and Allison gained a friend for life.

The commissary on wheels known as the chuck-wagon was Goodnight's gift to trail drivers. Whether or not he is the originator of the sour dough biscuit as some claim, he certainly brought it to perfection. For this he merits the undying gratitude of the American cow-boy. The chuck-wagon served as a moving van for bedding and a cafeteria for grub. It was also the pantry for the green berry coffee, salt pork, corn meal, flour and beans. Contrary to popular opinion, neither cook nor trail boss slaughtered beef from the herd. Strays from the herd ahead, crippled cows, bothersome mothers in search of their young and others left behind supplied meat in abundance. In isolated cases the trail boss ordered killed any steers habitually slowing up the progress of the drive. Attached to the lid on the chuck box was a wooden leg which served as a prop to give the lid usefulness as a table.

The wagon itself was loaded with bed rolls, slickers, clothing. A water barrel was always in evidence. The cook made it a point to roll out before daybreak. When breakfast was ready, he aroused the men with cries of "Rise and shine. Give glory to God." "Come and git it 'fore I throw it to the coyotes." Other expressions had a more salty flavor. Trail boss and cowboys went out of their way to keep the cook in a happy frame of mind. If crossed, he showed it plainly in the meals he served. He was the factotum—doctor, veterinarian, dentist, seamstress, guardian of the chuck wagon, undertaker, advisor, repair man, letter writer, custodian of personal belongings, friend of every cowboy in the outfit.

Roundup over, the drive north began just as soon as the Brazos was fordable, for it was a bad omen to have a herd water-bound at the very outset. The remuda (horse herd handled by a wrangler—as necessary to the drive as a spare tire to a car) was less difficult to handle in water than cattle. Horses were always better swimmers. As a rule the drive consisted of about three thousand cattle, eighteen cowboys, cook, chuck wagon, remuda of one hundred and fifty horses, wrangler, trail boss. A lead steer usually headed the herd. Like humans, steers often formed friendships and would be inseparable throughout the drive. The cowboys flanked the herd. Drag riders brought up the rear. Fifteen miles a day was considered good travel. At night the cook made as little noise as possible, with his pots and pans, especially the skillet. A falling skillet sufficed for a stampede, the only thing as frightening to a cowboy as an Indian attack. It was at night that the cowboy crooned to the cattle to quiet them down. The more mournful and doleful the song the more docile the cattle. But of this came the heritage in American folk song as we know it today.

The daily routine was enlivened by the prankster. There seemed to be one in every outfit. Clay Allison was a natural. He could think up more tricks than many. He lived before his time. TV and the screen would have proven happy mediums for his talents. He caused confusion by mixing up bed rolls, boots, loosening saddle girths, sending cowboys on impossibe errands. He had a pleasant singing voice, and was often called upon to cheer up the boys huddled about the camp fire. He told jokes, swapped yarns, needled a wrangler, enlivened the cowboys' spirits on glum, rainy days. He never bothered the cook—at least not during the drive. It has been said that he never made an enemy in any outfit he was with. The boys just took to him, avoiding him only when he was drunk. While he was known to be fast with a gun as well as a bowie knife he does not seem to have built up a reputation for gunplay during these Brazos days.

Several factors helped make the term cowboy synonomous with Texan. The Chisholm Trail, the fact that the majority of cowboys were Southerners or sons of veterans of the Confederate Army. Nor did the word Texan necessarily mean that the cowboy was a native of Texas. It merely identified him as working (with a herd) on a drive. The herd could be from the Nations Territory, Arizona, New Mexico, Colorado, but in Abilene, Newton Wichita, Ellsworth, Caldwell, Hunnerville, Hays, Dodge, they were all known as Texans. In Kansas the cowboys relished the idea of fighting the Civil War all over again. The men they found at the end of the trail were usually

Northerners. All during the trip they made plans for hurrahing the town. That meant shooting out lights, racing up and down the main street as they shot their six-shooters into the air, or took pot shots at stope-pipe hats, aimed at glasses and bottles in saloons, took a girl from the arms of a Northerner as he danced her, egged them on to a brawl, visited bawdy houses, gambling dens, discomfited the peace officer, especially if he were known to have served in the Federal Army during the late war, and rioted in the best hotels. These men from the Brazos country ushered in an era. They gave spice and flavor to the history of the West that would be utilized in another generation of pulp magazines, stage sets, turning cameras.

While it may be true that every male child (and many a female) was taught to shoot and ride from the time he was able to talk, this is not a right held exclusively by Texans. Wild Bill, Buffalo Bill, Pawnee Bill, Doc Holiday, Billy the Kid, Dave Rudabaugh, the James Brothers, Pat Garrett, Wyatt Earp, and many others were not native Texans, and many never lived in Texas. Being a Texan, as cow towns understood the term, did not mean being a gunman. The cowboys went wild because this was a form of relaxation after months on the road away from wine, women and dance. Of songs they had plenty. But singing in a bar room or to a dance hall girl was quite different from singing to cattle. At last they reached the end of the trail where they would have money to spend and plenty of women to spend it on. When they took over the town no one disputed nor challenged their audacity. Boot hill was too close. Later on men like Earp, Masterson, Webb, Gillett, Tighlman, and other lesser lights were to restore order out of chaos. But during the first few years of the drives the cowboy ran the show pretty much his own way.

In the end the so-called Northerner won. He ended up with the most important thing of all—the cowboy's money. They, too, made plans. They imported the dance hall girl, the orchestra, the piano player, the gambler, whisky, honky-tonks, bordellos, keeping everything moving around the clock for the full twenty-four hours, never closing despite gun play, fist play, or horse play. One reason for this was that after the cowboys spent all their money they returned to camp to relieve those guarding the remuda, the chuck wagon and equipment. Very few returned to the Brazos country with anything more than they had at the start.

Clay shared in the fun at Abilene, Newton, Caldwell, Ellsworth. He was one man peace officers sought to avoid, especially when he was "all likkered up." Then he was downright insulting and cowboys crowded around him just to see what he would do much to the embarrassment of the officers. "That Clay Allison fellow," they would say to one another, "Let's stick with him, and, sure 'nuff something will happen. Man, jest don' yer try to drink wid him. O'nery? Man, 'tain't no Yankee he wouldn't go after."

So, they made the rounds—shouting, bullying, laughing, drinking, shooting, loving, spending—content to be led by the tall cowboy from Tennessee who jocosities were as colorful as they were numerous. In time Clay came to know these people at the end of the trail by their first names. Butler, Good, Webb, Masterson, Webb, Peshaur, Kane, Hungerford, Harris, Short, Thompson, Brown, Bassett, Mather, Clements, Foy. Allison never missed an Eddie Foy show when he was in town. By the time he managed his own spread in New Mexico his name was a by-word with all these and more.

Meantime many of the cowmen were moving from the Brazos country to the Pecos and Cimarron valleys of New Mexico. More and more caravans were moving over the Santa Fe Trail through the main road and its various cut-offs, moving over Rabbit Ear Mountain, the Raton Pass, San Luis, to bring goods to Taos, Rayado, Fort Union, Fort Bascom, Cimarron, Las Vegas. Thousands of others were using the same routes in quest of gold. Maxwell was frantic. Prospectors swarming all over the Grant without so much as by your leave. Whatever Maxwell's efforts at keeping the miner out no one could gainsay that the mining camps were an immense help to both stockman and cattle buyer. Cowboys liked this lush land which compensated for the drought in the Brazos country. It was also closer to the railhead. The Federal Land Office in Santa Fe made it so easy for you to claim and own the land that an exodus started from the Brazos country which filled northeastern New Mexico with cattle it otherwise would not have had. There was the added advantage of selling at the camps and forts as well as reservations without having to drive the steers clear to Kansas. The wealthier stockmen kept ranges along the Brazos as well as the Rayado, Cimarron, Ute, Red and Canadian rivers. This as well as the coming of the railroad was to change the course of the cattle empire. How early this movement started we know from the affidavit of Thomas H. Dawson found in the Colfax County archives at Raton:

"Thomas H. Dawson, being first duly sworn, in his oath deposes and says that he is a resident of Colfax County and Territory of New Mexico, and that he has resided in said county and Territory since the year 1867; that prior to moving to the said county he resided on the Clear Fork of the Brazos river in the State of Texas, and was there engaged in the cattle business; that on or about the month of August, 1867, he started to move with several of his neighbors, from Texas to New Mexico, with their families and cattle, and that among his neighbors who accompanied him were Joel W. Curtis and Jasper N. de Graftonreid...." He said that Curtis and Graftonreid had cattle and horses which they joined in one herd in order to drive the same from the Clear Fork of the Brazos river in Texas to New Mexico, having with them their families and some men hired for the purpose of aiding in driving and caring for said stock.

"They drove toward their destination for about fifteen days, until they came to a place known as Fanthom Hill, which had been at one time a government post in the State of Texas, on or near the Clear Fork of the Brazos river. On reaching Fanthom Hill, the party encamped for the night, and resumed their journey toward New Mexico the next morning, and continued on all day when they again camped for the night. The next morning, quite early, some of the men were holding the cattle hereafter described; others of the party were in bed; some were getting breakfast, when a party of Comanche Indians made a dash upon the party and carried off about two hundred head of cattle besides four oxen and five head of horses belonging to Dawson, besides taking off a large number of cattle and horses belonging to the other members of the party." Dawson further states that the said dash made by the Indians was sudden and took his party completely by surprise, and, before he could do thing the Indians drove off the stock. As quickly as he could get ready, Dawson and five members of his party followed the Indians, but as the Comanches had taken all the horses belonging to the said party except six of inferior quality, they were unable to overtake the Indians. They followed the trail for about twenty-eight miles and finally got within sight of them. The Indians moved rapidly, killing much of the stock on the way to accelerate their speed and dead stock was seen all along the trail. The Indians moved rapidly to escape. Due to the inferiority of his horses as well as to the lack of knowledge of the country they were unable to overtake neither the Indians nor the stock, which were a total loss.

"Of the two hundred head of cattle, forty were two-year-old steers, sixty were three-year-old steers, the remainder were stock cattle mostly females of various ages. The cattle driven away by the Indians were a good class for that country, partly graded up. Dawson was moving them to New Mexico intending to sell them there because they commanded a good price. At that time there was a great demand for stock cattle in New Mexico and there were ready sales at good prices in Colfax county, to which place Dawson was going. Two-year-old steers of the class he lost were worth about thirty-five dollars per head, and three-year-old steers were worth about fifty dollars a head. The oxen were worth one hundred dollars per pair, or yoke. Dawson said that in Texas they were not worth that much. The prices on the Clear Fork of the Brazos being about eighteen dollars per head for two-year-olds, twelve dollars and fifty cents per head for three-year-olds. It cost two dollars and fifty cents per head to drive the cattle from Texas. Dawson was in the hopes of making some profit. The horses were worth about sixty-five dollars per head. Dawson said he was satisfied that the Indians committing this depredation were Comanches and reservation Indians because they were well mounted, had saddles and blankets and were armed with government guns, and the members of his party were familiar with the appearance of the different tribes of Indians.

Curtis and several other old timers about Cimarron were interviewed regarding this affidavit. Many have since passed away. Curtis, almost a hundred, and a cowboy at one time for Clay Allison, says that his memory is dim and he is not too sure as to whether or not Clay Allison was one of the cowboys who came with Dawson on this trip. It was the consensus of opinion of the others that Allison made this trip because he had some cattle belonging to the new firm of Lacy & Coleman which he hoped to dispose of at Cimarron. Dawson seems to have been the only one the Indians robbed, possibly because his herd was bedded down apart from the others. As Allison made a number of drives for his brother-in-law before settling in the area, it is not unlikely that this occasion was another incident in his life.

Life does not always seem to have been rosy and smooth between Allison and Coleman, as we gather from this item in the *Las Vegas Optic*: "Clay Allison, who has a flair for getting his man, is on the rampage again. His intended victim on this occasion is said to be his brother-in-law, Coleman, who has incurred his ire." His sister evidently cooled him down, for the shooting never took place, or perhaps he thought better of it as Coleman's place was northwest of his and gave him plenty of time to reconsider.

Allison's niece was of the opinion that this brother-in-law was known as "South," for she remembers distinctly that her mother always referred to the cattlemen as South and Lacy, and she often visited their homes, which were near the site of the city of Dawson.

Allison did not leave the Brazos country directly for the Cimarron. He worked for a time in Lincoln county, possibly for Chisum or grazing cattle for Lacy & Colman. While at Lincoln he became acquainted with all the principals who were soon to figure prominently in the Lincoln County War, with the exception of Billy the Kid, who was still a lad in Silver City at the time, or already on the loose elsewhere. As far as can be ascertained, Billy the Kid and Clay Allison never met. Clay knew Murphy, Sweeney, Emil Fritz, Brady, McSween and others whose names are familiar to those acquainted with the details of the Lincoln County War.

Chapter Four

NEW MEXICO

The California Column that marched east with Carleton and west in a desperate dash to save Canby embarrassment at the hands of his brother-in-law Sibley, was stalemated. The column found itself out of touch with the main force of the Union Army, and a step behind the retreating Confederates. The next few years were to be spent fighting Indians. Sons of Forty-Niners and prospectors for the most part, their conversation had little to do with the war. Possibility of gold strikes were never a threadbare, vapid topic. On a scout after redskins they kept one eye peeled for the enemy, the other sized up hills and dales as possible mining sites. Many traveled with gold pans. Every stream and watering place brought these pans into action. The task of rounding up tenants for the Bosque Redondo reservation irked them. Friction developed between the natives and the garrisons at Loma Parda, Fort Union, Fort Craig, Las Vegas, Paraje, Albuquerque and Santa Fe. Collecting Navajos and Apaches seemed to be a fetish with Carleton. The soldiers murmured constantly. They resented the idea of policing Indians, instead of battling Confederates. They did not look upon themselves as part of the great Army of the Union but rather as frontier fighters, doomed to protect life and limb against the forays of Cochise, Delgadito, Victorio, Red Sleeves, Alexander, whose fight was not so much against the California Column as against the people of New Mexico. The soldiers insisted that they were doing the work of the Territorial militia. At times they were at the point of open rebellion until Carleton spread the propaganda of gold. He permitted passes to be issued whereby the men had ample opportunity to live the dual role of soldier and prospector. Claims were staked which would be worked following an honorable discharge. Many never returned to California. A few struck it rich.

There are those who will argue that Sutter was more sinned against than sinning in his determination that his losses be compensated, his right to fight the invasion of his privacy and domain be protected by law, that he be left in peace. Maxwell, the Sutter of New Mexico, had even more cause to complain. The government recognized his Grant as valid. He had left Illinois as a young man venturing into the fur trade, the path inevitably leading to Taos, the headquarters for that virile breed known as Mountain Men. Attracted to Kit Carson they fell in with Fremont, receiving national recognition as scouts. He married Luz Beaubien, daughter of Charles Beaubien, co-owner with Miranda of the controversial Beaubien-Miranda Grant. Eventually Maxwell acquired the tract working it very much like a feudal baron. Settled on the Rayado at first, he eyed the richer soil of the Cimarron, where he built his famous mill. He was fortunate in obtaining beef contracts for the Cimarron Indian Agency, Fort Union, Fort Stanton and other garrisons.

Over at Fort Union, at the sutler's store, William Kroenig, W. H. Moore, John Buck, did business with the Utes and Jicarillas squatting on Maxwell's Grant. These Indians usually brought in gold nuggets they picked up along the streams mostly because they were amused at the way the men acted every time a nugget was placed in their hands. As far as the Indians were concerned, the funny colored stones were of no value since you could not eat them or even sharpen them into arrowheads, hatchets or knives. The white men gave calico, beads, blankets, knives and food in exchange. Realizing the value of these nuggets to the soldiers the Indians never divulged where they picked them up. They were magic with a purchasing power the likes of which they had never experienced. Time and again Kroenig sought to beguile them into vomiting up the metoposcopy of their reserve but they would not be bamboozled. Soldiers trading at Moore's store were aware that the yellow metal passed hands, making a mental note of it, hoping to succeed where others had failed. Bronson, Arthur, Brown, Robinson, Hamilton, they bunked together and talked of the oddity that only Utes and Jicarillas brought in the gold, not the Pueblo Indians, which meant that it was to be found in the vicinity, or the Maxwell Land Grant. They decided to take advantage of the passes permitted by General Carleton. Bronson made the observation that the Indians always came in from the direction of Mt. Baldy. Thus, on their first trip out they headed in that general direction. Like the Indians, they picked up nuggets found in the streams but they made no general strike. Bronson took his findings to Moore in settlement of his debts. Kroenig was confident that the hills would yield fabulous wealth if sufficient time were allowed to dig. He asked Bronson if he would undertake the task, grubstaked by the store. Of course Moore, Kroenig and Buck would have to be counted in as partners. If he found nothing, he owed nothing. Bronson readily agreed taking Kelly and Kinsinger along with him.

Forty miles west of the site of Maxwell flowed the clear stream known in Fort Union as Willow Creek. It babbled along to meet the Moreno, having its origin in the Baldy watershed. The trio camped at the conflux of the Willow and the Moreno. Too tired to start the climb up Mt. Baldy, where Carleton had already planted an American flag, they decided on supper and bed. Kelly, selected for K.P. duty, decided to do some panning as the meat boiled. He dipped the pan into the stream close to the bank, scooping up as many pebbles as it could hold. Supper was forgotten that night. Swearing an oath of secrecy they broke camp and returned to the fort. Gold, like murder, will out. In the spring of 1867 it seemed that the whole nation beat a path to the Maxwell Land Grant. There were more towns on the Grant than were ever seen before or since. Maxwell's efforts availed nothing. The hordes tramped down his No Trespassing signs. Since he could not beat them he decided to join them. He had about as much luck prospecting as he did staying off the prospector. Virginia City, Discovery Tree, Baldy, Elizabethtown, Moreno, Willow Creek, Ute, Prairieville—all gone now—gave hope to the stockmen of the Brazos country, looking for closer markets. Lacy and Coleman were among the first to try the possibilities of these mining towns. Goodnight, Loving, Dalton and others had already opened the trail leading to Maxwell's so those following several years later were not actually pioneering.

All this was too much for Maxwell, who bemoaned the fact that the greedy prospector infringed upon his way of life and his peace. His daughter Virginia dealt a further blow by marrying a dashing young officer named Keyes without consulting him. Nestors, squatters and miners were carving an empire out of his land as if the United States Land Office never recognized his claim. Western migration was the handwriting on the wall. All because Bronson, Arthur, Brown, Robinson and Hamilton shouldered picks rather than guns, marched to Willow Creek, measured claims in a westward direction from the big tree known as Discovery Tree, to turn a nation of gold-happy prospectors loose on his land. Talk about the early Spaniards! Coronado, Alvarez, Onate, Espejo, Penalosa must have turned in their graves.

The government came up with the answer for Maxwell. He would capitalize on the strike. There must be some people in the world anxious enough for gold to buy the whole Grant. In the Pecos valley the government was ready to shake itself of the dust of Fort Sumner. If he could find a buyer he would rid himself of the grant and end his days in peace at Fort Sumner. Little did he suspect that this new home would be immortalized by Pat Garrett and Billy the Kid. The world would have long since forgotten that he lived here but for the tragedy that took place one night in his son Pete's bedroom. The old military cemetery that was to house his mortal frame was also destined to be the final resting place for Billy the Kid and several of his cronies.

Satisfied now that the Grant would never be the veritable kingdom of old, Maxwell dropped hints that he would like to sell. One day during a poker game at his mansion he turned to Miguel Otero, saying: "Why don't you go up to Colorado and push Chaffee, Waddingham and a few of the boys about taking this place off my hands? Gilpin doesn't seem to be interested." Elkins, Thompson and Watts, also enjoying the game, thought it unbusinesslike to sell at a time the greatest gold rush in the history of the Southwest was taking place. Maxwell was not interested in neither profit nor gold; all he wanted was cattle and sheep ranges and peace of mind. If prospectors kept digging holes on every acre of his land, he would soon have to rid himself of all live stock for lack of grass. But the men he mentioned were interested in gold and anything profitable.

Wilson Waddingham had left the largest tavern in San Francisco to invest in the Colorado gold fields; Chaffee left Niagara Falls for the same purpose. This latter was partner in the ownership of a stamp mill, bank, and the Little Pittsburg Mine in Leadville. George B. Chilcott, Charles F. Holly, Gilpin, had mentioned to lawyers Elkins and Catron that they were interested in buying the Grant but they were certain Maxwell would sell. The option was turned over to them on May 16, 1869, signed by Holly and Maxwell. By April 20, 1870, the Maxwell

Land Grant and Railway Company, sponsored by English and Dutch interests, projected a large scale colonization program which was to cause miner and squatter to fight back. The Maxwell Land Grant War brought about more deaths than the Lincoln County War. Allison took up the cudgel in favor of the opposition. McMains looked upon him as the commander-in-chief of those refusing to agree that Dutch and English capital had legitimate purchasing power. Some authors have placed the death toll in this war as high as two hundred, allowing for the many natives killed but whose names were never recorded.

About the time Clay Allison accompanied his first herd into New Mexico, Tom Stockton came up from Texas, bought land from Maxwell and built the famous Clifton House located several miles east of the Red River Peak, on the west bank of the Red river (Canadian), about fifteen miles south of the Colorado line. He was later joined by his father, W. H. Stockton, and his brother Mathias. Other cattlemen settled about the area to give Clifton the appearance of a thriving little community. There was the spring round-up, cattle drives commencing east of the Dry Cimarron and ending up near the base of the Raton mountains. The cattlemen came together at Clifton House to do their branding and to relax. Lacy & Coleman were not unaware of the bustling activity near the Colorado border. Trailing a herd to Clifton they sold to Stockton and a man named Wilburn. The trail boss was Clay Allison. The following spring he handled it alone without Coleman and Lacy. He was also given the chore of collecting from Stockton and Wilburn.

Stockton had a good enough reason for stalling and Allison trusted him, but every time he went to see the cowman living near the Dry Cimarron, he was always told to come back in a day or two. His bill at Clifton House mounted. Allison finally came to the conclusion that Wilburn had no intention of paying. He tried a game of his own. He gave up going to Wilburn's and had it noised abroad that he had returned to Texas. Relieved, Wilburn came to Clifton House, entered the bar and ordered a drink. As he was about to raise the glass, Allison stole behind him, pointed a six-shooter at his head, saying:

"No more delays. Pay now or be shot."

"How can I pay now? I don't carry such sums with me. Let me go home and in a few hours I'll return with your money."

"Make sure it's just a few hours, for when I come to your place again it will be to blow your brains out."

Wilburn, a squatter on the Maxwell Land Grant, hastily packed a few belongings and disappeared. He was never seen again in that part of the country. Allison, suspecting he had been gudgeoned, rounded up his cowboys and rode to the Wilburn dugout only to find it abandoned. There was nothing else to do but round up the cattle for sale elsewhere. Fortunately, a rancher on Crow creek was in a buying mood. Stockton paid up, and Lacy & Coleman commended Allison for a job well done.

Ritch, the prosecuting attorney during the Cooper murder trial, brought up an accusation which while not proven true at least proved interesting. He charged that before returning to Texas Allison engaged in rustling mules.

The mule herds brought over the Santa Fe Trail from Missouri and points east were valuable to the miner as well as to the native New Mexican, to say nothing of the frontier army posts. Some day a move will be forwarded commemorating this sturdy, if stubborn, animal's place in pioneer history. One of the mule men to cash in on the demand was General Granger of Missouri. He was known throughout the mining district for the number of herds he brought over the trail. He might be called the Charles Goodnight of the industry. Whether it was because he was a "Damn Yankee' or because of the profit, or both, Clay decided to take over. He stationed his cowboys at a strategic point along the Raton Pass, attacked the herd guards, took the animals to Texas where a business transaction transpired, no questions asked. As the prosecuting attorney could produce no witnesses, Judge Waldo ruled that the accusation be scratched from the record.

Either because Clay was dissatisfied with the Pecos country near Fort Stanton, in Lincoln county, or because Lacy & Coleman had something better to offer, his stay in New Mexico was short lived. Back in Texas again, he found out that Lacy & Coleman had bought land of the Maxwell Land Grant Company, up along the Vermejo in Colfax county. Munroe (also spelt Monroe) and John Allison were with Clay on this drive. It had been agreed that at the end of the journey they would receive their salaries in steers. Coleman kept his promise. He allowed them to cut out one head in every ten. As there were three thousand, Clay took three hundred to the Ponil country, where he built his first dugout. Coleman built his home between Speilman creek and the Vermejo river, grazing his stock on what later became known as the Maxwell Land Grant Company Beef Pasture. Coleman canyon perpetuates his name in that area. Lacy built south of Dawson's at the end of the Vermejo, east of Van Bremner canyon. Allison's place was M. M. Chase and Marion Littrell's and closer to the town of Cimarron than either Lacy or Coleman.

From the very first the cowboys that came to "hurrah" Cimarron looked to Clay as the leader. Within a few weeks every rancher in Colfax county called him his friend. Nor was Cimarron the only place Clay and the cowboys "hurrahed." Elizabethtown came in for its share. Saturday night was stay-at-home night for the element interested in peace and order. One might say law and order, but the law had not yet come to Cimarron and Elizabethtown. Sheriffs like Littrell, Hixenbaugh,

Bowman and Lambert were still off in the dim horizon. Six-shooter law was in evidence during these early days. Saturday night may have been appreciation night for the bar keep, gambler and dance hall girl, but it was a night of terror for the rest of the citizens. Miners usually added to the confusion by blowing in their gold dust and nuggets.

The cowboys came swooping and hooting in a cloud of dust, punctuating their fierce rebel yells with pops from their six-shooters. Streets cleared, the rounds were made—saloons, painted ladies, gambling halls, dance halls. At no place they visited did they ever let down on the drinks. At every place they shot at lamps, lanterns, mirrors, glasses, dudes in high hats. Clay had his own brand of sport: shooting at the heels of the deputy, the marshal or the sheriff, whichever was unfortunate enough to be on hand. He took particular delight in searching out the tenderfoot or newcomer who overly dressed in frontier fashion. There were times when it backfired and the tenderfoot returned with a six-shooter to make him dance. And dance he did, for the worm that turned was not as accurate a shot as Clay. It would be well to remember that at this time Allison was not lame. The Maxwell Land Grant Company was not at all impressed with this rowdyism and sought to overcome it by the introduction of order and culture. Civilization, emendation, elegance, must triumph over the boisterous, impetuous, unsavoury, plebian, tatterdemalion saddle-master and polemic whose only claim on society was that he could shoot straight, ride fast and furious, curse like a trooper, drink like a fish and love like a Don Juan. John Collinson, president of the Maxwell Land Grant Com,-pany sought out Alexander P. Sullivan, a newspaper man in Santa Fe, with whom he drew up a contract for the publication of the *Cimarron News and Press*. The first issue appeared on September 22, 1870.

Henry Lambert, who once walked in the shadow of the great put to use his culinary art by personally supervising the restaurant connected with the hostelry he operated in Elizabethtown. When Maxwell Land Grant officials found out that he once cooked for General Grant and for the Great Emancipator himself, they induced him to come to Cimarron, where he continued to serve the public at the St. James. The hotel boasted a bar which is credited as the scene of twenty-six killings. The Grant Company's plan for civilization evidently backfired. The first question usually asked around Cimarron in the morning was: "Who was killed at Lambert's last night?" Another favorite expression following a killing was: "It appears Lambert had himself another man for breakfast."

Allison and his cowboys frequented Lambert's Inn, as it was then called. After a few drinks, out came the six-shooters, out went the lights, down came the glasses, bottles, mirrors—lead poured into the walls, ceiling, woodwork. Then they marched out in search of the sheriff, his deputies or town marshal. Anyone unseasoned enough to permit himself to fall into their hands was escorted back to the bar where he was plied with whisky enough to drown in. Failure to comply with their invitation to down another meant dancing to the tune of singing bullets, coming from all directions. He drank, and drank, and drank, until he rolled to the floor babbling incoherent sounds; then the cowboys paid for the damage, and the drinks.

Streets were usually empty along about this time, as the boys jumped on their horses, riding up and down shooting and yelling. If they spotted a light coming through a window, they shot at the window, in the hopes of putting out the light. Every bar in town that preferred specie to unbroken glasses welcomed them. Gambling tables were turned over, dance hall girls invited to drink, demireps lifted to horses to carouse with the amorous rider and take the last of his money. Allison, always shy of women, even when in his cups, usually left them to the boys. He usually did a war dance around some luckless victim, shooting at his feet until he tired of the game, then went to his hotel room to sleep it off.

Associated with Clay in these escapades was young Davy Crockett (not to be associated with the Crocket of Alamo fame but a relative), also a native of Tennessee and a desperado of sorts. He endeared himself to Allison because he was especially vitriolic against the negro troopers stationed at Fort Union. One night at Lambert's he killed four of them because they crowded the doorway as he was leaving. He insisted that putting uniforms on former slaves was adding insult to injury. Merchants were unequivocally circumspect, in taking cognizance of their antics. Allison and Crocket loved to lasso a miner, prospector or dude, drag him to the nearest mercantile store, deck him out in the store's finest, and force the merchant to take the bill to the sheriff, at that time also collector of taxes. When the sheriff voiced objection, they told him that they paid for the clothes anyway since he overcharged in taxes and this was a way of getting back what was due them. The sheriff usually ended up paying the merchant.

The sheriff at this time was Isaac Rinehart. He had come to Cimarron at the invitation of Lucien Maxwell, who was looking for a good miller to run his grist mill. Maxwell later treated him coldly because he and his wife stood as witnesses for the marriage of Virginia Maxwell to Captain Keyes. As the ceremony was performed by Rev. Thomas Harwood in the mill, Maxwell suspected Rinehart as projecting the elopement. General Keyes of World War II fame was a grandson of this union. Maxwell forgave his daughter before he died; it is doubtful whether he ever forgave the miller. Shortly following the sale of the Grant, Rinehart sought the office of sheriff, rather reluctantly, according to some; because of the cut derived in collecting taxes, according to others. The law permitted the sheriff to retain ten percent of all taxes collected. Rinehart's name is intimately connected with the history of the Washita country in Texas, Amarillo and Tascosa. The Rinehart Addition in this latter place was named for him. He seems to have been especially successful in real estate and banking. He visited the Allisons often when he lived in Mobeetie, the humiliations suffered at the hands of Clay forgiven and forgotten.

Not far from Elizabethtown, one Charles Kennedy built a cabin which often served the wayfarer as a hotel. It was built near the branch of the road that led up the mountain side to Taos, the other trailing off to Black Lakes, Guadalupita and Mora. Whether Kennedy bought the site of Maxwell or squatted is a matter of dispute. He was a trapper by trade when he worked at it, and seems to have been a friend of Kit Carson and other famous Mountain Men. On one of his trapping expeditions he met Dulcinea Maldonado of Arroyo Seco and married her. The solitary cabin in such an isolated spot was not to her liking but she felt she was stuck with Kennedy and made the best of it. Her wretched existence was made even more pitiable by her husband's heavy drinking. Travelers from Taos to Elizabethtown took to stopping over at Kennedy's and it was noticed that some never arrived at their destination. The remains were buried under the dirt floor. Pelts, horses and other effects were taken to Anton Chico, Las Vegas or Loma Parda and offered for sale. To take them to Trinidad, Cimarron or Elizabethtown would be to invite compromising questions. As Dulcinea knew no English she had no way of warning off the traveler. Usually her husband compelled her to accompany him on his trips for fear she would inform the authorities. After the birth of her child he warned her that if she ever attempted to report him he would kill both child and mother.

One night a young trapper sought lodging. When Kennedy went out to stable the horse, Dulcinea tried signs to warn off the traveler. When Kennedy returned the stranger repeated the signs asking him to explain what they meant. The look in her husband's eyes told her that she was doomed. He told the man that his wife was a simpleton, not responsible for her actions. Satisfied, the man went to bed. His body was buried alongside the others. He took the baby, dashed it against the wall and buried it. He would have killed her also had he not felt that a traveler was more inclined to spend the night if he saw a woman about the place. After killing the child Kennedy settled down with his liquor. Satisfied that he had drunk himself into a stupor and would not awaken for some time she unlatched the door and stole out into the night.

September nights in that part of the country are not known to be balmy. They are cold, raw and chill to the marrow. Allison, Crockett, Goodall, Heifner and several other cowboys were whiling away the hours at John Pearson's saloon. They were surprised when Dulcinea stumbled into the place. Helped into a chair she told her ghastly story in rapid-fire Spanish. Some of her listeners knew enough of the language to understand what she was saying. Allison and Crockett did not believe a man could stoop so low. They decided to ride out to verify it. As Kennedy was too drunk to answer their questions they put him in jail until he sobered up. Meantime several lawmen went to the cabin and began digging. A kindhearted native rode to Arroyo Seco for Dulcinea's father. It has been said that Kennedy burnt the flesh off his victims, burying the charred bones. This may be true, for the men returned with two sacks of bones. When news of this evidence circulated a mob gathered to hang Kennedy, but Justice of the Peace Benjamin F. Houx and a law-abiding citizen named C. N. Story persuaded them to break up and return to their homes.

As Kennedy's trial would be something out of the ordinary a large hall was rented as the courtroom. Allison and Crockett favored immediate hanging; the justice favored a trial. Reluctantly, the pair agreed. Only because Houx pointed out that Dulcinea might be lying and the bones might prove to be animal bones since no skulls were found. The woman opened herself to suspicion because she refused to testify at the trial. Her father knew nothing of Kennedy or his living habits and thought his testimony would have little bearing on the case so he, too, refused to testify. The answer must be found in the bones. The two sacks were emptied on a table and five doctors from Elizabethtown and Cimarron were summoned to testify and examine them. Dr. Bailey and Dr. Le Carpenter said there was not a human bone in the pile. Dr. Steinberger and Dr. Bradford said that one bone was a patella or human knee cap. The other doctor was not certain. Still unconvinced Justice Houx ordered Kennedy to be bound over to await further trial and ordered that one hundred pounds of iron be riveted to each leg by some blacksmith. The verdict was contrary to public sentiment. The crowd in the courtroom stood up, booed the justice and yelled: "Hang him. Hang him." Guards surrounded Kennedy and he was ushered out of the room and back to jail.

Unfortunately for Kennedy this was the time of the year when most of the men of the area took their families to the fiesta at San Geronimo de Taos. Young men who could guard him effectively were not about to forego the opportunity of enjoyment at Taos merely to protect a man destined for a necktie party. Reports vary as to what happened on that thirtieth day of September. Allison, Crockett, Goodall and several other cowboys are said to have forced the jailor to give up his keys, took Kennedy out and hanged him to the nearest tree. Whoever was responsible, when the people returned from the fiesta it was all over for Kennedy. Again, Allison was the one, rumor claims, who cut off his head, put it on a pike, and stood the gory mess in front of Lambert's Inn as a warning for anyone else playing Kennedy's game. A few days later Lambert tiring of complaints from his guests took the head to the farthest corner of the corral fence in the hopes that the cowboys themselves would tire of the sight and bury it. Dr. Bradford took it to his office, boiled off the flesh, wired it to the skeleton which he already had and sent it to the Smithsonian in Washington with this inscription: Charles Kennedy, Murderer of Fourteen Human Beings. The doctor, a student of phrenology, thought the institute would be interested because of the prominent back head. Later when the excitement died down it was agreed that Kennedy killed only one man and that was an Indian who assulted him when drunk. The knee cap belonged to that Indian. Houx questioned no suspects, nor did anyone dare approach Allison or Crockett. The incident was soon forgotten. Crockett became involved in further difficulties with the law and was eventually shot to death.

Horse racing was periapt with Allison, A good judge of horseflesh he always managed to have one in the running at Elizabethtown, Taos, Mora, Las Vegas, Loma Parda, Rayado, Clifton House and Cimarron. His entries rarely lost. It was at such times when people were crowded together that they usually asked him to give a display of his shooting ability. Some one would throw a can into the air and before it started its downward course, he would whip out his six-shooter, sending the lead through at dead center. Several sought to equal the record but all attempts failed. Such marksmanship would hardly be left unchallenged in a day when the gunfighter was fast replacing the Mountain Man as a special even if lawless breed. Gunfighter meant exactly what the word implied. A man fast on the draw sought out another man with a reputation for speed. They shot to kill. The winner went on to find another thus building up his reputation as a gunslinger. These men lived violent lives, dying just as violently. For every name known to the reader of gunfighter folklore there are ten lesser lights whose grandiose ideas of a reputation were more flashing than their guns. Wistful thinking was not for the gunfighter.

Allison's dexterity piqued a desperado of sorts at Trinidad, Colorado. He boasted that he could outdraw outshoot and outfight Allison anytime, anyplace. He, too, was a horse fancier and had his own scheme for drawing Allison into a gunfight. He gasconaded with big talk regretting that he had only killed six men and he was still below his father's mark. He bragged at every opportunity that Clay Allison would be his seventh. His seventh proved to be other than Allison. Taking his race horse with him he crossed over Raton Pass into New Mexico, one jump ahead of the sheriff. Chunk Colber' shared a room with a waiter friend at the Clifton House. This waiter had come to the southwest for his health, working his way from place to place in the hopes of curing a lung ailment. He struck up an acquaintance with Colbert in Trinidad. The sheriff wanted Chunk bad enough to pay no attention to the fact that Clifton House was out of his jurisdiction. One night he made his appearance at the hostel and asked Stockton if Colbert was asleep in his room. Stockton told him that he felt certain that Colbert was nowhere near Clifton House. Actually the desperado was enjoying himself in a cantina in Cimarron keeping an eye cocked for Allison and an ear open for any talk that would help his strategy. The sheriff ignored Stockton's answer saying he would have a look into the room anyway just to make certain. He took the precaution of lighting a candle and made for the room pointed out by Stockton, Slowly, nervously, he opened the bedroom door left unlocked by the waiter who did not wish to be disturbed upon Colbert's return. The sheriff tiptoed to the bed. He fired at the prone figure. He later told Stockton: "With killers like Colbert you shoot first and investigate later." The waiter's grave was the first in Clifton House Boot Hill Cemetery. Although Colbert continued to stay on at Clifton House the sheriff failed to put in his second appearance possibly because on his second try he would not find a prone figure.

Just south of the Barlow & Sanderson stage stop (pre-railroad years) Tom Stockton had built a quarter mile straight race track. Here Chunk practised his horse. Tom told him that this horse would never stand a chance against Allison's but that he had a fine Kentucky sorrel which stood a better chance. He would give Chunk this horse in exchange for some work. He was short of hands and Colbert was an expert cowboy. Several days later Allison received a message that Chunk Colbert had a horse that would beat any Clay Allison chose to race. Allison brought a horse to Clifton House. Hoping for gunplay before the race Chunk became abusive. Allison refused to draw. He came to race a horse. The other would be settled later. He took a twenty dollar gold piece and a five dollar bill from his pocket. If Chunk would match this the race was on. He did.

Two Englishmen over from England in the interests of the Maxwell Land Grant Company were rooming at Clifton House at the time. These were drafted as impartial judges for Stockton sought to prevent wholesale bloodshed between Allison's cowboys and Colbert's adherents. The judges hoping the pair would bury the hatchet if neither won declared it a tie although Allison's horse was half a length ahead of Colbert's. Gillespie, a friend of Allison's, witnessed the race. He told the story many times before his recent death in Raton. He said that Allison remarked to him after the decision of the judges that he never saw a man so anxious for gunplay as Chunk Colbert. He felt that neither he nor Colbert would know peace until one proved he was faster on the draw.

The decision of the judges satisfied Colbert who promptly invited all to join him in a drink at the Clifton House. Several drinks later he again related his father's exploits regretting he had yet to equal the record set by him in the number he sent to Boot Hill. Chunk could count only eight, the last being the actual reason for his hurried departure from Trinidad. Chunk liked Clifton House and hoped to be there a long time. Of course while he was there he would have to send Boot Hill another tenant. Allison turned to Gillespie with the remark that he had no intentions of being Colbert's next victim. To leave Clifton House now would be a living death—to his pride. Every cowboy in the country would shun him as a weakling and a coward. It was the code of the era in which he lived. Gillespie cautioned him to be careful, a needless admonition since Allison watched Colbert's every move with the intensity of a falcon after the prey. For all his bravado Colbert knew he was better off that day shooting off his mouth rather than his six-shooter. The more he talked the more he sought to convince the gathered cowboys that the judges rendered their decision in fear of Allison but anyone who saw the race knew that his horse beat Allison's by at least a length. To celebrate the victory he was arranging for a big dinner. All were invited, even the loser.

It was a special kind of dinner. The host would not be with the guests. They would eat in the main dining room of the Clifton House which was usually reserved for passengers coming in on the Barlow & Sanderson stage. Next to Clifton House stood a one room adobe structure where Mrs. Gonzolez of Cimarron served short orders and kept a steaming pot of chili going at all times for the cowboys favoring this dish above others. It was a busy little place for all the travelers to and from Wooten's toll road above Clifton House availed themselves of native dishes. Colbert arranged to have the tiny cafe all to himself. Two special guests were invited to dine with him. Clay Allison and a man by the name of Cooper. Chunk wanted Clay to have all Mrs. Gonzolez had to offer. It would be terrible and unfeeling to send a man to Boot Hill on an empty stomach. Why Chunk wanted Cooper around has never been explained. He was Chunk's friend and Clay felt he could dispose of two as easily as one. He was convinced that Cooper was invited to no good purpose.

The tables in the small room were tiny, booth-like affairs hinged to the wall. Colbert waved Allison into a seat as he took the bench opposite him. Cooper sat on a chair facing the wall.

"Sort of inconvient for gunbelts," commented Colbert. Allison concurred. By mutual consilience they put their six-shooters in their laps. Colbert asked Mrs. Gonzolez to bring a pot of coffee. She brought the pot, poured out three cups, took the orders for enchiladas, placed the pot close to wall near Allison's left elbow. Calmly Colbert reached the cup to his lips sipping the black contents with the easy air of a well satisfied man. He made a few remarks to Cooper as Mrs. Gonzolez placed his meal before him. Dinner well under way he reached across his plate stretching out his left hand as he passed the empty cup to Allison for a re-fill. The pot was of refractory nature, flipping its lid every time the act of pouring took place. Clay could either take the lid off and pour, or he could pour with one hand and engage the other to hold the recalcitrant lid in place. Colbert had heard that Allison was at all times a gentleman and counted on his pouring to make his move. Allison disappointed him.

"If it's coffee you want, you know where it is."

As Allison was still talking, Colbert made for his gun with a quickness that alarmed even Allison he had the gun up, and fired. Later on in discussing the affair with Gillespie he said that Colbert did not brag when he claimed to be fast with a gun. Chunk was too fast for his own good, not on the draw, for possibly Jim Courtright is the only man in frontier history who was quicker on the draw than Clay Allison, but in his movement. So anxious was he to get in the shot that the muzzle of his six-shooter did not quite clear the table. The bullet passed through the table board ranging upward as it deflected over Allison's head. Chunk never got to fire the second shot. Allison's bullet entered his brain just above the left eye. A fresh grave was dug next to the waiter's and it pleased the sheriff at Trinidad to learn that he would not have to make a second invasion of Clifton House. The cowboys having had food and drink from Colbert thought it fitting that they should attend his funeral.

One thought occupied Allison now—what would Cooper's story be? A justice of the peace would come in from Cimarron and it would be Cooper's word against his. On the surface it seemed that Allison courted trouble knowing that Colbert was gunning for him. Besides, why did he bring the race horse to Clifton House? Could he explain to the justice that none of these things mattered? That Colbert would search him out no matter where he was, like a contender in a ring seeking to floor the champion? What about Cooper? He looked like he was willing to perjure himself in favor of his deceased friend. The cook was no witness since she was screened from view in her little kitchen. After the funeral Allison approached Cooper.

"I'm going for a ride. I'd like you to come along."

Did Cooper expect Allison to bribe him? Did he feel that he would lie next to Colbert if he refused? Whatever raced through his mind went with him. That was the last time he was ever seen at Clifton House or that part of New Mexico. Allison returned home from the ride alone. Tongues began to wag, to loosen a flood of suspicion that was to culminate in a murder trial. For all the men Allison shot, or was suspected of shooting, the only one he would be brought to trail for would be this one last seen riding off with him from the Clifton Country towards Cimarron. Did he murder Cooper? If so, where was the body? Did he merely put such a scare into him that he made tracks never to return? The mystery has not been solved to this day. Nor did Allison confide the secret to his friend Gillespie. The justice ruled that Allison killed Colbert in self defense. But this was before the days of the Santa Fe Ring, the Maxwell Land Grant, when Allison's name graced all the "Wanted" posters in the Territory and it would take two companies of soldiers from Fort Union to place him under arrest. Gillespie and others who knew Allison said that he was never known to lie. If he said that he did not kill Cooper but merely put such a scare into him that he shook the dust of Colfax county forever they took his word for it. They would have to take it in either case and the fact that he was brought to trial several years later proves that some very interested people were not taking his word for it nor did they ever give up the search for the body. Perhaps this amused Allison. Or did it? Quien sabe? He took his race horse back to the ranch and went about his business. Many were of the opinion that when Cooper saw Allison in action against Colbert it was enough for him. He might have bowed from the scene even without invitation from Clay Allison.

Allison had his Achilles' heel not because he met his Paris who knew where he was vulnerable but as a proof that no matter how fast or good you are with a gun you are never above an accident to yourself. Lord Byron walked with a limp which was overlooked in favor of other engaging attractions. Clay's titubate walk lessened him not in the esteem of friends, of which he had many for he was a leader of men and his cowboys remembered him to their dying day. The few who are left speak loyally of him insisting always that he never killed anyone who didn't need killing. There were those who thought that the floundering right foot added a certain charm to the forceful personality of the man. The accident took place in the Ponil country of the Maxwell Land Grant, centering around General Granger and his mules. No proof has come to light that Allison ran off the general's mules when he returned to the Lacy & Coleman outfit in Texas. One can hardly conceive of the general's idleness as rustlers worked against him at will. He was known to be contentious, agressive and fearless. The trail of a stolen herd of mules would not be hard to follow, and, if he was unfortunate enough to lose one herd he would take double precaution against losing a second. Nor did he ever come gunning for Allison which he would have done had he suspected him of rustling his mules, or at least have brought him to justice. The Colfax county docket records reveal no Granger vs. Allison judgment. Perhaps the general was too busy rounding up more herds for New Mexico. He evidently was a man to make the best of his opportunities. Let everyone else handle cattle, he was doing all right with mules.

George B. Shepherd who was deputy sheriff of Colfax county at the time Allison shot himself in the foot told the prosecuting attorney that the general corraled this particular herd at Lear's ranch on Crow Creek, south of Red river. Allison stood guard while his cowboys entered the corral to let out the mules. The military escort that had accompanied the herd over the Santa Fe Trail, alert to peculiar noises in the night, came running to the corral, and, in the resulting confusion Allison shot himself in the foot. This was the only casualty. The would-be rustlers escaped to a hideout along the Red river. Crockett wrote a note asking Dr. Longwell (some authors use the spelling Longwill) of Cimarron to come attend Allison's wound. He dispatched a cowboy to deliver the note and not to come back without the doctor. The doctor read the note and demurred. How did Allison get this wound? Was it reported to the authorities? Conquering his reluctance he decided to ride to Red river where he found Allison in agonizing pain. Crockett learning of the doctor's hesitation chided him for permitting so much time to elapse before deciding to perform his duty. After dressing the wound he told Crockett that he took exception to his remarks adding that Allison would not now be suffering if he had behaved himself. Looking up from his bed of pain Allison said that this was uncalled for and he would even the score just as soon as his foot was healed.

The doctor ignored this as part of the suffer's delirium. Instead, he had some cowboys lift Allison into his buggy and took him to his home in Cimarron where Mrs. Longwell would give him the attention he needed. As he lay there in bed it was suddenly brought home to him that if he were a married man all this would have been unnecessary as his wife would perform the services administered by Mrs. Longwell. Also, she would cook, keep house, do his laundry and make him feel wanted. At no time in his life did he feel so lonely and alone as those days spent in Dr. Longwell's home. Again his dreams came to him—of the home, the ranges filled with livestock, his standing in the community. Many things filled his thoughts as the foot slowly healed. The doctor never questioned him. After all, Allison's cattle were grazing in the Red river country where the accident occurred. The mishap could have taken place on his own range. A week later Allison felt improved enough to return to the Red river country.

The early criminal and docket records of Colfax county are in the handwriting of court clerk Lee. It is large, legible, straight, almost a woman's hand. As Lee was also a rancher he made notes of what was to go into the registers copying them into the books at his convenience. Sometimes a year or so elapsed before an incident found its way into the records. Allison chanced to be in his office when he noticed Lee recording something concerning him to which he took exception. Lee answered him with such vitriol, bitterness and sharpness that Allison pulled him out of the chair in which he was sitting stood him up against the door, reached for his bowie knife and pinned Lee's coat sleeve to the framework. Allison was adept at this sort of thing. He could throw the knife across a thirty foot room, pin a man to the wall without touching so much as the clothing. Men have testified that he was so accurate that he never once drew blood nor so much as scratched his victim at any time.

Expecting to be shot, Lee ducked and wiggled out of the coat and made a dive for Dr. Longwell's office, yelling at the top of his voice that he was being murdered. The doctor tried to calm him down. Allison pulled the knife out of the wood and noting W. W. Mills, a young attorney, eying him suspiciously from the next office he suddenly let the knife go again pinning the lawyer against the wall. Mills likewise wiggled out of his coat and joined Lee in the doctor's office. He was calmer than the county clerk and attributed Allison's actions to his drinking. He told the doctor that when he looked into those bloodshot eyes he thought he was looking at a devil. He could not understand why Allison picked on him. He had done nothing to arouse the man's anger. It was getting to where a man couldn't sit in his office anymore without someone trying to murder him. Mills asked the doctor if he had a gun.

"What do you want with a gun," asked the doctor?

"Under the circumstances I think I may have to shoot Allison in self defense."

The doctor, aware of Allison's prowess with both knife and side arms, smiled at the lawyer's presumption. Hickok, yes; Mills, no. And he was doubtful if even the famous Wild Bill could outdraw Allison. There was a gun on the doctor's desk. Quickly Mills slipped it into his pocket. The doctor came over, extended his hand, palm upward and asked for the gun.

"Be reasonable," he pleaded. "You don't stand a chance with Allison, and you know it."

"If you won't let him kill Allison, then I will," said Lee still smarting under the scare thrown into him.

"Listen to me, both of you." The doctor spoke sternly. "Everybody in this town knows both of you. No one considers either of you a coward. You have both faced danger time and again; but you are both inviting death if you think you can go in there and ask Allison to draw. Be reasonable."

"He is a desperado. He needs killing." The doctor did not know whether the lawyer was saying this because he actually believed it or because his feelings were ruffled.

"I have known Allison some time now. I do not regard him as a desperado needing killing." The words were almost whispered.

Glancing out the window he noticed Allison coming out of the county clerk's office, jump on his horse and steer it across the street to his office.

"It looks like Allison's on his way here. I may be a doctor but I do not like wiping up blood. Your blood."

"If it will make you feel better, we'll go," said Lee.

"That's the wise thing to do. Use the back door".

To prevent Allison from coming in to look for the pair the doctor went outside. Allison greeted him from his horse bidding him the time of day. The doctor instead of answering asked him why he mistreated the lawyer and county clerk and in a manner unbecoming a Southern gentleman. Clay threw his head back and laughed. He made no effort to dismount. He told the doctor that he had no fight against neither Lee nor Mills but against a man named James Wilson. It seems that he and Wilson were at Lambert's where, after a few drinks, they became involved in an argument. The bartender managed to quiet them down and Allison left. Wilson said aloud that the only reason he did not kill Allison was that he did not want to take advantage of a man unsteadied by liquor. Lee and Mills who were also in the bar agreed that Allison should be killed but not to be taken advantage of when drunk. When Clay found out what transpired after he left he decided to put a good scare into Lee and Mills. The bullet he would reserve for Wilson.

"Doctor, you know me well enough. If I wanted to kill Lee and Mills I had the opportunity. Perhaps I don't even want to kill Wilson. I might just cut off his ears. It will be something to remember Clay Allison by for the rest of his life." He saluted the doctor and was off. When Wilson heard that Allison had plans for him if he ever met him in Cimarron he said that he held Allison in contempt and would have shot him down under more favorable circumstances. It was noticed, however, that when word spread that Allison was on his way in from the Red river country Wilson was nowhere to be seen, and, like Cooper, he was never seen again.

The cooks in the eating establishments of Cimarron were especially fond of Clay Allison. They stored away all the empty oyster cans for his visits. After they had fed him or talked to him the same invariable question was asked: Would he mind shooting through the center of the bottom of the cans if they would throw them up in the air? They also liked to watch him hit the bull's eye with the bowie knife. He always obliged.

No matter how the frontier pushed forward; in spite of Indians, dust storms, drought, sickness, hardship, rustlers, land thieves, gun slingers, cattle drives, end of track towns, there were always the lucid intervals for frolic and the good old Saturday night dance fast becoming an American institution. People might be said to live in the wilderness but they knew how to gather for the occasion. Cowboys might envision the girl of their dreams under starry skies but they knew how to slick up over and against the possibility that such a girl might be found at the dance. It was still the day of chaperons. The fast talking for dates usually came during a fast polka, a mazourka, a quadrille or a schottische. The Saturday night dance at Cimarron was attended by all the families for miles around. Clay was particularly interested in the Bishop girl from up along the Vermejo. He eventually took to calling at her home until her mother told him in no uncertain terms he was not welcome. When he again made his appearance she emphasized her edict by use of a broom. Always shy and uncertain when it came to women Clay decided that such tartness would be reflected in the daughter. The last thing he intended to do would be to tie himself to a scold whose waspish asperity was hardly conducive to domestic tranquility. He could not understand why they looked upon him as a rustler and a gun fighter. His next venture was the Holbrook girl. This never proved very serious and the needle of time pointed very much to his living out his days a bachelor. Then he met Dora McCullough. Whatever the town folk had to say about Allison as a tough hombre, she had a chance to observe and study the deeper qualities—his honesty, politeness, sincere and genuine respect for womanhood. One secret she found out: He often sent money anonymously to people in need. Hardly the trait of a killer. Allison felt in no way encouraged as far as she was concerned especially after two failures. His reputation as a destroyer of men must have reached her ears since his exploits made the rounds even faster than the whirl of the dance. She was a rather attractive young miss from Sedalia, Missouri. Her father died during the late conflict; her mother shortly after. She and her sister were taken into the household of Mr. and Mrs. A. J. Young. Just what the relationship was no one knew for certain although a few have ventured to say that Mrs. Young was sister to Dora's mother.

In the beginning Mrs. Young looked at Clay with an eye of disapproval which gave him a sinking sensation. John Allison made it very plain that he was very much taken up with Dora's sister. The feeling was mutual. Mrs. Young had no objections to the younger Allison having heard that he was very level headed, a good man for business and vastly different from his brother. He was interested in tilling the soil, always up with the sun and full of dreams of golden wheat fields, dew on the earth, corn belts. Stock raising was not his idea of farming. But it was what his brother liked; that is what he did. No man was ever as close to Clay as his brother John, the recipient of his confidences. Thus when Clay told him how he felt about the tall dark haired Dora the younger brother took upon himself to play the knight errant in whispering to his friend how his brother was striken with her sister but dared not hope. He was surprised to learn that Dora was very much in love with Clay. It has been said that Clay Allison married a childhood sweetheart. This is far from the truth. While Clay knew a number of McCulloughs in Tennessee he did not go back to marry one, nor did he invite any to come to New Mexico for the purpose, not an uncommon occurance in those days. From the time he lived in New Mexico to the date of his death Clay Allison never went back to Waynesboro.

Mrs. Bourne of Raton remembered her two cousins quite well although she was a mere slip of a girl at the time the two brothers and two sisters took to courting. Their father (J. McCullough) was her mother's brother. He died when they were quite young. Mrs. Bourne did not know what the relationship was to the Youngs but they were brought up as members of that family. Clay was in his early thirties when he first met Dora; she was considerably younger. The Youngs lived on the Vermejo near the conflux of Wet Canyon creek and Gonzolez creek. Later, due to Maxwell Land Grant agitation, the Youngs sold to Beal who in turn sold to Bartlett. This latter developed the homestead into one of the show places of the nation. The Bartlett Ranch made headlines in the Roaring Twenties as a resort for the popular set of movie stars anxious for a reprieve from the artificial life of Hollywood. None of them was probably ever aware that they were on the site of the Young Ranch where Allison played his romantic role under the lights of Dora's eyes, for in her love Clay was to find himself. She was his salvation. That no one can take from him— or her.

While all these palpitations were set in motion, as is usually the case, everybody in the neighborhood knew of the dual romance save Mr. and Mrs. Young, who, while they observed that John was rather over friendly and sweet on the younger girl, did not think that Clay would be brazen enough to seek permission to attend Dora. She was too good for the likes of him. Absurd. That is the word she would have used had anyone turned informer. This was not the first time opposition to a marriage served to bring it about. Here was a situation and a crisis. Dora wanted to marry Clay. Allison certainly was in love with the girl from the Vermejo. If he could not marry her then he intended never to marry. But he wanted her enough to brave the wrath of the Youngs which was an experience indeed. Had Mrs. Young taken a shotgun rather than a broom he still would have returned for his lady love. She did neither simply because she belonged to the class of the uninformed.

During one of the obreptitious meetings talk turned to marriage. At last those dreams in Tennessee were becoming a reality. Why seek to emulate Loving, Goodnight, Coleman or Lacy if there be not a lady fair to share the estate of the cattle baron? The realization that someone did not shy from him as a gun man and killer did much to flavor his decision and direct his course.

He was accepted as a woman accepts the man she wants to marry. While all this was beyond his comprehension he still would make the best of it before she changed her mind and would be lost to him forever. Marriage definitely agreed upon Clay bought up a squatter's rights near the junction of the Vermejo and Red rivers, property that was ultimately to come into the hands of Captain French and near the site of the village bearing that name, more readily identified today as between French and Maxwell, New Mexico. Allison knew this spot for he often grazed cattle here as well as up near the site of Otero. French and Otero are ghost towns today and practically nonexistent but in their heyday they had all the gun smoke and exuberance of Cimarron, Elizabethtown, Las Vegas and Raton. What frontier town was without its gamblers, taverns, dance halls and the disorders of a turbulent age? At first Allison built a dugout. As the romance progressed he built a home. One day the Allison boys brought home their brides.

Mrs. Bourne was of the opinion that the double wedding took place before Rev. Thomas Harwood, the circuit rider of the Methodist church. Mrs. Lucy McReady, an aunt of Dora's, was of the same opinion. The Youngs were a religious people who would not have forgiven the elopement—for that is what it was—had the couples consented to wedlock before a justice. The marriage took place in 1873. One day the four went to visit the Youngs to beg their forgiveness and their blessing; both of which they received, learning in time to evaluate the husbands through the eyes of the wives. Clay had often heard his mother use the expression, quite common in Tennessee, "Bitter pills have sweet effects," which he sincerely believed since the Youngs were bitter towards him for his attentions to Dora, then hurt because of the furtive marriage but now reconciled because he was not the terror the people of Cimarron painted him to be. They soon observed that he never went looking for trouble nor did he shirk it when it came his way. They agreed with him that he never killed a man that didn't need killing. That Dora was reconciled with the Youngs we learn from the *Trinidad News* of July 20, 1888: "Mrs. Clay Allison, widow of a noted character in the earlier days, was booked to arrive here on the 21st. She will visit the family of Mr. Young on the Vermejo." The object of Dora's visit was to have her foster mother attend her at the birth of Clay's second daughter. Dora never had cause to regret the marriage. It has been said that when the cemetery in Pecos, Texas, was removed to a new location, she had Clay's remains taken to Fort Worth. Newsmen often hounded her for stories concerning him but held his memory too sacred to vouch any information, and was known to have run them off with a shotgun if they became obnoxious.

Before building his home Clay had a dugout west of Red river, seemingly projecting out of the hillside. It was about forty feet back in the hill and consisted of one large room. C. B. Thacher remembered the place well having often been a guest there. The cowboys working for Allison stored provisions in the cabin and lived with Clay during round-up and branding season. The men particularly liked to work for Clay because he was never niggardly about whisky. He usually kept a five-gallon jug on hand for their consumption. Each evening the men would wash up, eat their supper, then while away the evening in drinking and dancing. Clay loved to dance. He always made it a point to keep a fiddler in his outfit. Since there were no women about to lend charm and reality to their world of make believe, the men often danced with one another, or stamped about the dugout in an Indian dance, much to the disgust of the fiddler who was hard put to change his tunes to their varying moods especially when the whisky made their heads lighter than their feet. At this stage of the drink it hardly mattered who they danced with. The cook for the outfit was a rather turgid individual who invented ways of being absent from these hilarious proceedings which usually ended on the rather sad note of nostalgia. One night Clay himself missed the cook and went in search of him. Found hiding in the tall grass by the river he was brought back and made to dance before the assembled cowboys only this time it was not the fiddler playing the music; never an obese man jumped so high as the whirling cook dodging the bullets rattling about his feet.

The man Dora married was tall; about two inches over six feet. He weighed one hundred and ninety pounds; eyes, blue; prominent face bones; square set jaw. He had the look of a man ready to spring into a saddle to lead a caravan ever further toward the setting sun. He had a Roman nose and wore his hair long in the fashion of the day. At times he wore a mustache which he permitted to grow so long that it curled into his chin. His hair had a tendency to form ringlets and was blonde as a youth slowly turning darker with the years to blend with a weather beaten face producing the deception of swathiness which accounts for the readiness of many to describe him as dark and a half breed. At times he permitted his beard to grow but never beyond two or three inches. His right eye was crossed ever so slightly so that the iris seemed to be just off the bridge of the nose. His ears were large and stuck out from his face a little but this was hardly noticeable since his hair was thick and curled. The part started from the receding high forehead straight back to the crown of the head, in line with the corner of the left eye and the bridge of the nose. The upper lip was thin without end curvatures, creating the impression of a rather large mouth. The nether lip was thick, solidly round without tapering as if a protrusion. He wore expensive clothes, the latest fashion if they were masculine looking; nothing to cut him out as a dandy. He had a penchant for shirts never resisting a sales talk whenever in a mercantile store. He prided himself on his neat appearance and never went to town after a cattle drive without first primping. Women considered him above the average in looks. He treated them with the respect common to frontiersmen, being as gentlemanly to the harlot he passed on the street as to the mayor's daughter. Women baffled him and drew him within himself possibly because his reputation with a gun eclipsed whatever spark or flutter his general good looks and fine manners, his manly appearance may have engendered. He ranks with Jim Courtright and Wild Bill Hickok as high, wide and handsome but dangerous with the six shooter.

All this Dora knew and more. Underneath the cold exterior was a warm heart ever searching to help the unfortunate. Anyone who has ever attempted an article on Clay Allison has only repeated what he read or heard from another concerning him boiling their facts down to his antics when drunk, his honesty in his statements, his respect for women, the various men he sent to boot hill, his fearlessness and cold nerve. All are agreed that he was not a gun fighter but fail to explain why they think so. The fact is they have no explanation. They have reiterated time and again that he was dangerous when drunk but overlooked the possibility of his being more so when sober. Until Dora accepted him for what he was, he might be said to have been a man in search of himself looking for the answer in establishing a reputation for fearlessness only to realize that he had to live with it or be killed. It was the law of a lawless age. It was the code of a raw breed of men whose only and ready answer for justice was carried about the hip like Justice with the scales in her hand. Like her they were often just as blind.

Shortly after his marriage Allison became acquainted with the only man able to out-draw him. He worked his gun differently than the normal run of gun toters, and certainly out of kilter with even the exceptional type. Allison's way was to let his hands fall loosely to the sides, jerk the gun hand up to the gun butt hooking the hammer of the single-action under the thumb and sliding the forefinger into the trigger-guard. As the gun cleared the holster he tightened his fingers on the butt, shooting away as the muzzle came into focus. This expert with the six-shooter had just come in from Texas. He was not above some rare antics himself so that soon the gossips of Cimarron classified him as a desperado but he was to prove himself a sheriff of no mean ability. Western Americana is too much taken up at the moment with Stoudenmire, Gillett, Garrett, Milton and Earp to reach out to Hixenbaugh, Littrell, Rinehart, Lambert and Bowman but some day they will find their Boswell. Some were marshals; others were sheriffs; a few were both. Mace Bowman was never a marshal. He was a born gentleman turned cowboy.

As a child he tired of fine schools, servants, wealth. The war was opportune for him. Shouldering a rifle at fifteen, he waved good-bye to doting parents, weeping slaves, barking dogs. He fought for the Confederacy as a matter of course rather than principle. The recklessness of youth made him brave. He was often commended for his daring and courage. A bullet penetrated his left lung and was to trouble him for years to come ultimately causing his death in Trinidad. His wife and Sister Blandina were at his bedside when the end came. Upon the advice of a doctor he came to Texas drifting into the Brazos country to work as a cowboy. In the spring of 1867 he and some companions found a wealthy stockman named Robert Lee bound to a tree in a lonely area, the work of some heartless highwaymen who hoped he would starve to death and become the prey of wolves and coyotes for they had relieved him of the receipts of a cattle sale.

Grateful for their providential arrival Lee asked them if they would not help him organize a posse to track down the thieves. Mace Timothy Bowman (to give him his full name—his friends called him Mason; in New Mexico he was known as Mace) joined forces with the rancher. Meantime the outlaws received word that Lee was recruiting cowboys to give them a bad time. Undismayed, their leader also organized a force to oppose him. During the next four months both sides engaged in three pitched battles, both sides losing heavily. In the next engagement Lee won a signal victory exterminating the gang to the complete satisfaction of cattlemen and citizen alike. Lee offered to keep Bowman working as range boss but Mace had other plans. The busy little town of Trinidad attracted him. Although he did not meet with the success he hoped for as a guide along the Santa Fe Trail he did serve as deputy sheriff for several years. Also, he married. Next he tried ranching in the Cimarron country, moving to Raton when that city was inaugurated by the Santa Fe Railroad. He was elected sheriff of Colfax county seven months before his death.

Meeting in Lambert's one evening, talk turned to Hickok's fast draw. Allison said that he had the same method of drawing and boasted that he thought he was even faster. Bowman begged to differ. Although he was five years younger than Allison and had less experience in handling guns he was willing to wager a gallon of whisky that he could outdraw Allison. They walked to the center of the room, paced off the distance to the wall and turned. Before Allison's gun was half out of the holster Mace's six shooter was pointed at his heart. Allison refused to believe it. Again they met, paced off the distance, and turned. Allison was amazed. Bowman's gun was again in readiness. He took his gallon, after which the pair went out into the country where Bowman taught Clay his amazing method. Allison worked at it until he mastered the trick and soon learned to draw with the same lightning rapidity. Jim Courtright, the marshal of Fort Worth, was possibly the only other man who could equal his speed. Had these two met and engaged in a trial of skill it would have been something for the speculation of lovers of Western Americana.

Several miles from the present city of Raton is the beautiful Sugarite country where settlers often gathered in a large barn-like hall for social amenities so often sought after by pioneers. The dance was the most popular diversion, although there were box suppers, dinners, and other forms of entertainment. Allison and Bowman attended one such dance but found the people rather staid, quiet and inactive. After a few drinks, they decided to put some life into the party. The people refused to co-operate. Angered at the rebuff they drew their pistols, driving everyone from the hall save the fiddler. Taking a stool from against the wall they placed it in the center. On it they laid their six-shooters, cocked and ready for action. Taking off their coats and boots they commenced a jig around the stool, each equi-distant from the guns. If one darted in toward the weapons, the other did the same.

Outside a blizzard raged. In this high altitude this was dangerous for people have been known to freeze to death in a short time due to the sub-zero temperatures encountered here from October to April. Teeth rattling, a few decided to brave the wrath of the dancing fools than freeze in the dancing snow. The two men were too intent on their game to notice the hall filling with half frozen people anxious to dance again if only to keep the blood circulating in their veins. At last one brave woman, tiring of what she called the infantile conduct of two grown men, picked up the guns, ran to the little room in the back of the building, lifted a trunk lid and placed them on some clothes. Had a man tried this, he would never have reached the kitchen. Clay's bowie knife would have stopped him in his tracks. Bowing to the fleeing figure they produced two more guns and went on with their act. Since neither seemed to gain the advantage they tired of the sport to devote their attention to the men. Whether one would have shot the other is a matter of conjecture. Possibly so, since they were both on the tipsy side.

Some of the men realizing that their fun had been spoiled decided to make a bed on the floor of the little kitchen. To venture home in the storm would be hazardous at best. They might even lose their way, and end up as stiff as boards. Bowman made all the would-be sleepers get up and return to the dance floor. Allison collected the others. All were required to take off their boots or shoes. To refuse meant death. Some pleaded that they were willing to comply if only the women folk were out of the way of the flying bullets. For they knew that they would have to dance to the tune of the six shooters. Those living close by were permitted to leave; the others were packed into the little room. Before this new game got under way the two decided that they were sleepy. They emptied the kitchen of the women, coiled up on the floor and were soon sound asleep much to the relief of every one. Many decided that they would never come to a dance again if Bowman and Allison were present, but the resolution was short lived. Two weeks later they were all back dancing away to their hearts content. It was the more enjoyable since neither Allison nor Bowman put in appearance.

Lambert's was not the only cantina in Cimarron that offered excitement. There was the Brick House at the present time still open for business by way of a garage perhaps because motors are found to be less recalcitrant than humans. Christmas Eve was like any other night at the Brick House save that the bartender would have welcomed more business. Too many of his customers were home attending to other chores in preparation for the coming day rather than drinking in the cheer dispensed in his establishment. But there were enough around to keep him active. When time had cut deep into the night the door of the tavern again opened. Clay Aliison stood as if framed in the doorway. For a moment he listened to the shrill, hollow laughter, stacado music from the man pounding away on the piano, ribald cries of the enchorial brigade gathered about him—like so many lost soul's seeking consolation in sound. He walked to the bar calling for attention by striking the butt of his six-shooter against the surface. Silence. All eyes in the room focused on his tall figure.

Injustice of any kind upset Clay Allison. It also made him fighting mad. This plebian vulgarity hardly fitted the tone on earth everywhere at a time when prayer was in order. Glaring at the upturned faces he said:

"Is this the tribute fitting the Babe of Bethlehem? This is Christmas Eve. Don't any of you forget it."

The wind outside seemed to be making a terrible racket. Inside it was a "silent night" indeed.

"This is no night to drown your sorrows. No one leaves. We might as well conduct our Christmas service here and now."

Looking to the man at the piano he said:

"A Christmas song, please. One we all know."

To the young man who had formerly served as a minister in the Episcopal church:

"Reverend, please lead us in prayer."

To the people:

"We will all be reverent, won't we. I have a friend here (lifting the revolver) that will help."

So, they sang holy songs and prayed. And they felt better for it. No more liquor was sold that night. Dawn came to Cimarron and all who opened the door of the Brick House paused in awe for religion somehow changed the aspect. The ex-minister was eloquent. Allison's head was bowed deeper than the rest.

Chapter Five

VIGILANTES

The next few years are full of incident and the most remembered in his life. His reputation keeps apace with his progress as a rancher, cowman and a law in his hands. Legends begin to make the rounds. Stories are rampant. He becomes "bigtime." The killing of Chunk, the fight with the ferryman, other incidents, rolled like a snowball downhill, gathering size as momentum pushed from mouth to mouth the daring deeds of a man nice to talk with but not against. He keeps busy trying to prove to Dora that he is the husband she expected him to be so that most of this talk is lost on him if he is aware of it at all. He is fast becoming a man of substance even for a hamlet larger than Cimarron. Dreams fade before reality.

Also an attempt on the part of the Maxwell Land Grant Company to colonize the vast tract, expand the industrial and educational facilities made Cimarron a veritable boom town. Melvin W. Mills hitched his wagon to a star and jumped on the bandwagon for a ride into politics to scramble his name with Elkins, Catron, Thompson, Ritchie, Prince and others said to have formed a ring in which they controlled Territorial elections; out of which were excluded everyone and anyone who refused to play ball. Charles Springer, fresh out of school, selected this town on the Grant as the place to inaugurate his law practice. Allison was to have reason for gratitude. Sullivan failed to come up to the expectations of the Grant people who had brought him out of Santa Fe to edit the Cimarron News and Press. Dawson succeeded him. And the new editor proved himself to be very-anti-ring. If this was not stew enough agitation fermented between the Grant officials and the squatter. Sheriffs served eviction notices. Retaliation. Grant pastures were fired; cattle rustling increased; officials threatened at gun point. Thunder heads gathered. Spokesman for the squatter was an unobtrusive man of medium height known at the time as a minister of sorts, a type setter on the News and Press staff, and for his bad teeth. He had been in town a year now, his voice still very dim on behalf of the squatter, but loud, clear and strong when he relieved Parson Tolby in the pulpit. He was a printer by trade; a circuit rider by choice. It is a fallacy to think that he came to Cimarron simply to investigate Parson Tolby's death. The parson's murder was merely to give him his battle cry.

Parson F. J. Tolby of Indiana came to Cimarron unannounced and uninvited. The town was in need of salvation so he enlisted with the Methodist Circuit Riders to chase the devil out of Elizabethtown, Ute Park, Ponil, Cimarron and Sugarite. He might have succeeded too, had he not decided that the ring needed a dressing down and he was all for naming names and quoting figures instead of biblical texts. Some politician whether local or Territorial decided that the parson was doing very little devil chasing and very much devil bringing. The parson was daring enough to cause some very important people to get more than their fingers burnt. Time and again he threatened to disrupt the political scene at Cimarron, as well as Santa Fe. So say they who seek an explanation for his murder. The only thing that can be said with certainty is that he was killed. It is still in the records as unsolved.

Recognizing him for what he was, Clay Allison was one of the first to welcome the parson. Men of the cloth never found him failing in respect. Things religious fascinated him. Luis Griego, son of Pancho Griego, who had no reason to say anything nice regarding Clay Allison paid tribute to his father's killer when he said: "Allison killed Chunk while eating at the house of a woman generally known as La Lauriana (Laurel lover). There was a picture of Christ crowned with thorns on the wall. Chunk made a blasphemous remark and took a shot at the picture. The shot went through one of the eyes of the pictured Savior. This highly incensed Clay Allison and without a warning word he shot Chunk through the breast, killing him instantly . . ." While we may not agree as to the version of Chunk's death we are not surprised that a contemporary gave it a religious twist, rather unusual for those wild and lawless days.

Parson Tolby loved Cimarron and planned to make it his home for a long time to come. He bought a lot in the new addition and contracted for a carpenter to build a home suitable for his wife and family. Meantime he continued to live at the place furnished him by the Grant company. Buzzards and bees worked not quite like ants and grasshoppers. The Santa Fe Ring had plans. Colfax county would be divided in such a way as to place the tremendous profits of the mining district in the new county under the thumb and graft of the big wigs from the capital. They thought nothing of it. The election ballots would be fixed. This was not something indigenous to the political circle at Santa Fe. It was part of the history of the era. Whigham, Sherwin, Donohoe, Griego, Rynerston, Catron, Owens, Elkins, Lacy, Dawson, Waldo, Otero, Thompson—moving shadows all. From their corners they whispered, their glances furtive, evasive, mysterious —lips moving without sound. Promises and a handshake. Brewing a stew, sewing a shroud. The Kingdom of Colfax brought more than one man to ruin. Letters passed from Santa Fe to Cimarron and back. Strange letters. Terrible letters with words of murder and payment.

Who actually belonged to the ring? Quien sabe, senor? Dis ring on my finger—dis I know. Is there another? Perhaps. Everywhere there is talk especially en de papeles. It ez not wise to ask, senor. The sky. She ez good. I like. Manana too. So, de ring. Bah. Why ask me senor? With a shrug of the shoulder he is off to gather wood wondering within himself if he will live to light it. Talk not to strangers. Beware.

One morning the people of Cimarron woke up very much like the residents of Paris during the early days of the Revolution to find themselves virtually prisoners in the hands of terrorists. And at such an inopportune time when the city was adjusting itself to prospectors, gamblers, religion, a boom, recognition in politics, a widely accepted newspaper, hopes and a brighter outlook for the future through the facilities of the Grant Company. The town was suddenly aware of mob rule, vigilantes and the Maxwell Land Grant War. Printer and Preacher Oscar Patrick McMains was to make the Lincoln County War seem like child's play by way of comparison. The unofficial number of dead had been tabulated as upwards two hundred. The official number definitely overshadows the Murphy-McSween fracas despite publicity. When time re-evaluates the two wars, Allison and the Maxwell Land Grant conflict will stand the test to outshine the other. The Maxwell Land Grant War (1875-1893) was probably the longest and most bitter fought on New Mexico and Colorado soil. It died only with McMains. The Russells, Bacas, Gonzolez' Colemans, Lacys, Stocktons, Gillespies—hundreds of others have left records gradually finding their way into print. In the not too distant future the full story will be pieced together as a wonderful adjunct of Southwestern Americana. Time and again McMains was to lament the fact that the loss of Clay Allison prognosticated the cause. He looked upon Allison as his right hand and felt that he could have smoked out the Grant Company if he had not moved to other parts. Allison denied this. He claimed that he took part in the war only until such time as Tolby's murderers were brought to justice. McMains jumped at the pretext to convert the parson's death into a cause—his cause. He had settled on the Crow Creek ranch and meant to stay on it. The Grant Company was to hound him at Crow Creek, Cimarron, Raton, Stonewall and Trinidad. He asked for it.

What, actually, did Parson Tolby know? What could he reveal that would implicate a person that he would have the minister dead rather than divulge information? Who was so scared that he had to engineer a killing without a shadow of suspicion falling on him? The price paid was good enough to buy silence forever. By this time the secret must be in the grave with the killer. Was it a cattle rustler caught in the act of changing brands? Was it some member of the political ring at Santa Fe? Who killed Parson Tolby? Answer that and pick up the reward money promised by New Mexico. The vigilantes, led by Clay Allison, thought they had the culprits and treated them accordingly, but even the vigilantes were forced to admit they were mistaken.

These were the desperate hours. Widows cried; children feared; men rode like avenging angels cutting down the just and unjust alike. It began on September 14, 1875. The body of the murdered parson was found in a thicket by cowboys out hunting strays. Placing the remains over a saddle they formed a funeral procession, riding one behind the other, Indian fashion. It is not certain whether Rev. Thomas Harwood or O. P. McMains conducted the funeral service. Perhaps both. The printer-preacher asked for and received the post vacated by the death of Tolby although Harwood was rather reluctant about it. He opposed McMains' investigation of the murder as well as his fight against the Maxwell Land Grant Company for which the battling parson never forgave him.

Allison developed a particular fondness for Tolby because he was rather liberal in his views not hesitating to enter a cantina to discuss religion and political matters although he always refused the drink Allison proffered. He was always willing and ready to discuss horse racing, gambling, dancing with the same fiery intensity as religion. Although a Union man Allison overlooked it in his favor, as he was to do with McMains, ministers being the exception since they were not supposed to preach Yankee or Southerner but heaven and salvation. Tolby often visited the law office of M. W. Mills to regale his audience with stories of his Civil War experiences. Sometimes Supreme Court Judge Joseph Palen was found with the group. Politically, Tolby favored the Copperhead Democrats while the judge was a staunch Republican. The discussion was heated at times but Tolby never left without shaking the judge's hand and calling him friend. Allison often invited Tolby to the horse races but the minister always declined.

Saturday, September 11—Rev. Tolby left his home in Cimarron for Elizabethton as he alternated Sundays between the two places. There was nothing in his sermon matter nor his delivery to indicate that he was in any way upset. The talk was of no particular significance then but the congregation sought to make something of it later—"Be not solicitous for your life, what you shall eat, nor for your body, what you shall put on . . . Seek ye first the Kingdom of God and His justice . . . Be not therefore solicitous for tomorrow, for the morrow will be solicitous for itself . . . Sufficient for the day is the evil thereof." The preacher took his text from the King James version of Matt. 6:25-34. Tolby found enough work to keep him in Elizabethtown until Tuesday morning.

Tuesday, September 14—Tolby started back to Cimarron. About a mile ahead rode Cruz Vega, a mail carrier employed by Florence Donahue who had the mail contracts for the area. Vega later testified that he saw the minister get off his horse about six miles out of town. As the Elizabethtown-Cimarron highway was south at this point it would place him about Willow creek where Tolby no doubt stopped to water his horse. Astride his mount again the minister continued on for another two miles before Vega lost sight of him. This would place him close to the creek that bears his name. From the day the cowboys found the body in some bushes near the water even to this the name Tolby creek persists. The horse was found close by, tied to a tree. Did Tolby tie the horse? Did the murderer? Was Vega aware of a horse and rider hiding in the thicket as he rode by? Tolby's horse might have made an interesting witness—if horses could speak. But, if they could, the animal might have met the same fate as the master. If ever circumstantial evidence pointed to a man that man was Cruz Vega. He picked the wrong time to carry the mail. He often said that. If only he had waited until the evening or the next day. He insisted he had nothing to do with the death of the minister. There were those who believed him. Donahue, Griego, Rinehart and Mills. So did the natives. Vega was lodged in jail. As the District Court was being held in Taos, a courier was dispatched to break the news to Judge Waldo. Mills, the defending lawyer, was calm when he received the news. In fact everybody was calm except O. P. McMains.

Vega steadfastly protested his innocence when questioned. Why would he want to kill Tolby? That is what McMains wanted to know. Following the funeral groups gathered here and there. Natives also gathered. They were in an ugly mood. The Tejanos would not give Vega a fair trial. They called everybody Tejano who was not one of them; hence that Mills, McMains and others were from parts other than Texas was not a matter of distinction—all Americans were Tejanos. Francisco Griego (better known as Pancho) a man not without courage decided to act as spokesman for the natives. He was well known as a business partner of Donahue having also served for a time as marshal in Santa Fe until difficulties with the law turned him into a gunman of sorts. He had several notches in his gun and was fast on the draw. Told that Allison was interested in bringing the murderer to justice Griego said he was not afraid of Allison and was willing to put him to the test anytime. He said Allison was fast with his tongue, not his gun. Rewards amounting to the sum of three thousand dollars were posted for the arrest of the murderer (or murderers). Most of this money was put up by the Masonic Lodge of which Tolby was a member.

Mrs. Tolby was a frail built woman, and timid. This country was new to her, and wild. The stories she heard made her long for her Indiana home but she weathered her fears for the sake of her husband and two little girls. The tragedy took the little bit of starch out of her so that she felt like a lost soul. Mrs. W. A. Crocker took pity on the widow and took her and the children to her home. Mrs. Tolby said she would return to Indiana as soon as relatives arrived to take her back. A day or two later a cowboy came with a note from Clay Allison. Frantic she ran to Mr. Crocker.

"Clay Allison wants to have a talk with me. I have heard things concerning him. He is a desperate character. What shall I do?"

"You had best receive him. If you say no he will probably come anyway. Can't say as he means you harm. I heerd he was right friendly with your husband."

So Clay Allison came. Mrs. Tolby and Mrs. Crocker attended him in the parlor quite a distinction in those days. His gentlemanly manner soon disarmed the nervous widow as he regretted the loss of his good friend. He gave her a purse of thirty-five dollars and told her that if she needed more she should not hesitate to call on him. He would do all in his power to track down the person who made her a widow. Not long after the visit Mrs.

Tolby and children departed from New Mexico forever.

Meantime McMains aligned his forces. A tenseness and bitterness pervaded the air about Cimarron. Stories were rampant. It reached the ears of Clay Allison that Griego hoped to shoot him on sight. Before working with Donahue, Griego had worked with W. W. Boggs and Lucien Maxwell as a cow hand and a driver along the Santa Fe Trail as well as the Chihuahua Trail. Natives clustered about by the score. Cowboys became alarmed and sent messages along the Vermejo and Red rivers for all available hands to come to Cimarron. McMains asked Allison to take charge of his ever increasing army. Although Clay soon found himself commanding two hundred men he did not let it interfere with business. Florencio Donahue ordered a wagon load of beef. Allison obliged, leaving disorganized Cimarron to cut it for him. He arrived late in the evening of the next day asking Florencio if he could not leave the wagon unpacked until the next day. Donahue said it was all right with him since he wanted to go to town that night anyway. He told Clay that if he came along he would treat him to a drink. Allison accepted. On the way into town they came upon Pancho Griego and his eighteen year old son, Luis L. Griego who were also riding to Cimarron. Donahue hailed the pair saying that he was going to Lambert's saloon. He invited them also. Pancho glanced from his partner to Allison, nodding his acceptance. He said nothing. Luis went along for the ride for young natives did not drink in public places when a father or uncle was present. This was considered a mark of respect and esteem.

Monday night, November 1, 1875—The four dismounted, hitched their horses to the post.

"After you," said Allison to Pancho.

"No, senor. After you." The native New Mexican is inherently polite.

At the bar Allison said to Poncho in Spanish:

"Pancho, quiero verte solo." Allison had a good command of Spanish.

"Muy bien, vamos."

Pancho walked ahead to select a spot. Florencio and Luis watched and waited as did several others in the bar. Lambert groaned but said nothing. He knew better. Off to themselves they made conversation.

"I hear that you have been looking for me, Pancho."

"Si, senor. You are a hard man to find."

"Is there something in particular you want?"

"Si, senor. I want to kill you."

"Now?"

"Now is as good a time as any. Let us drink up. We will keep our hands above the table. We shall keep drinking until one or the other finds an opportunity to draw. Is that not fair?"

"Fair enough."

So they drank.

"Rather warm in here," remarked Pancho.

Allison agreed.

"I think I will fan myself with my sombrero."

"As you wish."

Pancho fanned.

Stealthily he worked towards his gun, the wide brimmed hat serving as a shield. Without seeming to move Allison had his gun muzzle above the table top. He fired three shots. Commented the editor of the Santa Fe New Mexican:

"On the night of November 1, Francisco Griego was shot and killed by C. Allison. Both parties met at the door of the St. James (Lambert's), entered, and with some friends took a drink, when the two walked to the corner of the room and had some conversation. There Allison drew his revolver and shot three times. The lights were extinguished and Griego was not found until the next morning. Francisco Griego was well known in Santa Fe, where his mother lives. He has killed a great many men and was considered a dangerous man; few regret his loss.''

Why was the body at Lambert's all night?

When news reached the cowboys that Griego and Allison were at Lambert's, many fearing trouble came to the saloon. They arrived too late. To celebrate the victory they began drinking and doing a war dance about the corpse. The more Allison drank the more he stripped until he was the Indian chief he made himself to be when drunk. His breech cloth was a little red ribbon. The prosecuting attorney was to make much of this dance during the murder trial. Young Luis went home to prepare for the burial. This home was to be a rallying place for the natives.

McMains was sick—very sick. Cruz Vega was released by the authorities for lack of sufficient evidence against him. Was this justice? A murderer on the loose! And poor Parson Tolby cold in his grave. It was the talk of the town. Quietly, like evanescent shadows, moving mutely in the night, the natives held their meetings. Fear marked their brows. Also determination born of fear. They had guns and ammunition, too. That chaparito called McMains, he was a muy, muy mal hombre, making everybody mad at them because a parson was killed. Caramba! Did not the padre at Mora drink poisoned wine at the Mass? He knew it was the drink of death. But he drank. He was brave. They gave him a grand funeral, the Penitentes did. Nobody made a fuss. Not the obispo at Santa Fe, not the sheriff, not even the Hermanos of the Morada. Why all this disturbance about un ministro from muy lejos? Perhaps the gringos plotted this to take their land away from them. Perhaps this was the work of Tejanos. Quien sabe? The Tejanos always wanted their land. Long ago their abuelos told them to be wary of the Tejanos. The gobierno gave good money to the Tejanos mucho tiempo pasado to keep them out. Said all the land to the Rio Grande was theirs. Now they wanted the land again. Maxwell said it was his. These bearded men digging so many holes in the ground said it was theirs. A compania called the Maxwell Land Grant and Railway Company said it was theirs. Everybody was looking for yellow metal. Fools. You couldn't eat it like chili. Now there was trouble again. They would sign no papers. They would fight. Up the Ponil, along the Red, the Rayado, the Vermejo rode their riders. So they gathered and whispered and waited.

McMains had riders, too. At Coleman's, Lacy's, Glutton's, Holbrook's, Young's—Crow Creek, Willow Creek, Grouse creek, Nigger creek, Humbug creek, Elizabethtown, Virginia City, Cimarron, Rayado, Ute, Prairieville— masked riders, vigilantes, a law in their hands. Of the two hundred cowboys that gathered, forty-five belonged to the Clay Allison outfit. McMains lived this night forever. Every action of the future was judged by the greatness of this night. There are pictures extant of his leading riders armed with Winchesters. He is older in the picture, a veritable patriarch with long, white flowing beard but never in any of those raids against Maxwell Land Grant partisans was he ever so triumphant as this night when two hundred men were ready to kill and plunder at his bidding.

Spies were abroad alert to every move made by Vega and the natives. The vigilantes knew where they could pick him up when they were ready. McMains had a corn patch on the Ponil. It was agreed that Vega would be offered the job of picking this corn. Unsuspecting and unsuspicious the mail carrier was only too eager to earn the five dollars promised since the larder at home was empty as he had not been paid by Donahue from the day of the murder. Also he hoped this friendly gesture on the part of McMains spelt the end of the affair. He picked the corn. He pitched a small tent near the cornfield. He slept. The Allison-Griego duel was yet to come but was not far off.

October 30—Noises. Shadows. Cries. Coyotes. Wolves. And men. Masked men. They surrounded the tent. Vega stirred in his sleep. Suddenly he was awake. What could one do against two hundred vigilantes? They formed a circle placing him in the center. McMains was masked, but his voice was recognized.

"Who killed Parson Tolby?"

"I do not know."

"Did you?"

"No."

"Who paid you to kill?"

"No one paid me to kill. I did not kill."

The circle formed ranks. The prisoner was marched to a tree.

"Boys, bring the rope."

A rope was placed about Vega's neck. A few men at the other end pulled. Vega's feet were an inch off the ground.

Confess," shouted McMains.

"I am innocent."

"Didn't Donahue, Griego and Longwill (this name is also spelt Longwell in the documents) pay you?"

"No one paid me. I did nothing. I know nothing."

Turning to the men holding the rope the masked leader said:

"String him higher, boys."

A foot from the ground, the rope was again let loose. Vega fell. Several buffaloed him (i.e. hit him over the head with the butts of revolvers.) at the same time call on him to confess to the crime. All he kept saying was:

"I know nothing. Nothing. I did not do it. I am innocent."

A third time, rougher than before. This time he almost choked to death. To save his skin he nodded affirmatively. Let down once again he confessed to whatever they wanted. Someone asked if a certain Cardenas was implicated. Vega said yes. In fact all he said now was yes, yes, yes. Satisfied that they had his confession most of the vigilantes dispersed leaving Vega half dead at the foot of the tree.

October 31—Vega's body was found swinging from a telegraph-pole. Upon closer examination a bullet was found lodged in his back. Again the natives assembled. The funeral procession was a long one and the marchers thought many thoughts as the Rev. Antonio Forchegu led them from the newly constructed church to the plot in the corner of the cemetery where the natives were buried. After the padre consigned the body to the grave, Pancho gave the funeral oration. He knew there would be more bloodshed. He would have to challenge the leader that others might live.

A bullet in the back. Allison shuddered. Hanging was bad enough. Why the bullet? And in the back. He decided that perhaps he was on the wrong side. He should lead the natives. McMains amazed him.

"And where was Parson Tolby shot?" boomed the minister, his voice as clear to the cowboys in the rear of the crowd as to the ones in front. "Is justice dead in this country?" he continued. "Is the giant fraud known as the Maxwell Land Grant to take over our homes, our country? This is war. Let the ring see and taste our power. Let the Dutch capitalists see that we plan to fight. They are responsible for all this trouble. An eye for an eye. Justice. If a man hung it is because he was a murderer."

A rider galloped in at full speed.

"The Mexicans are arming. Griego says he will lead them. He blames Allison for the death of Vega. Looks like he plans to kill Clay."

McMains smiled.

"Are you left with a choice?" he asked Allison.

"Griego I can take care of in my own way. We will have to meet face to face like Chunk Colbert and I suppose there will be others anxious to go down in history as stopping Clay Allison. Perhaps it is best this way. Lives will be saved. Besides, he needs killing. Have I ever killed a man who didn't need killing?"

"Never," answered the cowboys.

"Have I ever run away from trouble?"

Again the answer: "Never."

"Then let us all go home. Pancho and I will settle the issue. Then peace will be restored to the valley. Besides, I have to cut some meat for Donahue."

"There will never be peace as long as foreign interests control the Grant." yelled McMains.

Allison knew he was looking into the eyes of a fanatic. He jumped on his horse and left. Other riders followed. McMains stood alone.

Vega said nothing to implicate either Doctor Longwell or Lawyer Mills. He did mumble something concerning Cardenas. The *Santa Fe New Mexican* regretted that it had published the rumor that Vega named the two professional men as implicated in the death of the minister. McMains turned this over in his mind and interpreted it to mean that actually the pair were guilty and the newspaper was trying to hush it up. Again he made the rounds. The death of Griego served as a chiasma and anastomosis to combine forces once again. McMains and Allison again had two hundred cowboys at their command.

Cardenas was a native of San Fernando de Taos (to distinguish it from the two nearby villages of San Geronimo de Taos and San Francisco de los Ranchos de Taos). In the summer of 1864 he shot an American after an argument over the attentions of a young senorita. Brought to trial he was convicted on September 9th and sentenced to be hung. Beaubien, Carson and other prominent citizens pleaded that the sentence be changed to life imprisonment. The judge agreed. After serving a short sentence he was given his freedom and he soon convinced the town that he was a kind, devoted and attentive family man. It is hard to explain why he killed the American, for he had an aversion to violence in any shape or form. He worked for Maxwell on the Rayado for a time and after the sale of the Grant settled along the Ponil, the passing years dimming the plot on his early life. At the time of the Tolby murder he worked for Florence Donahue, taking care of his alfalfa and corn fields. He and Vega were close friends. It is possible that Vega, unconscious before death, brought in the name Cardenas in his ravings. At any rate he mentioned this name, which was enough for McMains.

Without stopping to realize the implication, he immediately sought out the sheriff and swore out a warrant for the arrest of the native. Rinehart could have asked how McMains knew that Cardenas was guilty but he merely swore in a few deputies and arrested Cardenas. That night the vigilantes surrounded the jail and marched the prisoner off to the same place, they questioned Vega. He told the masked men that he was innocent of any implication in the death of Tolby.

"Donahue and Griego were shooting at some Americans who came upon them changing brands. Tolby saw them and was coming in to report. Isn't that why they paid you to kill him?" The leader was a short, squatty fellow and Cardenas had the impression that he had seen him often in the newspaper office.

"No."

"How much were you paid to kill Parson Tolby?"

"Nothing."

"Who hired you to kill him?"

"No one."

"Boys, string him up until he confesses."

So, the terrified Cardenas "confessed" that he was paid by Longwell, Mills and Donahue. Given his freedom, he immediately retracted, saying that the vigilantes had forced him to say what wasn't true. Angered at this turn of events, Sheriff Rinehart went in search of his prisoner and restored him to his cell in the stone jail. That night the vigilantes again hauled him out, exacting another "confession." As they were taking him back to his cell one of the masked men shot him. From that moment on no native appeared in Cimarron without side arms. The same held for the Tejanos. Dawson wrote some scathing remarks in the Cimarron paper pointing a finger at Clay Allison as a leader catering to mob violence. Allison went to the news office, punched Dawson in the nose and told him in very meaning words that he would not be so gentle the next time.

McMains was restless and discontent. The culprits were still at large. When would Donahue, Mills and Longwell be brought to justice? Since the courts seemed uninterested it was up to the vigilantes to act. The natives, having read the newspaper, came to the conclusion that Allison was not their friend, but an enemy. Some even insisted that he was responsible for the deaths of Vega and Cardenas. Fearing they would gang up on him, as Dr. Longwell later testified, he went about Cimarron a walking arsenal. He was usually accompanied by his forty-five cowboys. McMains made daily trips to the sheriff's office to bring about the arrest of Longwell, Mills and Donahue. The sheriff was more interested in arresting Allison, Carey, Wrigley, Young Howard, Allen and some other cowboys with Allison, but he valued his life too dearly. He appealed to the Territorial governor and to the commander of the military garrison at Fort Union. The natives smoked the peace pipe with the Utes and Jicarillas, asking them to don war paint in their behalf, for they were few against the Tejanos. McMains hearing that the Indians were ready to help the natives enlisted the aid of the settlers and squatters, telling them that this added chicanery was the work of the Maxwell Land Grant Company. He urged them all to place themselves at the disposal of Clay Allison. Guards were posted at all entrances to Cimarron. Nor was anyone permitted to leave town without Allison's permission. Three hundred men called him leader. Everyone attempting to walk the streets was questioned—natives, business men, even the sheriff and his deputies. No two people could stop to pass the time of day. The only ones permitted to drink in cantinas or to play cards were members of the vigilance committee. By November 9th the *Santa Fe New Mexican* was able to inform the public that Cimarron was in the hands of a mob that would not be satisfied until it tasted the blood of Mills, Donahue and Longwell.

November 9th—Allison went to Dr. Longwell's home. Dawn had not yet dusted the horizon. Mrs. Longwell answered his knock. Was the doctor in? Certainly, the doctor was in. In bed with smallpox. Fearing a plague the cowboys made tracks in a hurry. Once out of sight, the doctor sprang out of bed, saddled his horse, not stopping until he reached Fort Union, where he explained the situation to Commander Curwen Boyd McLellan, who immediately telegraphed the governor. He readied the troops.

Meantime the reign of terror continued in Cimarron. All the civil authorities at the county seat were forbidden to act without permission of the vigilantes. Violence, lawlessness, apprehension fed the residents. Many packed their belongings and shook the dust of the city. Those that remained ganged together to defy the mob. They sent a spokesman to McMains and Allison to say that only after the death of the last Indian, native and citizen would Donahue, Mills and Longwell be taken. In the hills the Indian awaited the signal to attack the vigilantes.

Mills was in Trinidad for an injunction before Judge Wells in a mining litigation. From what some friends learned over busy telegraph lines they warned him not to return to Cimarron. The vigilantes were gathering by the hundreds. They came from all directions—Rociada, Las Vegas, Sapello, Rayado, Loma Parda, Buena Vista, Santa Fe, Pecos, La Cueva, Golindrinas, Los Luceros, Guadalupita, Mora—horse and rider; rifle and six-shooter. The governor stormed at the audacity of the vigilantes.

"Who is their leader?" he demanded.

"They say Clay Allison."

"Then post a reward for him. Five hundred dollars, dead or alive."

"Ridiculous! Ridiculous!" Mills would not be stopped. "Get my team and buggy ready. I'm going to Cimarron."

"You'll be killed."

"Absurd."

"Allison is a tough hombre."

"Hitch my team. I'm going to overtake the stage for Cimarron."

The horses raced, strained, pulled for dear life as the summit of Raton Pass was reached. Then came the mad dash down the pass for Clifton House, where Mills caught the stage for Cimarron.

"What about your horses and buggy?" asked Stockton.

"The devil with my horses and buggy. I just want to get to Cimarron."

The journey continued. At Cimarron the vigilantes already notified that the lawyer was on his way, assembled in the plaza. They let the stage by, then surrounded it. Mills was jerked out and a rope thrown about his neck.

"Hang the murderer! Hang all the murderers!" Cries came from all sides.

Suddenly, above their cries another voice was heard. The spokesman for the natives made a bid for a part in the drama.

"Yes, hang him. If you so much as throw the rope to a telegraph pole you will all be killed. Look about you."

Indians—Utes, Jicarillas, Taos, Jemez, Isletas, all fully armed. Allison was quick to grasp the situation.

He called upon the men to pick a jury of twelve men. The lawyer's friends were to do likewise. They would parley and decide whether or not Mills was guilty of the murder of the parson. All day long they interviewed and interrogated witnesses. Mills seemed doomed. As the dusk of evening began to gather an officer rode into the midst.

"Everybody with a rifle or pistol, drop them at once," commanded McLellan. The garrison from Fort Union had surrounded the town. "My men have orders to shoot down the first man refusing to drop his firearms."

Disgusted, the Indians broke ranks and returned to their pueblos and tepees. The natives quietly returned to their homes. Only the cowboys stood uncertain as to whether to open hostilities and fight the Civil War over again, or to obey McLellan. Looking to Allison he told them to obey the Yankee officer. They dropped their guns. Interrogation of the witnesses continued. The soldiers camped in town. The governor sent Judge Henry L. Waldo up from Santa Fe to look after Mills and see that he received a fair trial. Longwell rode from Fort Union to Santa Fe where he remained until peace was restored. Later he made Santa Fe his home and became the leading surgeon at Sister Blandina's St. Vincent's Hospital. Mills never forgave him for not returning to Cimarron to face the music. Tempers flared and shootings occurred despite the presence of the troopers. McLellan made no attempt to turn Allison over to the Territory, saying that this was the function of the sheriff's office. But the sheriff's office took one look at the cowboys and decided it didn't need five hundred dollars that bad. There were losses on both sides, but the twenty-four continued to guard Mills lodged in jail. Every eight hours another twenty-four went on duty, the twelve citizens always careful not to antagonize the twelve cowboys, who were anxious for a pretext to start shooting. McLellan permitted the guards to retain their rifles. Allison, aware that the losses on both sides did not solve the mystery of the murder of the parson, asked the justice of the peace to declare Mills innocent. Taking the paper the justice gave him, Allison went to the jail and read it to the guard. They turned Mills over to him. Allison put Mills on his horse and told him to ride to Santa Fe, where he belonged. The lawyer had been elected to the Territorial Legislature but a few days before. The governor telegraphed that the troops remain in Cimarron until further orders. Judge Waldo took no offense at the action of the justice, glad to be relieved of a chore that might have meant his death. Allison maintained to the end of his life that he saved Mills from the vigilantes. The lawyer gratefully compensated him by spending the next few months in working up an indictment against him and O. P. McMains.

Rev. Thomas Harwood was annoyed at this turn of events. He acknowledged McMains to be a fine preacher and often said that he made a better preacher than pastor. If ever a man lived who had the happy or unhappy faculty of getting people into trouble that man was O. P. McMains. Harwood admitted that the former printer was not safe as a leader and too headstrong to be led. Nor would McMains be advised by Harwood, his superior. The self-appointed commander of the vigilantes asked his superior to lend his moral and financial support in ferreting out the murder or murderers of Parson Tolby. Harwood refused to do so, whereupon McMains called him a weakling and a coward without backbone. He would do without Harwood's help. Talk turned to the part McMains played in the deaths of Vega and Cardenas and Judge Waldo was all for putting the rabble-rouser in jail. Harwood, who had taken over Tolby's duties when McMains proved recalcitrant, decided to ride to Santa Fe to plead with Attorney General William Breeden to admit McMains to bail rather than the ignominy of prison.

McMains misinterpreted the action and sent one of his pugilistic looking subordinates to chastise the minister. Harwood succeeded in talking him out of it, even making a friend of him, proving to him that he was acting for McMains' good rather than against him. Judge Palen survived Tolby a little over two months. On his death bed he thought he was trying Tolby for murder and at times the scene reversed itself. Tolby was his judge. McMains sought to make something of this but no one would bite. He was to be a scourge to the Maxwell Land Grant for the next fourteen years, carrying death and destruction from Springer to Stonewall despite imprisonment, threats, fines, starvation. Time and again he was to lament the loss of Clay Allison. He often remarked that if he had Allison at his right side during his raids, he would have brought the Grant Company to its knees.

Meantime Mills at Santa Fe kept talking. He sought to convince the governor that Allison was a dangerous man. Questions were asked not about Griego nor Colbert nor Wilson nor Vega nor Cardenas but Cooper. Where was Cooper? Did Allison kill him and hide the body? This was a new twist, surprising even Allison himself. Governor Axtell caused new posters to be circulated. The reward for the capture of Clay Allison still stood at five hundred dollars but he was wanted for the purpose of answering questions concerning the disappearance of one Cooper, last seen around Clifton House the day Chunk Colbert was killed. Mills took a poster to the governor, flung it on his desk, and asked:

"Governor, do you think any man is silly enough to risk his neck for five hundred dollars?"

"Do you mean that this Allison is that dangerous?"

"Dangerous enough to cut a dozen to pieces if they ever attempted his capture."

"What do you advise?"

"Send three companies of soldiers to surround his house. He wouldn't dare fire a shot for fear his wife might get hurt. The imposing number of soldiers would keep his men from starting anything. Snare the lion in his den.''

The soldiers surrounded the house. No Allison. Dora told them that he was over at Isaac C. Lacy's to close a cattle deal. Again the men marched. At Lacy's Allison laughed at the idea that it took three companies to take him prisoner.

"And how will you divide the reward money?"

The captain merely shrugged his shoulders. McLellan would probably pocket it all. Allison surrendered without resistance, mostly to keep Lacy from becoming involved.

"If the governor wants me that bad, I'll go."

Allison was turned over to Sheriff Rinehart, who sought a change of venue to Taos for fear the vigilantes would storm the Cimarron jail and liberate him. Rinehart asked the soldiers to accompany him.

"It's the Territory that wants him, not the army," said the captain. He turned, mounted his horse and headed his columns back to Fort Union. Allison's cowboys were all for shooting the sheriff. Restrained by the prisoner they decided to sit around to watch the sheriff's next move. At the time Allison was to be tried at Taos, McMains would be tried at Mora. The vigilantes decided to wait in Cimarron. If anything happened to Allison at Taos they would ride in and take over. When Governor Axtell heard that the soldiers rode back to Fort Union, he went into a rage and telegraphed the commanding officer to keep the three companies in Taos throughout the duration of the trial. Hence it was that soldiers surrounded the courthouse at Taos while Allison was on trial for the murder of Cooper. Just how Mills was able to work this is hard to say, since the body was never found nor was it ever proven that Clay did away with Cooper in the first place.

Allison made life very uncomfortable for the sheriff. Passing a water hole polluted with dead skunks and other debris, Allison, who had refused to turn over his guns to Rinehart, forced the sheriff to fill his hat with water and then place it on his head. At Taos he called to by-standers about the plaza to witness the fact that he was under arrest. Again asking the sheriff for his sombrero he entered a cantina, filled it with foaming beer and forced the lawman to put it on, yelling gleefully to the mob:

"Look, boys, I'm under arrest."

Allison was asked to pay bond and make his appearance during the next term of court. At Cimarron the sheriff made no effort to collect bail any more than Allison attempted to pay it. The offer of the five hundred dollars was never recalled. During the following weeks Allison continued to work on his ranch as if nothing had happened. All Cimarron waited. He mulled over in his mind the fact that the governor valued him at merely five hundred dollars. He kept abreast of the news from Santa Fe, hoping to catch the governor alone some time to question the reason. His patience was rewarded. The governor was on his way to Trinidad.

June 3, 1873, Governor Axtell boarded the mail coach. There were two other passengers: Justice Waldo's sister-in-law and a lady traveling companion. To avoid any discomfiture at Cimarron it was arranged that the coach would arrive at night. After a short delay in changing horses, the mail was on its way again by ten. The next stop would be Clifton House where the steeds would again be changed for fresh mounts, due to the arduous climb over Raton Pass. Three miles out of Cimarron a lone rider dashed from behind a clump of shrubbery and ordered the driver to halt.

"What do you want?" asked the startled driver.

"Passage."

"We can't take on passengers. Wait for the next stage."

"I want this stage and no other."

The six-shooter in his hand emphasized the fact. Clay Allison climbed aboard, told the governor to push over. Making himself comfortable he ordered the driver to carry on. As they rolled along Allison introduced himself to the governor.

"Understand you have a five hundred dollar reward for me. Why?"

"Because you are one of the leaders of the violent mob at Cimarron."

"What has that to do with the disappearance of Cooper?"

"We had to charge you with something and Mills thought that would be as good as any."

"Why consult Mills? Has anybody bothered to consult me? What about my side? Was it necessary to send soldiers to arrest me? Why the change of venue to Taos?" (See 2 Ex. Rec. 244.)

The governor recovering from his surprise and putting on a bravado for the sake of the two frightened young ladies asked Allison how he dared make him a quasi-prisoner. He was interfering with his personal liberty, which amounted to kidnapping or imprisonment. Allison apologized for frightening the ladies but he said that this was as good a time as any to have a parley with the governor.

"And what would you have done if I walked into your office at Santa Fe to petition an audience? You would have had me thrown out."

The governor agreed that this was possible.

"Yet you have the affrontary to take a seat with me in a carriage given over exclusively to my use."

Allison pointed to the ladies.

"Are they included in exclusive use?"

"Don't be vulgar."

"I intend to ride. If you do not like riding with me

I'll have the driver stop and you can walk to Clifton House.''

The governor did not like the alternative one bit. He remarked later that the prospect of hoofing it at night resolved him to treat Allison civilly. Gradually, the governor took to studying the man. At Clifton House four mules replaced the horses. Still Allison continued with the governor. The more he talked the more the governor was pleased that he sought him out.

"Governor, I give you twenty-four hours from the time you return to Santa Fe to recall those posters."

"And if I refuse?"

"You won't."

"How can a man so courageous as you—for I am forced to admit it takes courage to do this—refuse to pay bail and refuse to stand trial?"

"Because the court at Taos would not give me a fair trial."

"You will receive a fair trial if I demand it. Consider me your friend."

"And the posters?"

"They shall be removed. The offer for the reward shall be withdrawn."

Trinidad reached, the governor and Allison shook hands. Allison tipped his hat to the ladies, smiled, and went in search of a friend for the use of a horse to take him back to his ranch. All the driver said was:

"I'll be d——d."

Allison was as good as his word. So was the governor. The posters were recalled and a young lawyer recently from Iowa was appointed by the governor to defend him. Charles Springer was to emerge as a figure in New Mexico history. He was clever enough to turn the case into a political battle, for he had just entered politics at this time, and sought to divert the trial into other channels. He made a good start with a corpus delecti plea, then followed through with the fact that everybody was guessing simply because Cooper was not seen from the day Colbert was killed. Because he was seen riding out of Clifton House with Allison was no indication that he was murdered. Allison could have intimidated him sufficiently for him to go to parts unknown. Intimidation was not murder and this was a murder trial.

Young, confident, tall before the jury, the eloquent lawyer planted his feet firmly before the jury box, ignored the opposition, addressed the twelve men:

"From what I know of this Allison; from what I am told by witnesses, Mr. Robert Clay Allison is a Southerner of resolute character, recognized as a leader among men, ever prompt to rescue those injured unjustly, ever ready to resist an indignity. He has been accused of escaping from his captors; it has been said that he would not face the legal consequences of his acts; but we know better. We know that a man keenly scrupulous in matters of courtesy would hardly work against the court in such a sacred matter involving his reputation and his honor . . ."

W. S. Ritch, the prosecuting attorney, later to become governor of New Mexico, jumped to his feet.

"Objection."

Judge Waldo: "Objection sustained."

Attorney Ritch: "Is it possible that a man being indicted on seven separate accounts, three of which are for first degree murder, be called honorable?"

Springer: "In each instance we must prove it is murder. Produce one body. Find one witness to any of the murders, so-called."

Cowboys in the rear: "Yea, produce the bodies."

Waldo, banging the rostrum with his gavel: "Order in the court. Order in the court."

One of the jurymen (in Spanish): "This is more fun than we have had for some time." (Giggles.)

Another juryman (also in Spanish): "Wonder why they are so afraid of this Allison. Three companies of soldiers have kept this courthouse guarded since the first day of the trial."

Another juryman: "I understand Axtell trusts Allison." (Laughs.)

Waldo: "Order in the court. I'll call a recess unless I get complete order."

Silence.

Ritch had also interviewed witnesses. One murder rap should stick. He wrote out a brief in longhand. Not content, he wrote out another. These were never destroyed. They supply his attitude and way of fighting the case. They leave nothing to the imagination and show him ready to believe anything about the prisoner, even the unimaginable. He addressed himself to the judge, not the jury.

Ritch: "This ambitious son of the Iowa (Ritch evidently had Indians on the brain—he called Allison a half-breed and now was calling Springer the son of Iowa Indians) seeks to paint a rosy picture. He would have the tiger-like proteges of the *News and Press* coterie gentlemen, a little below angels, and harmless sort of people. This 'Mr.' Allison, if we look for the facts—and we do—would make one of the most thrilling, blood-curdling chapters in marauding, murder and savagery that has ever found a place in frontier literature. . . . "

So the voice droned on through a whole litany of crimes from bush-whacking days during the Civil War in which the prosecuting attorney claimed that Allison fought for neither North nor South, but for Allison, and his band of cutthroat guerillas. Either Baxter County Allison was well known in New Mexico, or in getting together his brief the lawyer confused the Baxter County Allison with the Wayne County Allison. He claimed that Clay Allison perpetrated every crime on the books and a good many not in the books. After the war he plundered from the disbanding Confederate Army to the extent that they were forced to send a company in pursuit but were forced to abandon the chase due to the fact that Allison had thirty of his cronies at strategic points to pick off the soldiers at will. Rather than answer for his crimes he fled to Texas. He sold General Granger's mules after first having rustled them. He threatened the lives of Dr. Longwill, Lee, Mills and others. He was a menace to society. Dr. Longwill was kind enough to treat a wound he had received as the result of an accident, taking him under his own roof until he was well enough to stand on the injured foot. In gratitude he sought to kill the doctor.

"... Are these the acts of a gentleman? Cooper was a kind, educated man, far above the average in intelligence. He remarked that under more favorable circumstances he would have shot Allison but was adverse to shooting a man under the influence of liquor. Griego may have had his faults. He may have murdered, but he was worthy of a better death than a shot in the back. He was murdered as was Cooper and Colbert. Who denies that the Texans revelled over the corpse left at Lambert's? (This shows the results of the questioning of Luis Griego, who maintained to the end of his life that Allison shot his father and all other victims in the back. Naturally, he was prejudiced in favor of his parent. He stands alone in this contension.) Did not Allison, stripped of wearing apparel, with only a ribbon to cover his extremities, dance like an Indian over his victim's body? (This testimony was given by the doctor, who was neither at the scene of the crime nor in a position to know, since he did not make Cimarron his home during the violent days the vigilantes rode.) Is not Allison the son of a Cherokee woman? Did he not bulldoze Sheriffs Rinehart and Burleson alike? How can my worthy opponent talk about an absence of legal authority under which to make an arrest? Did not the citizens themselves come to the recognition that Colfax county could never be peaceful so long as Clay Allison was left to roam the country at will? They sought his arrest. They want him to leave the county for the county's good. And did he not threaten the editor of the *News and Press* with the butt end of a rifle until restrained by Wallace? And was he not, during the time he was wanted for murder, a traveling arsenal stalking the streets of Cimarron? Springer, with affrontery equal only to that of Allison's, seeks to induce this highly respectable court to believe that there is no bona fide cause for this trial. Springer, the man who works with the *News and Press* coterie ...

"... Look at Allison. Six foot in height. Look at his main features. Blue eyes, black hair, rather aquiline nose, thin lips. Are not those eyes rather restless? Do not his cast of features denote firmness? (The lawyer meant to say cruelty.) His countenance is one of melancholy rather than vivacious. He is well skilled in the use of the rifle butt and knife, as Lee, Mills and Dawson can testify. Did not this ambitious Springer write that there was a political scheme afoot to divide Colfax county? Did not Governor Axtell say: 'I know nothing whatsoever of a political scheme to divide Colfax county? The whole truth is that this system of the *News and Press* coterie literature is one of systematic detraction, lying by suppression, misrepresentation and stringent lying, and to this end nothing in the catalogue of crimes is left which can be made to say the detestable coterie of the *News and Press* ...''

Springer: "My worthy opponent confuses the issue. Is the *News and Press* coterie on trial? Is my political affiliation on trial? Is the issue concerning the division of Colfax county? On what does he base his statement that the defendant is the son of a Cherokee woman? And if such were the case, is that why he is on trial? I ask that the case be closed as too ridiculous of the name.... Let it be struck off the books, for the citizens of Taos refuse to be the laughing stock of the Territory...."

When it was all over and Allison was a free man he remarked: "As sure as nails and taxes, lawyers have powerful imaginations." While he resented the unjust remarks of the prosecuting attorney he was sensible enough to recognize that the attorney was merely overzealous to the extent of over-stepping himself. Axtell, true to his promise, declared Allison a free, honorable citizen.

Meantime McMains, over in Mora county, was not faring so well. The accusations were more specific and concrete. Hundreds of witnesses had seen the body of the murdered Vega. His salvation was due to an oversight on the part of the recording clerk. The word "murder" failed to appear in the indictment. Up to the very date of the trial he stormed up and down the valley with invectives against the Maxwell Land Grant Company. His trial took place at Mora on August 25th and 26th, 1877, about the time Clay Allison decided to move for other parts. The lawyer representing New Mexico was William Breeden; the defending attorney was Frank Springer; the judge, W. D. Lee. It was a mixed jury that finally agreed that McMains was guilty in the 5th degree and the judge fixed his fine at five hundred dollars. The fact that a number of natives served on the jury proved that they sought to be fair despite memories of Griego, Cardenas and Vega. The jurymen were: Pedro Moris, Juan Ortega, Benjamin Lornenstein, Concepcion Trujillo, Norbeto Saavedra, Nestor Maes, Sacramento Baca, Jose M. Cacenias, George W. Scroggins, George Cashmere, Candelario Bustos and Juan Solis.

Nor was McMains grateful. He denounced Springer, the *News and Press,* the Maxwell Land Grant Company, and dedicated the balance of his life in keeping alive warfare and hate against the latter. In Washington, where he had gone to plead his cause, it was feared that he had the life of a Chief Justice, if not the Chief Executive, in mind when the pistol he was brandishing popped off accidentally just outside the door of the Supreme Court chamber. Barns, homes, out-houses, crops, fenses, all came under the torch as McMains sought to bring the Grant Company to its knees. Time and again he was heard to say: "If only Clay Allison were here. Like in the old days. He could lead these men to victory. I'd give my right arm for another Clay Allison." When questioned about this by the editor of the *Las Vegas Optic*. Allison denied that he had anything to do with McMains. He said that he acted to help Mrs. Tolby and also to check the political party that sought to run the public and private machinery of the county.

"Clay Allison, so well known in Colfax county, is in Las Vegas and on Wednesday (May 9th) said to the reporter of the *Las Vegas Optic* that he wishes to deny emphatically that he is in any sort of sympathy with O. P. McMains in his incessant agitation of the Maxwell Land Grant question. And he especially desires to contradict the report originated by either McMains or his followers that he would go to Mr. Wigham, agent of the Maxwell Land Grant Company, and attempt to intimidate him in any way whatsoever in the discharge of his duties. Mr. Allison has concluded that the law should take its course, and from present appearances he says there is no doubt but that the best policy for the settlers on the Maxwell Land Grant is to make compromises with Mr. Wigham, secure their homes, and end this eternal litigation warfare on the Grant of which old man McMains is the chief promoter and instigator. Allison wishes to distinctly disavow any sympathy whatsoever with McMains and his present policy of senseless agitation. Allison also desires to say that he held to these same views with reference to old man McMains and his Maxwell Land Grant agitation three years ago, and was only restrained from making them public by his brother-in-law (Lewis G. Coleman), who thought it might be wise to keep quiet on the subject for a while. Old man McMains ought to take a tumble by this time as he can no longer rely on Allison as his right bower." (*Live Stock*

Journal of New Mexico as quoted from *Las Vegas Optic* —May 14, 1888.)

Allison reacted violently to the editorials concerning him published by Dawson's successor. He warned the editor, who refused to be intimidated. Rather than dampen his comments the editor chose to be vitreous. The editorial simmered. Late on the night in question, Allison broke into the news room, accompanied by J. Curtis. One side of the week's issue was already printed, so Clay utilized the blank side to write in red letters: CLAY ALLISON'S EDITION on every copy, gathering them up between them they hawked them about the streets of Cimarron, selling them for two-bits (twenty-five cents to you) a copy, more than the paper ever brought before or since. The press itself, they dumped into the river. The Maxwell Land Grant Company did what it could to salvage the press and type. Later when McMains founded *The Comet* in Raton he bought this press and much of the type. *The Raton Daily Range* is an outgrowth of the McMains paper. When the *Cimarron News and Press* made another short-lived bid for life, Thursday, January 10, 1907, the editor informed his public:

". . . On one occasion the *Cimarron News and Press* was put entirely out of active service by the unkindness of certain citizens of the locality. Many of the older inhabitants of the town remember the incident well. Clay Allison was a well-known character who was connected with a number of exciting events during the 70's—the times which tried men's souls, and brought out all the good or bad in the character of the individual. In some manner the *News and Press* incurred the displeasure of this gentleman, and one night, accompanied by some half dozen of his friends (a number differing from the *Live Stock Journal* report, which mentioned only Joe Curtis—and is a good example of how these things get rolling along—everybody quotes the 1907 version—nor would it be practical to ask them to believe otherwise. Collectors of outlaw Americana are never primed for the truth but look for and accept the exaggerations. They would argue a half dozen until blue in the face—so, a half dozen it is.) Allison paid the town a visit. They stopped a few moments at Lambert's Hotel where they put a few marks on the blackboard, and then went across the plaza to the newspaper office. The editor and those connected with the paper at the time were absent, but the door yielded to a few well directed jars from a pole, and the party entered. When they got back to Lambert's again they were covered thoroughly with printer's ink. Whether they believed in the efficacy of this medium or not, they were daubed with a goodly quantity of it. Lambert's facetious query as to their having been to the printing office was cut short by the threat that something would happen to him if he mentioned the occurrence, and the party left. The press of the Cimarron newspaper was found battered to pieces and every movable thing in the office, including cases, stands and type, were found dumped in the Cimarron river. Years after when the youth of Cimarron wanted ammunition for their bean shooters they went down to the river and gathered up silent messengers of thought ruthlessly scattered among the sands. . . . ''

It was not as bad as all that. More of the press and type were salvaged than the public suspects. Nor was the complete press thrown in the river but only such part as Curtis and Allison could comfortably travel in several trips. Allison wasn't that anxious. The distance from the plaza to the river discouraged too many trips. Even had there been half a dozen men, the weight of the press would have disuaded them half way. Let us say that Allison dumped enough into the stream to make it impossible to carry on for a while. Several months later we find the paper in circulation again with Frank Springer at the helm. The lawyer's star was in the ascent.

Chapter Six

COLORADO

1842. George R. Smith of pioneer stock felt he couldn't breathe in Kentucky. Getting too crowded. He moved to the Georgetown area in north central Missouri. Civilization hounded him. Complacently he accepted it, permitting himself to be elected to the legislature and to advance in military life to the rank of general. He sought to interest the citizens of his community to diverting the Pacific Railroad from its proposed course, in an effort to attract it to their town. Georgetown was not interested. As a member of the State Legislature he was appointed to the board of directors of the railroad and was successful in inducing the officials to map out an inland route across the prairie. On November 10, 1857, the general bought one thousand acres along the right of way, paying thirteen dollars an acre for it. He recorded the plat of a town which he called Sedville in honor of his daughter, Sarah known to everybody as Sed. On October 16, 1860, he filed a second plat including the original Sedville, and called it Sedalia. Merchants came in from Otterville, Syracuse, Georgetown and other places. During the Civil War it was a military post. The county seat was removed from Georgetown and the town became a social and economic center. It later became famous for the number of newspaper men and writers it produced. Smith served as its first mayor. It was also the home for one summer of the Clay Allison family.

Whether because Dora had relatives in Sedalia or perhaps Clay wished to live the life of a gentleman, the summer following the trial at Taos they moved to Sedalia, Missouri. John and Munroe were placed in charge of the Allison interests in New Mexico, with brother-in-law Coleman close by to look in on their efforts. These two Allisons were farmers at heart with but little interest in the cattle industry. Within three months Clay recognized the move as a mistake. His affairs in New Mexico were badly managed and to save his stock he gave up the idea of social life in a busy railroad town. How much the idea was Dora's in the first place is a matter of conjecture. Considering how high she climbed in the social scale following the death of Clay and her second marriage leads one to suspect that she was in pursuit of culture, refinement and education not so much for her own sake, but to afford these advantages to the children born of this marriage. Also, it may be attributed to Clay's own roving spirit. He was not the man to settle for long in any one place. Indeed, the surprise is that he stayed in Colfax county as long as he did.

Clay Allison left the Cimarron county without misgiving. Tolby, McMains, Rinehart, Springer, Griego, Colbert, Crockett, Kennedy, Lambert—so many shadows of the past; dreams vanishing at the waking hour. The sinuous advance of the Santa Fe Railroad along the Arkansas valley of Colorado, as it moved anamorphously toward the Raton Pass brought into being other "end of track" towns that influenced his career. Allison did not concern himself with the fight of the railroad with the Denver & Rio Grande for right of way over the famous pass. He left that to Bill Tilghman, Bat Masterson, J. J. Webb and others who carved out names for themselves in Western folklore equally as famous or infamous as his, depending on which eye you keep closed in viewing the subject. Clay was now to be seen frequently in Trinidad, Granada, El Moro in his new role of cattle buyer. He divided his time between Las Animas (Bent county) and El Moro (Las Animas county), leaving his cowboys to guard the herds as he completed negotiations with prospective buyers. It was a lucrative business stepped up since the disappearance of the immense buffalo (bison) herds upon which the railroad gangs depended as the source of their meat supply. Cattlemen were just as guilty as foreign noblemen in the wanton slaughter of this unique animal. The scarcity of buffalo meat was now paying off, even if such meat could be obtained, the railroad tracks were pointing away from the bison habitat, smack into the center of the beef markets. So, our cattle buyer roamed Southern Colorado, where in a short time his name was a by-word and his deeds were recounted in the saloons, at the breakfast table, along the right of way, at the end of the track. Often men greeted each other with: "Did ya hear the latest 'bout Clay? Happened last night."

"No, can't say as I did."

"Well, 'pears that he made a fellow dance to the tune of his gun, at the Green Lantern. What a sight 'twas, too. It were like this . . ."

So the story runneth. No question but that Allison's jacosities, as colorful as they were in a turgid era, impressed the bystander as well as those who chanced upon them through hear-say. Among those who witnessed Allison's antics during these Colorado days was the future governor of New Mexico, Miguel Otero. At the moment he served as clerk in his father's seemingly mobile mercantile business, for the store had a way of skipping along to the end of the track as the railhead shortened the gap into New Mexico. Allison came to know Otero very well. He once offered the New Mexican his best horse, which bespeaks the esteem and regard Allison held for him. It has been said that Clay had horses for various moods and rode them accordingly. He used a certain horse when angry, another when out to settle a dispute, and still another when out for a good time. He hoped some day to own a horse racing and breeding farm but procrastinated until death overtook him, his dream never materializing.

John Allison came often to be with his brother at Las Animas. When the Allisons decided on a spree most of the bartenders in town closed the cantinas because the jacosities of the pair embarrassed their customers. Also they were fearful of tragic consequences, for what often began as fun ended in tragedy. Las Animas, El Moro, Granada, Trinidad in those days were pocket-sized editions of Dodge, Abilene, Hays and other frontier towns sandwiched between the web of trail driving days and rail-driving days. Change is never complete and at once; it evolves; the transition period always produces the heroes and the villians after a dose of upstarts and crusaders. Until stabilization, men took the law into their own hands. The six-shooter was the court of justice, or raw injustice. Those were the times that tried men's guns and nerves. To relive those days with a 20th century mind would be to fail dismally in comprehending attitudes and a way of life. These men were a breed apart, like miners, fur trappers, mountain men, pioneers, rail workers, gamblers, frontier lawyers and frontier doctors. Today, like the lawman, they work by science, Earp, Garrett, Bowman, Slaughter, Hickok, Courtright, would never have graced the pages of Western folklore had they lived in the 20th century.

Allison was a product of his time. The mind must be transposed and transported to those times if his actions are to be comprehended and a grasp of feeling apprehended. Many seek to lay the blame to the door of the late conflict. This is a fallacy. Billy the Kid, Joel Fowler, Dave Rudabaugh, did not place the blame on the Civil War. Indeed, Billy the Kid was a baby learning to walk when the war broke out. On the other hand, men like Allison and Courtright, who fought in the war, are not classified as trigger-happy outlaws. When saloons closed because Clay was intoxicated it showed the hand of change already writing on the wall. The transition period is about over, for in an earlier day the barkeep would have enjoyed a possible shooting scrape as well as the next. It really helped business for the curious would come to ask what happened and the next thing you know they were ordering a drink. Only a phychiatrist can explain why too much liquor converted Clay Allison into an Indian chief. In such a state he insisted on divesting himself of wearing apparel, wearing only a loin cloth, and giving out Indian yells and performed war dances. It might have been a fixation. From boyhood the free life of roving bands always impressed him. He may have had secret inhibitions to imitate the natives of the forests, and the relaxed mind under the influence of liquor brought them to the front. Whatever the reason there is no denying that the stripping took place only when he was drunk. This is brought here in the light of what follows.

On the particular afternoon of the Allison celebration, Frank Riggs, a liquor salesman (better known as drummers), came to Las Animas, arriving on the afternoon train. His first care was to procure a room at the hotel since experience taught him the folly of delay in this regard in a boom town. On the way he met Clay Allison, astride a horse. He had known Clay for a long time and decided to greet him.

"Hi, Clay. Quite a horse you have there."

"Sure is. And to prove it to you just give me the word and I'll command him to kick your hat off."

Riggs, fearful Allison would force the horse to do just that, hastily assured him that he was sure the horse could do all he said it could and more. Seeking to divert his mind from the animal he invited Clay to a place he had in mind where they could enjoy drinks on him. He was shrewd enough to surmise why the taverns were closed. Allison told him that the only way he could get into a cantina at the moment would be to break in, which would be a felony.

"There is a better way than that," said Riggs. "Tie your horse to the post. We will walk. I'll leave my traveling bag here with the druggist."

Allison agreed. They repaired to the back door of a cantina. The salesman knocked.

"Who is it?"

"It's me, Riggs. Bill, let me in. It's the whisky drummer."

Satisfied it wasn't Allison, Bill opened the door. Riggs offered an explanation.

"I just met my friend, Clay Allison, and invited him in for a drink with me. Noting a number of other customers at the bar, he added: "It's my treat, boys. Let every man in the room drink with me to the health, happiness and long life of my friend Clay Allison."

Taking a bank note from his pocket, he handed it over to Bill, telling him to hold on to the change until he returned from the druggist with whom he left his valise. He would be back immediately. He picked up his bag and headed for the depot, where he boarded a freight for the next town. He avoided Las Animas until he found out Clay moved to other parts. Meantime Allison took Bill in tow. He insisted that the bartender carry out a pint of beer to his horse. The mare took one sniff of the contents and upset the pail, whereupon Allison ordered Bill to carry out another. He dared not refuse. Several attempts proving vain, Allison became convinced that the horse was not in a drinking mood. He rode off, much to the relief of the harrassed Bill who anxiously awaited the return of Riggs to throttle him.

It was while Clay Allison was at Las Animas, so the story goes, that he disturbed a court session, riding his horse directly up to the judge's rostrum, asking his honor to suspend all judicial procedure while he was in town. Some even go farther by saying that Allison assumed charge of the district court. As foreman of the grand jury, he arranged that all the grand jurors be treated to all the whisky they could hold. As court was in session almost a month, the jury proved quite an expense to the county. During his stay at Las Animas he was called to Trinidad to defend a helpless young woman and her father.

An old man named Shaw had moved in from a farm near Lawrence, Kansas, hoping to profit by the boom brought about by the advance of the railroad. He met with some success in procuring a small adobe home —furnishing it to suit his daughter's taste. She had no difficulty in being placed as a competent seamstress and the poverty of Kansas days seemed a thing of the past. Trinidad, unlike Dodge, Raton, Otero, and other "end of the track" towns did not owe its origin to the advance of the iron horse but rather to Gabriel Gutierrez and his nephew, who built a cabin on the site in 1859. Others followed from Taos, Las Vegas and Octate. The community had its rip-roaring days before the rise of the trail driver, cowboy, railroader, especially in the hey-day of the Santa Fe Trail. Trinidad, named for Trinidad Baca, daughter of one of the early settlers who came from Taos, was the county seat.

The big "politico" in this town of two thousand at the time was one Brigido Cordova, town marshall and dictator. One day when Geraldine Shaw went off to work she chanced to meet Cordova, who was rather a handsome cabellero as well as a gay lothario. Pleased at the attention bestowed upon his daughter by the town's most prominent citizen, Shaw encouraged his visits. One day, either to spite Cordova or to protect the girl, a neighbor informed Josh that his daughter was playing with fire, and might get burnt. Cordova was a married man, the father of four children. When he called that evening Shaw ordered him out of the house. Enraged, the marshall demanded to know why. Josh called him a cad and told him to go back to his wife and children; to leave his daughter alone. Brigido said he would return whenever he felt like it. He had the grace to leave immediately. But this was a ruse. He hoped by so doing the girl would plead in his favor. He avoided the Shaws for a week. One evening he was suddenly knocking at the door again. Old Josh opened the door. Seeing Cordova on the other side he let it slam in his face *muy pronto*. The anxious lover next tried gaining entrance by force. When he opened the door he gazed down the barrel of a Spencer rifle. One look at the face of old Josh and Brigido knew he would be blasted to Kingdom Come if he stepped over the threshold. It was his turn to slam the door *muy pronto*. Shaw set the latch. The amorous lawman began beating on the door with the butt of his pistol. Josh warned him to desist. Told him if he didn't quit he'd blast away. Cordova put his pistol away and tried kicking in the door. He thought the old man was bluffing. This was more than Josh could take so he let him have it, right in the chest, killing him instantly.

Several people, attracted by the marshall's insistent pounding, had gathered to encourage him. These carried away the corpse. Shaw's luck was short lived. Feeling ran to fever pitch. Cordova's friends returned with threats and a rope. Shaw, ever alert, held at bay. Resorting to a ruse they called upon the old man for a parley. He opened the door, finger on the trigger of the Spencer. Taking advantage of the open door a number of the determined citizens threw fired turpentine balls into the room. Shaw jumped back, shut the door and stomped on the balls. While he was thus occupied several climbed to the roof and began hacking away at the adobe. Others, less scrupulous, poured coal oil down the chimney, sending a few fire balls to follow the stream. But old Josh was not without friends. Martin Arbuckle and Francis Wallace armed themselves with a brace of six-shooters, pushed people aside, gained entrance into the house, brought out father and daughter and dared anyone to lay a finger on them. They arrived at the Wallace mercantile store in safety.

Egged on by a few leaders, the mob marched to the store and surrounded it. Wallace climbed to the roof to address the crowd:

"Did you think we were sleeping? Once, in a situation as serious as this the people of Trinidad sent to the Maxwell Ranch for Utes. That was ten years ago. Have you forgotten? Peace was soon restored. We have sent for Clay Allison and his cowboys. They will arrive any minute. They will come shooting. If you value your lives get off the streets. Go home! Clay's men will show you no pity. The innocent will be killed along with the guilty. Remember what happened when Parson Tolby was killed. Go home! We want no bloodshed."

Even those who knew no English understood the name Clay Allison. The crowd dispersed. When Clay arrived with his men the town was quiet to the point of friendliness. The old man and his daughter were left in peace. No one was willing to gamble on what Clay would do if they were molested. This was one occasion at least when a reputation such as Allison's proved an advantage to good.

While at Las Animas Allison took exception to the antics of a certain Le Fevre, a rival buyer, and he called him down publicly. LeFevre said he wouldn't talk to him like that if he weren't wearing a gun. Clay took off his gunbelt and administered as sound a thrashing as ever a man received. LeFevre later remarked philosophically that he learnt his lesson, for a larger man could be whipped by a leaner but more agile opponent. He later married a native Trinidad girl and moved south to Manuelitas, not far from Sapello, where his grandchildren may be found among the Tafoyas, Pereas and Montoyas. He lies buried in the old cemetery near Salazar, the colonel who had charge of the Texans following their surrender during the ill-fated Texas-Santa Fe Expedition of 1841-1842.

All day Saturday Clay and John Allison made the rounds in Las Animas, toasting everybody's health. That night there would be a dance. Sheriff John Spear dreaded it. The Allisons would be at that dance. Trouble. The only sensible thing to do would be to have a posse in readiness. Deputy Charles Faber welcomed the prospect of the dance. Gunmen were not the only ones anxious to cut down another more famous marksman. Lawmen were sometimes bitten by the bug. Charles Faber was such a one. Faber had several reasons for wanting to get Clay out of the way. He resented the way Allison selected anyone he chose in a cantina, forced him to kneel in the middle of a room as he gulped all the whisky he could hold. A six-shooter was always a good persuader. The fact that the Allison boys attended the dance did not deter others from having a good time. When the dance was well under way, Clay being well under the weather, began his Indian chief act. He started peeling off his clothes, firing his revolver now and then to keep the dancing couples on the floor. At this point it was decided to send for Faber and his men. Twenty men marched behind the deputy to the dance hall. At the entrance Faber called out to the Allison boys to drop their guns.

"I see plenty of boys with their guns on. And you do, too. If you want us to take off ours tell them to take theirs off."

Realizing he might encounter stubborn opposition, Faber let go with his shotgun, aiming a little high but not high enough, for some of the shot hit John just off the right shoulder. It was a flesh wound but all Clay saw was blood streaming down his brother's arm. In a flash his six-shooter was up and Faber was down, killed by the first bullet. Spear, the posse and a few others who came along for the excitement (actually only fifteen had been deputized) beat to quarters. Impervious to those about him Clay dragged the dead deputy by the hair of the head to where John lay bleeding.

"John, this is the s.o.b. who shot you. I got him all right. Everything's going to be all right. Don't you fret. Everything's going to be all right. You will be well soon." At the same time he snatched up his clothes, tried to dress himself, stop the flow of blood, crying at the hurt caused his brother. He finally agreed to have the wounded man conveyed to Fort Lyon, where a doctor attended him. Clay was with him all the time. At the trial, judge and jury ruled self defense since Faber fired without notice of any kind and Allison made no threats, merely offered what they considered a reasonable argument. At a public dance all the men should have checked their guns. Also witnesses testified that Faber had declared that he hoped to shoot it out with Allison for the distinction of being faster on the draw.

At El Moro, above Trinidad, Clay fell in with Buckskin Charlie, a former mountain man who had worked for Charles Beaubien at Taos but was presently occupied as hunter for the New State Hotel, the Palace, and other eating places in El Moro, Trinidad, Granada and Las Animas. He supplied the kitchens with deer meat, quail, antelope, and bear meat. Rufe Harrington, formerly connected with the Santa Fe railroad, gave up his job to build the New State, to which was attached the inevitable New State Saloon. Beginning as the best of friends, after a few skirmishes with the bottle Clay and Charlie took to arguing the best way of stalking a deer. Charlie invited Clay to a fight. It was agreed that neither knives nor guns would be used to settle the argument. Allison's fists were so furious that Charlie was taken to the Trinidad hospital for treatment. When Allison later learned what he had done he made a special trip to the hospital to offer his sincere apologies. Fortunately there were no drinks at the hospital to seal the renewal of friendship.

Sister Blandina must have smiled. Allison was such a gentleman.

One of the wonders of El Moro was Doctor Menger's tall stovepipe hat. While it was the doctor's pride and joy, the beaver was a source of loathing and horror, and every time he saw it Clay plotted a way to rid the town of its sight. He noticed that the doctor passed by the hotel every afternoon at a certain time. He borrowed a sawed-off shotgun, loaded it with bird shot and when the medical man sauntered by peppered the tall beaver with bird shot. Taking the startled doctor by the arm, he led him to Otero's mercantile store and fitted him with the best Stetson in the place. Next he took him to the New State cantina, where they celebrated the demise of a relic of by-gone days.

Above the tavern was a room used for recreation. One day while Otero was engaged in a card game, Allison entered the tavern below and started shooting through the ceiling to break up the poker game then in progress. The bullets struck so close that the players felt safer on top of the large Charter Oak stove in the room which would have been a picture indeed had a photographer been present, knowing the players. Pete Simpson, future sheriff of Socorro county, who was to play a major role in the Lake Valley War; Miguel Otero, future governor; Jacob Gross of the firm of Gross & Kelly; Blackwell, lawyer and real estate agent; Frank B. Nichols, known to anyone who has read the story of New Mexico politics. Clay would have enjoyed the scene. The week that he stayed at the hotel kept everyone on edge. He was too free and easy with his guns but behind the trigger finger was an awareness and an alertness. In all his wild shooting he never once hit anybody. Even drunk he was a better shot than most crack shots sober.

During these Colorado days Clay Allison made frequent trips to Dodge and other cattle markets in Kansas. The Wyatt Earp and Bat Masterson episodes took place during this interim. These incidents split the pro and con camps of armchair outlaw and Western protagonists. There are those who are one hundred per cent pro Wyatt Earp and Bat Masterson, thus making Clay Allison out to be a weakling. On the other hand there are parlor authorities who are for Clay Allison. This much must be remembered in judging the episodes: Earp and Masterson were each their own authorities whether dictating to S. Lake or writing their own stories. Also their stories appeared decades and decades later. Time could cloud a man's memory, especially if it be a man who had a high opinion of himself like Wyatt Earp, who never seems to have done a wrong thing in his life—sort of a patron saint of frontier marshals. There are those who will tell you otherwise. This is not the story of Wyatt Earp any more than it is the story of Bat Masterson, but most authorities in the know seem to rate Allison and Courtright as quicker on the draw than either Earp or Masterson. However, that is neither here nor there. Allison had no reason to cringe every time he entered Dodge City so long as Earp was around, as the good marshall would lead us to suspect from his words to Stuart N. Lake. Earp is not without his fans or worshippers any more than Bat Masterson. One thing is certain: the Clay Allison side of the encounter with Wyatt Earp in Dodge has never been printed, simply because neither John nor Munroe nor Dora ever hoped or cared to be the Boswell or Lake to gratify Allison's devotees. All eye witnesses have long since ridden the Great Trail. Only the few who have read a great deal (never ever having left their homes to investigate primary sources) will argue. Nor do we care to become involved. We do not paint Allison to be a hero but we do insist that he was not cowed by the mighty Wyatt Earp.

Robert Wright was a partner in many enterprises in Dodge, the more notable being Wright & Beverly's fine mercantile, haberdashery and fine liquor place on the corner of Second Avenue and Main Street in Dodge. The year Clay Allison turned cattle buyer, the cattle drive to Kansas fell off, which really hurt the owners of the immense herds driven in under contract. Dodge became the principal depot for the sale of surplus stock. Buyers and drovers made contact at this point, purchased and received purchases to avoid undue delay, thereby facilitating business and bringing quick returns to both owners, cowhands, merchants, dance hall girls, cyprians, cantinas, gambling dens, hotels and merchants. It was a fairly established practice in Dodge to see how soon a cowboy and his pay could be parted. Wright, well known to Allison, sent for him, ostensibly to discuss a deal telling him that they were friends and he wished him to make a kill as a cattle buyer. In the light of what followed Allison accused him of sending for him not to buy cattle but for ulterior motives.

In order to get a picture of Dodge as Clay saw it, here it is as described by a reporter of the Topeka *Times* (1878):

"During the year 1873 we roughed it in the West. Our first stopping place was the famous Dodge City, at that time a perfect paradise for gamblers, cut-throats and girls. On our first visit the buildings in the town were not buildings, with one or two exceptions, but tents and dugouts. Nearly everyone in town sold whisky or kept a restaurant, perhaps both. The A. T. & S. F. railroad was just then working its way up the low banked Arkansas, and Dodge was the frontier town. Its growth was rapid, in a month from the time the railroad was completed to its borders, the place began to look like a city; frame houses, one story high, sprang up; Dodge became noted as the headquarters for the buffalo hunters, and the old town was one of the busiest of trading points, and they were a jolly set of boys there. They carried a pair of Colt revolvers in their belts, and when they died, did so generally with their boots on.

"It wasn't safe in those times to call a man a liar or intimate that his reputation for honesty was none of the best, unless you were spoiling for a fight. In those days Boot Hill was founded, and the way it grew was astonishing to newcomers and terrifying to tenderfeet. We all remember but now forget the date, when a party of Eastern capitalists came out to look around, with a view of locating. They were from Boston and wore diamonds and kid gloves. The music at one of the dance halls enticed the bald-headed old sinners thither, and what with wine and women, they became exceedingly gay. But in the midst of their sport a shot was fired, and another, and, in a little time the room gleamed with flashing pistols and angry eyes. This was enough. The Eastern capitalists hurried to the depot, where they remained until the first train bore them to the classic shades of Boston. But with all its wildness, Dodge could then, as it does yet, boast of some of the freest and whitest boys in the country."

The Dodge City reporter himself wrote (1877):

"Dodge has many characteristics which prevent its being classed as a town of strictly moral ideas and principles, notwithstanding it is supplied with a church (taken care of by Father Wolfe with whom Clay Allison was often to ride the stage, from Dodge to Camp Supply in the Nations Territory, on to Commission Creek, where E. E. Polly had his store, to Fort Elliott, the Sweetwater country of the north plains of the Texas Panhandle). Allison first encountered the padre in Dodge in 1877 when the Dodge City papers advertised Masses for the 2nd and 4th Sundays of the month, and scolded the people for not giving the priest better financial support or at least sufficient to cover his expenses. Fr. Wolfe and Clay Allison held many a religious discussion during these trips), courthouse and jail. Other institutions counter-balance the good works supposed to emanate from the first mentioned. Like all frontier towns of this modern day—fast men and fast women are around by the score, seeking whom they may devour, hunting for a soft snap, taking him in for cash, and many is the Texas cowboy who can testify as to their ability to follow successfully the calling they have embraced in quest of money.

"Gambling ranges from a game of five-cent chuck-a-luck to a thousand-dollar poker pot. Nothing is secret, but with open doors upon the main streets the ball rolls on uninterruptedly. More than occasionally some dark-eyed virago or some brazen-faced blonde, with a modern sundown, will saunter in among the roughs of the gambling houses and saloons, entering with inexplicable zest into the disgusting sport, breathing the immoral atmosphere with a gusto which I defy modern writers to explain. Dance houses are arranged along the convenient distances, and supplied with all the trappings and paraphernalia which go to complete institutions of that character. Here you see the greatest abandon. Men of every grade assemble to join in the dance. Nice men with white neckties; the cattle dealer with his good clothes; the sport with his well turned fingers, smooth tongue and artistically twisted mustache, and last, but not least, the cowboy, booted and spurred as he comes from the trail, his hard earnings in his pocket—all join in the wild revel; and yet with all this mixture of strange human nature a remarkable degree of order is preserved. Arms are not allowed to be worn, and any noisy whisky demonstrations are promptly checked by incarceration in the lock-up. Even the mayor of the city indulges in the giddy dance with the girls, and with his cigar in one corner of his mouth and his hat tilted to one side he markes a charming looking officer.

"Some things occur in Dodge that the world never knows of; other things occur that leak out by degrees, notwithstanding the use of hush money. That, too, is perhaps for the best. Men learn by such means. Most places are satisfied with one abode of the dead . . . yet Dodge boasts two burying spots; one for the tainted whose very souls are steeped in immorality, and who have generally died with their boots on . . . Boot Hill is the somewhat singular title to the burial place of the class just mentioned. The other is not designated by any particular title but it is supposed to contain the bodies of those who died with a clean sheet on their beds . . . the soul in this case is a secondary consideration. . . .''

Wyatt Earp, Jim Masterson, J. J. Webb, Charles Bassett, John Brown, Bat Masterson, and other good city policemen, marshalls, county officials, were the particular reason why a heterogeneous, miscegenate populace decided to check its guns if they would enter the dens of sin. Gypt, Joe, Jim, Mannen Clements; the Thompsons among others resented the custodians of the law as well as the law itself. They especially sought to rid themselves of Earp—or, at least, so he said. Men like the Clements were not choosy. They resented anyone wearing a badge. It has been said that they were willing to pay a price to see Wyatt Earp carried to Boot Hill. With the following they had it is a wonder they did not perform the task themselves.

Allison, the cattle buyer, was an impeccable dresser. Neat and clean at all times he requested of Wright & Beverly nothing but the best. Even on this trip he wore black and white from the toes of his fancy boots to the tip of his huge sombrero, through the full array of white buckskin and silver-trimmed accouterments (see Lake *Wyatt Earp*—page 180—Earp is giving this description about fifty years later. He either had a good memory or Allison must have really impressed him). When he arrived at Dodge, Wright told him that Earp had killed a friend of his in the line of duty. The lawman and the cattle buyer met between the Long Branch Saloon and Wright & Beverly's. Neither had ever laid eyes on the other before, hence Allison briefed by Wright, asked Earp if he was the man who killed his friend a few nights before. In talking to Earp, Allison actually leaned against him, leaving his right side free for gun play. Whether Allison actually had his thumb on his Colts hammer and half out of the holster when Earp's 45 was jammed into his left side is a matter of dispute. The question is, if Allison's left side was pressed against Earp's, as witnesses looking out of the Long Branch testified—everyone made it a point to be off the street at the moment—couldn't Allison have detected the slightest move Earp made for a gun, since he had his opponent's gun side covered? Earp knew Allison was in an ugly mood. He said he had heard Allison was gunning for him. Bat Masterson was across the street in a doorway, armed with a shotgun to prevent any of Allison's friends from interfering. Allison knew this. He also knew that Bassett had him covered. If he dropped Earp he would caught in a cross fire from two Winchesters. He valued life too dearly to get the drop on Earp for no particular reason. In a flash, too, he recognized that he was acting like Chunk Colbert. What if he killed Earp, who would gain thereby? Clements? Wright? Not Clay Allison. He would be a dead duck, but not from a bullet from Wyatt Earp's gun. It would be better to have the public think that Earp outsmarted him and live than for them to say he outdrew the famous marshall and died. Earp was twenty-seven at the time (born March 19, 1848), eight years younger than Allison. Allison was admittedly faster on the draw. Why did Allison permit Earp to draw a forty-five? Did he see the rifle across the street and sense the one at his back? Something must have come to his mind or he could not have spoken to Wright the way he did. Yet he was gentleman enough never to mention his suspicions.

With a gun in his ribs Allison is supposed to have remarked that he was going around the corner and Earp says he told him to go ahead and not come back. Allison backed out of sight beyond Wright & Beverly's. Masterson said that he ducked into a side entrance where twenty men were ready to do his bidding. Erp, Harris, Beeson, and Luke Short, a gambler, the killer of Jim Courtright, waited to see what would happen next. Beeson gave Earp Bill Thompson's double-barrelled shotgun and told him to use it. It seems that everybody in Dodge wanted both Earp and Allison out of the way and the best way to do it was to set them on each other like a pair of fighting cocks. Why didn't Beeson use it? Earp seemed in control of the situation. Bill Harris insisted that Earp use the shotgun, but he sure made himself scarce when Earp needed him. Wyatt said something to the effect that Allison's six-shooters were no match for a shotgun, and he wanted a fair fight. Just then Allen came out of Wright & Beverly's. Beeson and Harris ducked into the Long Branch. Allison called out Wright by name. Evidently he had been promised protection from interference on the part of Earp's men. Clay rode his horse toward Earp, who felt sure that now the showdown had come. What made Allison suddenly reel his mount and take his leave of Dodge? Was it the realization that he would be killing a law enforcement officer? Could he plead self-defense? Was this his fight or Clement's? He always claimed to be on the side of law and order, would a cold-blooded killing —in the event he won—justify his ever saying that again? Or did he make a promise to Dora before leaving Las Animas not to get himself into trouble? Who can explain his strange behavior? He never did. The only ones explaining it were his opponents—wouldn't they be just a wee bit prejudiced in their own favor? Some have called him a coward. Was racing his horse toward Earp, Masterson, Bassett, Harris, Short and other armed men at the Long Branch the act of a coward? It may have been the act of a fool but hardly a coward. He raced toward certain death. The onrush was sufficient. When Earp called to Bassett and Masterson to watch the store, saying: "I'm going to get him," why didn't he shoot as Allison came riding? Perhaps he, too, realized that

Clements, Wright and others were using Allison to do their dirty work for them. The real men that needed killing were watching from the window over at Wright & Beverly's—and possibly the Long Branch. No matter what the ifs and whys, wherefores, buts—the fact remains—neither shot the other.

By the same token Bat Masterson is placed in an unfavorable light because it is said he backed down from Clay Allison. Studying the circumstances, Masterson (who was much younger than Earp) did not back down before Clay Allison any more than the cattle buyer backed down before Wyatt Earp. Allison was the type to take up for the under-dog. He hated gunmen who went about boasting their prowess and had no use for marshalls who believed they could best accomplish their purpose in keeping law and order by killing every gunman in sight. When Clay, with McNulty, owner of the Turkey Track Ranch in the Texas Panhandle, and some twenty-five armed cowboys, went from cantina to cantina hunting down policemen, city marshals, or any lawman, possibly over the death of George Hoyt, who once worked as one of Allison's cowboys, and said to have been killed by Earp while firing his pistol in the street, or perhaps because he was drunk, Masterson—whose name Allison called repeatedly—decided that discretion was the better part of valor. A man with as many drinks in him as Allison had, and with a small army at his heels, could cause hurt to a lot of innocent bystanders. Masterson did not avoid Allison for fear of consequences to himself, but rather to save many unsuspecting people from bloodshed. Fortunately McNulty was able to get Allison into bed before any blood was spilt. The little army of cowboys, deprived of its leader, dispersed. When Jim Masterson was city marshall, Allison disobeyed the law by going about wearing side arms. Jim called his attention to it, took his guns and arrested him. Allison appeared at the police court, paid his fine, and left without threats.

The law was the law. Jim was later to have trouble with the vigilantes in Raton, New Mexico. Curry, later governor of the Territory, took a prominent part in this affair because of the murder of his brother.

Following these incidents Allison left Las Animas for Hays City in Kansas, where he continued the role of cattle buyer. It had changed considerable since Mrs. Custer first saw it. She noted that there was scarcely a building in it worthy of the name except the Station House. In her book, *Following the Guidon*, we come across these remarks about the place Clay was to call home for the next few months before moving to the Washita and Gageby country of the Texas Panhandle.

"A considerable part of the place was built of rude frames covered with canvas; the shanties were made up of slabs, bits of driftwood and logs, and sometimes the roof was covered with tin that had once been fruit or vegetable cans, now flattened out. . . . The carousing and lawlessness of Hays City were incessant. Pistol shots were heard so often that it seemed a perpetual Fourth of July. . . . The aim of the border ruffian is so accurate that a shot was pretty certain to mean death, or at least a serious wound for someone. . . . Our men knew so much of the worthlessness of these outlaw lives that it was difficult to arouse pity in them for either a man's or a woman's death in the border towns. . . . There was enough desperate history in that little town in one summer to make a whole library of dime novels. . . . Boot Hill was the cemetery in which all of the dead of the town were buried until about 1879 (the year Clay Allison lived there). The number of natural deaths during the first ten years were exceeding small. . . . It was in Hays City that the graveyard was begun with the interments of men had died violent deaths. There were thirty-six of their graves before we left (in 1869). I should not have heard much about these things had not the men delighted to shock the three women in camp with tales of bloodshed."

She goes on to relate how the soldiers at Fort Hays, near Hays City, studied methods as to how best to evade the vigilance of posted sentinels in order to go on wild rampages in the city. Two or three would get into a fight over a girl, or a card game, but mostly over North-South relations, and fight the Civil War all over again. Overwhelmed by sheer force of numbers they would return to the post to arouse the whole company and renew the fight in the hopes of cleaning out the whole town. Once in January, 1869, a squad of riotous Negro soldiers killed a white man named John Hays. The next day three soldiers were arrested and lodged in the guard house, then taken to jail. On the following night they were taken from jail by an angry mob and hanged. Governor Harvey wrote Col. Nelson, then in command of the fort, asking him to place Hays City under martial law. Asked if he had complied with the governor's wishes, he replied:

"Fort Hays has been the depot of supplies for General Sheridan's forces in the field, and consequently it sometimes happens that three or four hundred wagon masters, teamsters, etc., are congregated here at one time. While here, numbers of these men in the habit of visiting Hays City after nightfall and what with the use of whisky and their revolvers the town was rendered very uncomfortable for the better class of citizens. It was upon the representation of such citizens that I sent out a patrol a few nights ago to stop the dangerous rowdyism going on. Nearly fifty arrests were made, and of that number there may have been five or six citizens.... I presume also you have been informed that three colored soldiers were very recently taken out of jail at Hays City at midnight and hung by the unknown inhabitants of that town...."

Ten months later in a resort sponsored by a desperado named Jim Curry (no relation to the New Mexico Curry) and a woman known only as Ida May, some Negro troopers having entered to partake of the pleasures of the house but were refused entrance by Ida May, saying that her place was off limits to them. Curry backed her up. The men decided to force their way in. Curry stood them off while the valiant Ida May went for help. In the fight that followed six of the soldiers were killed despite the fact that they were armed and not averse to taking a life or two themselves. That was late in the afternoon. By nightfall a mob had collected and rounded up every Negro in Hays City. None were permitted to remain save a harmless old man named White, and his wife.

Tommy Drum kept a better cantina than Jim Curry. In fact, it was the best in town. Drum came in with the railroad and remained. Despite the many and diversified brawls, killings, fights, that took place in the tavern he was in a perpetual state of calm to the extent that he earned the nickname "Gentleman Tom." Allison frequented his place often, shooting at the glasses, bottles, making tenderfeet dance to the music of his six-shooter. He was ever particularly anxious to catch a soldier at the bar to force him to drink until the whisky was flowing out of his ears. He never actually mellowed towards the North although he did make an exception in the case of Tolby, Springer and possibly McMains. When prohibition went into effect (December 31, 1880) Drum gave away the unused portion of his stock and opened a fruit stand in Indiana. Clay continued to visit Hays City despite the drought in hard liquor. Perhaps it was this prohibitory law that caused Allison to give up the cattle buying business and return to ranching along the Washita and the Gageby. Or it may have been McNulty's picture of the Panhandle that caused him to suddenly emerge as a cattleman near Fort Elliott.

At Hays City Allison became acquainted with the editor of the newspaper and kept the Kansans informed as to his progress in the Washita country. The editor did not intend to let the Hays City citizens forget that Allison once resided there. Nothing remarkable seems to have transpired during the Hays City days other than what has already been said.

It is interesting to note that E. E. Polly, who was to sign many of the Allison papers on the Gageby when he was judge of Hemphill county, was a soldier and hospital steward at Fort Hays and Clay saw him often during the Las Animas and Hays City days. Mrs. Polly, a wife of eleven days, was one of the first victims of cholera. When she was dying she requested that she be not buried in the regular military cemetery plot but on the hill southwest of the fort, where she might overlook in spirit the activities of the garrison. Her request was fulfilled. Her remains still rest on that hill where she keeps watch over her beloved military post and Hays City. E. E. Polly settled eventually in Canadian, Texas, after operating a trading post and stage station on Commission creek, and the Morgan creek ranch; he never tired of telling the story of that lone soul on the hill waiting to see who would be carried off to Boot Hill next. Allison passed the grave many a time and often discussed it with Polly. It always left him sad and he hoped that he would go before Dora. This wish was granted six years after he moved to Texas.

CHAPTER SEVEN

THE TEXAS PANHANDLE

A mile and a half from Fort Elliott in Wheeler county of the Texas Panhandle, the forceful impact of the buffalo hunter and the buffalo hide trade brought the town of Sweetwater into being. This was the supply depot for the hunters and the only trading point for nearly two hundred and twenty-five miles north and south. The town boasted its quota of stores and saloons, dance halls and gambling spots. It was a while before law and order scratched the surface. A post office gained recognition as George Montgomery took over as postmaster. The knowing ones of officialdom changed the name from Sweetwater to Mobeetie, which actually was an Indian name for the same thing. Killing off the bison in the Panhandle may have brought the Comanches swarming down to Adobe Walls to avenge what they considered an infringement on their hunting rights, but it also brought a sigh of relief to the cattlemen of Kansas and southern Texas, who were anxious to open new ranges for their ever increasing herds as well as to be closer to the railheads and beef markets.

Anderson, Tuttle, Rhodes, Aldredge, Morgan, Mose Hays, Hopkins, Polly, Frye, Parsell, Dubbs and others located along the Washita and Gageby where the tall grasses grew. Here was real cattle country. For a time longhorns replaced the Buffalo until Goodnight, Allison and others showed the way with whitefaces. Dodge was humming with talk. Charlie Myer, Charlie Rath, J.

Wright Mooar, J. W. Mooar, Tom Dixon, Billy Tilghman, Bat Masterson, had the cow town all agog extolling the glories of the Fort Elliott area known as the Sweetwater country.

As regrettable as the annihilation of the buffalo may have been to some there was no denying that their extermination hastened the colonization of the Texas Panhandle. So long as the Comanches, Kiowas, Apaches, Cheyennes and Navajos depended on the buffalo as a meat supply there was little point in inviting a scalping party by defying them to build your dugout in the heart of their hunting grounds, especially since they were protected by the Federal government, due to the Council Grove Treaty. Now with the food supply gone, thanks to the buffalo hunters, the Indian would prove more amenable and permit himself to be led off to reservations. With Fort Elliott in the vicinity the ranchers of the North Plains felt reasonably sure that their interests would be protected against the remaining few refusing the amenities of reservation life.

If the Indian proved less of a menace after Adobe Walls, another scourge blighted the Panhandle to plague cattlemen and soldier alike: the rustler. Yet, despite his activities or in spite of them, the Turkey Track, P.O., C.T. and other outfits were to survive the hazards and risks. Added to the rustler there was the fight against the Scotch and English cattle kings who sought to corner the market after exports of canned beef flooded the English ports, English businessmen resenting the huge profits that remained on this side of the ocean. These English men helped make ranching a civilizing agency. In many instances if they did not bring culture they certainly taught the cowboy to love books and the ranchman to live in large houses like barons rather than in dugouts like gophers.

A regular trail led from Mobeetie to Dodge. Polly established a stage at Commission creek; Charles E.

Jones and J. H. Plummer of Wolf creek organized the Plummer-Jones Trail. When they dissolved partnership on June 28, 1878, Tuttle continued it as the Tuttle Trail (see *Ford County Globe* for that date). Six-yoke teams freighted from Mobeetie to Dodge, which gave a glow of contentment to the tradesmen and merchants Rath and Hamburg. At this time Clay Allison was living in Hays City, his reputation as a cattle buyer quite widespread.

Founded in 1867 as an outgrowth of Fort Hays, a frontier military post, it was a gathering place for scouts, cattlemen, soldiers, desperadoes. Within ten years it boasted a population of six thousand and showed a liklihood of becoming the city of Kansas. Allison thought it had a future, hence he changed from Las Animas to the cattle town. If you ever stand on the corner of 18th and Fort St. in Hays, you will be on the location of old Boot Hill. It has been said that a few of the seventy-five occupants of the cemetery were sent there by Clay Allison, but this has never been proven. Some writers place his notches at forty, others half the number, and some at eleven. The only one who knew the exact number was Allison himself, and he was not the talkative type.

At Hays, Allison met Buffalo Bill and other notable frontiersmen of the day, who seemed to be attracted to the town. The townsite promoters sought in vain to de-rail the trade that persisted in coming to the very gates of the city but somehow by-passed it for the towns to the east and north. Whatever hopes the newspapers built up for the town were dashed to the ground when the editors finally conceded that it would never amount to anything more than a trading center rather than the cattle center of the state they looked for. Despairing of ever becoming a wealthy cattle buyer under such a gloomy outlook, Allison took the $3,200 he had left to buy a herd of cattle and headed in the direction of the Sweetwater country. There must have been something about the man that attracted for he was long remembered, and well remembered. The editor of the *Sentinel* boasted: "Allison was a Kansan—one of us." That sentence packs a lot of friendship and pride. From the day Allison enlisted in the Confederate Army to the day of his death he never lacked for friends. He had a pleasing, engaging personality although no one ever saw him laugh must but he could manage a pleasant smile.

His features underwent a change as he grew older. While his eyes remained blue, the hair became increasingly darker, as did the texture of the skin. Cowboys and riders of the open range do become leathery. No modern skin lotion for them. The sun, wind and rain, and the cloak of the open prairies. He had the habit—a good one —of looking straight into your eyes when he spoke to you, as if attempting to scrutinize your real thoughts. When discussing business his express was impenetrable, observant, calculating, dead pan. He spoke little, preferring to listen. He secretly hoped you would be his friend, but would not put himself out of the way to show it. He enjoyed the conversation of Englishmen and others with a command of the king's English. He encouraged reading and "book-learning" among his cowboys. He never lost contact with his family, encouraging his brothers and sisters to come out West, where opportunity never slept. His mother seems to have passed away some time after 1867, or certainly before his move into the Texas Panhandle. His sister Mary was married to a Coleman from Tennessee who gave Clay his start in the cattle business and seems to have had grazing interests at least along the Washita and the Gageby. Clay's niece distinctly remembered the Coleman home near the site of Dawson (a future coal mining town of note that has since joined the ranks of ghost towns). Often this niece sat in Allison's lap, never able to live down those blue eyes and windblown handsome features. During an interview in April, 1948, she said that in 1873, when Allison bought up a squatter's rights near the Ute Park area, a Mr. A. J.

Young bought up the squatter's rights to the property that was later to become the famous Bartlett Ranch. She did not think that Clay knew Dora McCullough from childhood as Otero said, but that there were families of this name near where he lived in Tennessee. Allison first met Dora after she came to make her home with the Youngs.

"Clay Allison, a man with a pretty well established reputation in New Mexico as a man of his word, in affairs of honor, seems to be thriving in his new home in Hemphill county, Texas. He bought a herd of cattle two years ago, paying therefore $3,200. At various times since he has sold beef to the value of $2,800 and he is now on the eve of selling out for $9,000." (Ford County *Globe* —March 15, 1881.)

The Allisons were ranching three sections of land on the Washita and the Gageby. Clay moved to the Texas Panhandle in February, 1880. On March 25th of that year he registered his brand as A C E, location of left side with the purchase brand the same on the other side. The ear marks on his cattle showed the right ear cropped, a slash, bent under, while the left ear also cropped at the extreme left end but without the slash. (Page one, Record of Marks & Brands, Vol. 11, Wheeler Co. Courthouse.) The purpose being to cut out his cattle in the round-up as well as along the trail to Dodge. It was while he was still in Hays that an incident occurred in East St. Louis which caused Allison to write a letter to the *Ford County Globe* that gives us snatches and straws to work with. He went to East St. Louis in July, 1879, on a cattle buying trip. While there he selected the Lone Star Saloon as his hangout. At the bar one Tisinger by name, hearing that this was the fabulous Clay Allison, decided to egg him on to see or test his metal, relying on his own ability as a boxer, since the six-shooters were checked according to ordinance. But even in the matter of a fist fight he decided that he should not attempt it alone. He confided in two buddies, who agreed to step in at the opportune time. Tisinger opened the way by remarking in a loud voice that he hated to drink with murderers; that the bartender had no right to serve drinks to killers. As Allison was the only other man drinking at the bar the implication was plain. He then said that he always heard that men who are brave with six-shooters look kind of sick unarmed and are cowardly without their guns.

Tisinger was a tall, burly, muscular fellow. A veritable bully, who depended on his size and weight to see him through. He boasted that no man in East St. Louis could stand up to him. And he could take on anyone in the cantina provided they were man enough to stick to fists. The more he thought of the help close by the more abusive he became. Before long it was known all along the street that it looked as if Tisinger and Allison were going to have it out. Allison was well known in East St. Louis since his New Mexico days, when he administered a severe beating—with fists—to one J. Ead, who, like Tisinger, thought that if he could inveigle Clay into a fist fight he might claim the distinction of licking a man said to the killer of fifteen gunmen of note. Concerning this fight, the *Ford County Globe* commented:

"Clay Allison, one of the Allison brothers from the Cimarron, south of Las Animas, Colorado, stopped off at Dodge last week on his way home from St. Louis. We are glad that Clay has about recovered from the effects of the East St. Louis scrimmage."

Regarding the result of the Tisinger affair, Allison proved himself to be as capable with his fists as with a six-shooter or a bowie knife. Here is his letter to Lloyd Shinn, editor of the *Ford County Globe,* published at Dodge weekly:

"About the 26th of July there appeared in one of the St. Louis papers an account of an altercation between myself and one Tisinger, in East St. Louis, in which account there appeared several gross misrepresentations which I desire to contradict. First: it was alleged that I was the murderer of fifteen men. In answer to this assertion I will say that it is entirely false, and that I stand ready at all times and places for an open inspection, and anyone who wishes to learn of my past record can make inquiries of any one of the leading citizens of Wayne county, Tennessee, where I was born and raised; or of the officers of the late rebellion, on either side. I served in the Ninth Tennessee Regiment, Company F, and for the last two years of the service was a scout for Ben McCullough (This was a mistake. Ben McCullough never served in Tennessee. As he was killed in the Battle of Elk Horn in Louisiana on March 7, 1862, he could hardly have been the man Allison scouted for in the last two years of the war. The McCullough Allison served under was not from Texas. The chapter on the Civil War days has already covered this), and General Forrest. Since the war I have resided in (New) Mexico, Texas and Kansas, principally on the frontier, and will refer to any of the tax payers and prominent men in either (i.e. any) of the localities where I have resided. I have at all times tried to use my influence toward protecting the property holders and substantial men of the country from thieves, outlaws and murderers, among whom I do not care to be classed. It is also charged that I endeavored to use a gun on the occasion of the St. Louis difficulty, which is untrue, and can be proven either by Colonel Hunter, of St. Louis, or the clerk of Irwin, Allen & Co. It is also stated that I got the worst of the fight. In regard to this I also refer to Col. Hunter. I do not claim to be a prize-fighter, but as an evidence of the correct result of this fight, I will only say that I was somewhat hurt but did not squeal as did my three opponents. My present residence is on the Washita in Hemphill county, Texas, where I am open for inspection at any time.''

The editor of the *Hays City Sentinel*, noting Allison's letter in the *Ford County Globe,* struck out in his defense:

"Clay Allison writes to the Dodge *Globe* in contradiction to the statement in one of the St. Louis papers that he had killed fifteen men. He admits that he may have incidently killed a man or two in the way of law and order, but he has no recollection of turning in fifteen. Allison was an old Kansas, new of Washita, Texas. The East never will do justice out here. We remember the last man we were compelled to lay out: The St. Louis papers branded us as the executioner of ten, and threw in the line that we didn't rank high as a killer either. It isn't fair in no wise, if a man can't kill a fellow or two without being branded a red-handed murderer. . . ."

The editor went on to complain against his minister who cut him off from the congregation after reading that he had ten slayings to his credit. He praised Allison for his stand and wished for a few more men like him.

"Clay Allison spent several days in the metropolis (Dodge City) last week, and during stay gave us (D. M. Frost and Lloyd Shinn) a pleasant call. He started for the Washita, Panhandle of Texas, Friday morning (Feb. 26, 1880)." A year later the *Globe* printed this item: "Clay Allison is thriving in a new home in Hemphill, Texas."

Lee and Reynolds operated the sutler's store at Fort Elliott, as well as the stage and freight depots on the trail to Dodge. Theirs was a thriving business and fearing that legal organization would serve to hinder rather than to help, they bitterly opposed the measure proposed for a new county. Despite their efforts Emanuel Dubbs was elected judge, Henry Fleming sheriff. Allison frequented the sutler's store and on one occasion was there when a wee bit on the tipsy side. Noticing some of the officers from the fort, he called on them to explain the treachery of the North in the late war. Allison drinking was one thing. Allison drinking and fighting the war over was something else and the officers decided to be as discreet as possible under the circumstances. They politely excused themselves, saying they had business at the post. Allison drew his gun, told them to sit down until he was good and ready to let them go, which he figured would not be for some time yet since they chose to ignore his questions. John Donnelly, the clerk, sought to intervene. Allison fired two shots at his feet and made him sit down with the officers. "Damn Yankees. All of you." He repeated over and over again. Several of Clay's friends sought to remonstrate. He glared at them, waving his pistol, warned them to mind their own business. Sheriff Fleming made several unsuccessful attempts at talking him out of his gun. Useless. If Fleming made so much as a move to disarm him, that would be the end of Fleming. An educated, decent sort of gambler—if you would call a gambler decent—before election to office, he still had enough of the gambler's instinct to recognize Allison's warning for what it was worth. He went to Colonel Davidson, commander of the fort. After all, soldiers were involved, so let Fort Elliott see what it could do. He reasoned that this was a problem for the Army. Colonel Davidson told him to leave the matter with him. He would take the mighty Clay Allison down a peg. He paraded to the sutler's store, walked up to Allison, pointed his large army Colt pistol to within inches of Allison's face and commanded him to leave the store at once and for good.

For a second Allison did nothing to show he comprehended. He merely stared at the brazen or foolish colonel. He was trying to figure how much was nerve and how much bravado. Suddenly he let out a string of abuse, calling the colonel every name in the book and a good many not in the book, ending up by saying that the colonel was just a blue-bellied, yellow-livered coward without nerve to pull the trigger. He, Clay Allison, would give him exactly one minute to put away his gun, or suffer the consequences. Allison pulled out his watch and started to count away the seconds. Davidson's future career as a soldier hinged on that minute. A soldier, he might explain in a report, but how would he explain a civilian to his commanding officer? Perhaps this was the sheriff's department after all. What if he pulled the trigger? Which way would Justice carry? Break him? Promote him? And for what? The glory of killing Clay Allison. What was that expression he had heard so often? Discretion is the better part of valor. Trembling with rage over the situation, he put his gun away and stalked out of the store. Allison felt that the victory called for another drink. He let the soldiers go and treated everybody in the house to free drinks.

The Thirty-Fifth Judicial District was created during these troublesome times and Frank Willis, who later practiced law in Canadian as well as publishing a newspaper there, was appointed District Judge. Court summoned for session, it was found that the jurors' panel lacked three men These were "summoned by order of the Court." The three were L. B. Lockhart, Emanuel Dubbs and Robert Clay Allison. Allison served on the jury several times, according to the Register of Warrants in the Treasurer's office of the Wheeler County Courthouse. He was paid for this service on January 21, 1881, and on February 19, as well as on April 9, when none other than the merchant and banker Henry Hamburg vouched for him in collecting the $7.50 due him. Allison also received $5.00 on February 12, but for some reason it is not clear in the records. The $7.50 was received for five days jury service. Another item in the books read— R. C. Allison—redeemed or cancelled—September 22, 1881—$2.00. No reason given. Allison served on the jury from October 21 to October 25 in the case of A. A. Parsell versus G. R. Elliott, the lawyer for the plaintiff being Moses Wiley; for the defendant, A. L. Neal. The record goes on to add: "The jury consisting of N. F.

Locke and five other good and lawful men being duly sworn to try the case...." It was a suit for the recovery of a promissory note made to the amount of $192.82, Clay Allison being one of the other "five good and lawful men."

The election of a sheriff did little to intimidate cattle rustlers. On the contrary it made them bolder. The citizens of Mobeetie (an Indian word for Sweetwater—name changed possibly because of the other Sweetwater in Texas, near Roby) petitioned the protection of the Texas Rangers. Furthermore, the Federal government still permitted Indians to leave their reservations in the Nations Territory and New Mexico to hunt on the north plains of the Texas Panhandle not because there were any bison left for their arrows but because the Indians insisted on their rights stemming from the Medicine Lodge Treaty which gave them this area as their hunting grounds and the treaty was never revoked. It was understood that they would return to their reservations after the hunt and settlers were in no way to be molested. What they did was walk into solitary ranch homes, demand to be fed, carried away all food in sight and threatened the rancher's wife and children if any protest was raised. The settlers became so vehement in their protests against such conditions that Major Jones of the Texas Rangers sent Captain George W. Arrington to Mobeetie to investigate.

Arrington, a product of Greensboro (December 23, 1844) Alabama, had served in the Confederate Army. After some exciting adventures he proved himself a daring ranger despite his shortness of stature. Major Jones trusted him and relied on him as a prudent, sensible, level-headed trooper during a crisis. His one failing was a quick temper which the major cautioned him to govern. During his declining years when he lived in Canadian he played checkers with as much zest as if in pursuit of a law breaker. His temper flared at the loss of a game.

It took him some time to calm down in order to ready himself for another. As sheriff he ranks as the greatest of the Southwest. He possessed a sixth sense in tracking down outlaws. Arrived at Mobeetie he favored the policy of killing off the Indians, for to him as to others the only good Indian was a dead one. Cattlemen were quick to back him. Colonel Davidson disagreed. He said his job was to protect the Indian. If the Texas Rangers so much as killed an Indian they would be responsible to the United States Government. Angered at the colonel's defiant attitude, Arrington turned to the next best objective: rustlers. These had been particularly busy that winter among Charles Goodnight's cattle. While the Ranger was in the area he learned that Ace Powell was operating in the vicinity. He had no orders concerning Powell but he knew he was wanted for rustling and other crimes. He decided to capture him and bring him to Fort Elliott. Arriving at the dugout Powell had built, he found him in conference with Clay Allison, who had just paid the wanted man a small sum on a cattle deal. They were to go to Mobeetie on the following day to arrange the bill of sale.

Arrington: "Powell, you are under arrest. I'm taking you to Fort Elliott."

Allison: "You will take him nowhere until I complete my business with him. I want him in Mobeetie tomorrow."

As Arrington could show no warrant for the arrest, he agreed to have Powell at Mobeetie at the appointed hour. Arrington sat down to drink some coffee. Allison decided to have some fun with him. He slipped behind the chair, jerked the Ranger's six-shooter out of its holster and asked Arrington what he would do if he decided to shoot. The Ranger, without turning around, asked Allison to replace the gun where he found it. Having no bones to pick with the cocky little ranger, Allison did as he was told. Arrington was not a man to joke with, nor could he take a joke. Angered, he stood up and told Clay that if he ever tried that again he would kill him. He was a disciplinarian and jokes were out of his field, especially if practised on him.

As the Rangers accomplished nothing to the satisfaction of Goodnight and the stockmen, a meeting was called to organize the Panhandle Cattlemen's Association to band together in their common cause against the rustler. All the ranchmen in the area were invited to attend the meeting, which was held in Mobeetie. This was Allison's first experience with an organization of this sort. He had heard of them but made no attempt to find out too much about them, feeling that he and his cowboys could take care of any rustlers that ever attempted stealing his stock. The rustlers knew this, too.

Perhaps more than any other cattleman in the Panhandle, Charles Goodnight realized that printed warnings in the newspapers were little noted nor long remembered by cattle thieves. He was particularly anxious because of his experimentation with Herefords rather than the famous Texas longhorn. Others were swift to follow and the longhorn was doomed. Rustlers were active with the whiteface because it brought a better price than the unpredictable longhorn.

The year 1883 was an unforgetable year—dry, dusty, hard. It was also the year the rustlers had their greatest successes. No one seemed able to stop them. Even Allison was forced to face the fact that his own herd was in danger and not out of reach of two brothers, residents of the Mobeetie area, who so managed to cover their tracks that no one was able to catch them red-handed. They seemed destined for the rope, and actually were hung by a mob in Oklahoma some years later. The cemetery in Mobeetie shelters their remains. Calves wearing mysterious brands grazed side by side with cattle of well known brands. Allison noticed this often as he rode the range. Then he knew.

The meeting was called to order. Charles Goodnight pointed out that there was hardly any reason to explain or to go into detail as to why they were assembled. As president of the Panhandle Cowman's Association he appointed "Pistol Pete" Eaton and his nephew, also named Goodnight, as cowboy detectives to trail the rustlers. For a time Allison sat in his chair, taking it all in, wondering when Goodnight would point the accusing finger at the brothers who had the affrontery to attend, even to the extent of offering a reward for the capture of the rustlers. Slowly, deliberately, Allison drew attention to himself.

"Mr. Chairman, are you interested in knowing who the rustlers are?"

"Mr. Allison, if you know, name them and do us all a favor."

Pointing a finger at the brothers seated near the door, he shouted: "There they are. The d——n cattle thief rustlers. It's the ——— (names withheld, as sons were promised) boys." And addressing them directly he added: "You d——d well know it."

The hand is quicker than the eye. The accused reached for their six-shooters, the first thought to evade capture. There was a moment of silence, like the calm before a storm. In that split second timing the brothers decided to make a run for it while they held the advantage. Their guns pointed at the startled men, they backed out of the door, slammed it shut, ducked around the corner of the hall. As agile as they were crafty, they soon gained the corner of the house where Allison at the moment was standing with his back to an open window. A flash warning from one of the men who saw them approaching the window sent Allison springing to the corner out of range. The unidentified rancher who shouted "Look out, Allison, they will shoot you through the open window," saved his life.

From his corner, Clay yelled out: "Come back here, you calf stealing rustlers. Come back and take what's coming to you." But the pair declined the invitation, taking advantage of the confusion to make tracks. When they did return it was in pine boxes and Allison was already beneath the sod on the banks of the Pecos. An Oklahoma rope hung you just as high as a Texas rope—that they would find out.

On March 12, 1883, President Kit Carter convinced that the "fence-cutting" war had reached a climax, called together the members of the Association in Jacksboro to notify them of the state of chaos that existed between the "free range system" and the influx of settlers better known as "homesteaders." Actually, barbed wire worked both ways. The rancher could fence out the settler, and vice versa. But it became customary to cut the neighbor's wire, stalking about in midnight raids, snipping, clipping, alert with Winchester. Cowboys were hard put guarding the lines ever alert for fence cutters. Colonel Tom Ball explained that the free range system seemed doomed. He asked the ranchers to face the inevitable, natural and necessary change that marched hand in hand with progress. Free range and open range, like the old longhorn, was becoming a thing of the past. A man would have to show a paper for his property, which would have to be fenced in. The frontier itself was fast becoming a legend. Elbow room where a man could breathe would soon be a figment of the imagination and something you read about like the deeds of the closing era. Cattle trails, the old Santa Fe Trail, the Chihuahua Trail, six-shooters, buckboards, the chuck wagon—lost substance to become ghosts of days that had been. New words were written into the cattleman's dictionary: property rights, fences, barbed wire, grazing taxes, public highways, rights of way, first, second and third class roads, windmills, pumps. You didn't fight over a water hole anymore—you dug a well and set up a windmill. The good old days—going, going, gone.

These encroachments spelt doom for Allison, who protected his range against the influx of homesteaders, nevertheless, refusing to put up fences where the land seemed to meet the sky. What would you fence in and what would you fence out? Did good fences make good neighbors? Here in this sea of grass the cattle waxed fat and strong. And there was water in the Sweetwater creek, the Gageby, the Washita, the Canadian. This was cattle country not meant for corn, potatoes, wheat, crops. At least according to the cattleman. Worlds were abuilding and worlds were atumbling. All this craze to possess the land; to inherit the earth; to build bath rooms in houses! No more guns; no more arguments. No more fighting it out man to man. See your lawyer. See my lawyer. I'll take you to court. Let the courts decide. Tumbling, tumbling, tumbling down. Going, going, gone. Perhaps Billy the Kid, Wild Bill, Mysterious Dave Mather, Chunk Colbert died in time. They took the glamor of the era with them. Masterson, Earp, Tilghman were to live too long. The charm wore off. They were too close to a generation that would hardly believe they were frontiersmen. TV, radio and the screen might vamp them for a while, but the public tires all too easily. With these, but not Billy the Kid, Jim Courtright, Clay Allison. Even Pat Garrett lived beyond his era, hence never really caught the public fancy. Wyatt Earp will never match the appeal of Billy the Kid simply because he lived to see the day of radio, the talkies and washing machines. Men of trail riding days will forever be part of a heritage. Going, going, gone.

Canned beef proved a success in London, Edinburgh and Amsterdam. The loss of these markets to the cattleman in Europe induced capitalists to finance cattle barons who wished to ship American beef to these ports, but also to pocket the resulting profits. The rise of the cattle baron simultaneous with the influx of the homesteader, the sheep herder, the windmill, the fence cutters, awakened the majority of the people of the Texas Panhandle to new trends. Governor Ireland would listen to the pressure from the now influential stockman. An emergency session of the Legislature was called in January of 1884. Laws were enacted making wire-cutting a felony, also requiring the frequent spacing of gates in all fences of any length to avoid fencing in anyone, and, by the same token, fencing out anyone. The Texas Rangers were advised to enforce these laws, a task which Captain Arrington, as sheriff of Mobeetie, took to heart. If Governor John Ireland sounded the tocsin, he had but to comply.

As if all this were not enough, what really made Allison see the handwriting on the wall was the arrival of surveyors and talk of a railroad. The windmill salesman proved to the cattleman as well as to the homesteader that water was where you found it. Townsite promoters, slick operators, in conjunction with the railroad, stressed the facility with which water could be pumped out of the bowels of the earth almost at any spot in the Panhandle wherever you chose to dig. The drought of 1883 was forgotten in the blessings of the rains that flooded. Settlers wrote home about the tall, lush grass, the wheat, the alfalfa, the corn almost as high as an elephant's eye; they wrote home about the Eden some newspaper men in the Panhandle call "the golden spread." There is a difference in spreading gold and in piling it. Allison was not a farmer. Corn he liked; juicy grass for silage he admired; wheat—golden in the sun, rejoiced his heart. It was all fine for the homesteaders from Nebraska, Iowa, Wisconsin. They were farmers. So the ache for the wide open ranges as they were, to see range meet the sky as cattle roamed, to get away from cultivated fields that helped spring dust storms at best; to be able to ride without having to make turns for wheat fields, corn belts, alfalfa. The old black magic.

He was restless. He knew the symptoms. He was looking for new horizons, far horizons that would shut out the forward progress of the Yankees. He wanted more than a home and a back yard. But who would let him have it? Towns were springing up all about him. Ranches were breaking up into sections, half-sections, quarter sections. You didn't take your cattle out anymore to the tall grasses—somebody owned that land—schools, railroads, town-site companies, individuals. He would fly the march of the despoiler. Surveyors, farmers, fence-cutters, sheep men, railroaders, soldiers, homesteaders, tax collectors, settlers, squatters—he would flee them all.

Wheeler county was organized in 1879, with Mobeetie (formerly Sweetwater) the county seat. Henry Fleming, the first sheriff, took his duties seriously. The first thirty-four men he arrested were charged with fighting, shooting firearms, drunkeness, disorderliness, and talking loud in public places, this latter especially displeasing to Clay Allison, who liked talking loud in public places—i.e., cantinas—when on a binge. In one particular instance he went into his Indian chief act again, riding the streets of Mobeetie dressed in only a gun belt and six-shooter, much to the consternation and horror of the ladies—dignified and undignified—who summoned the sheriff to do something about it. All authors place this incident as happening at Canadian. Allison had moved out of the Texas Panhandle several years before Canadian was founded. Besides, he was dead. Canadian was founded July 4, 1887. Allison was twenty-four hours in his grave. The author regrets that he foolishly followed the mob in having Allison riding up and down the streets of Canadian with his Lady Godiva act, because that was what all authors said. After a thorough investigation and search of the records, which is what he should have done in the first place, nobody contested. The mistake advanced by Clark and others had taken such a hold that no one would believe otherwise. Even now, in the face of new evidence.

The sheriff called upon Allison to get down from his horse and quit disturbing the peace. Instead of complying, Allison spurred the steed to full speed up and down the main street of Mobeetie, giving the rebel yell and shooting off his pistols. Then he got down from the horse, leveled the gun in his right hand at the sheriff's head and marched him into the bar, where Jim McIntyre served as bartender and monte dealer. He forced the sheriff to drink until he couldn't stand up. Satisfied, he went back to his horse as undressed as when he went into the saloon. However, there is no record of his arrest, nor does a search of the dockets at both Wheeler and Canadian show that Allison was ever arrested at any time during his Washita and Gageby years.

Mobeetie was a rip-roaring, wide open town. It was more than a miniature Dodge—it was a whole history-making town that hummed to the tune of wine, women and song. Lee & Reynolds kept it supplied with the most modern conveniences from the East as well as contact with Dodge. It was a town that could talk of its own white way, white slaves and white gamblers. The shyster lawyer also gave the honest-to-goodness one a rough time. Mobeetie was so many things wrapped in one. As Jim McIntire later said:

"Mobeetie at this time had only three or four residences and a couple of stores, but there was one vacant building and we rented it. There was another saloon in the village, and that was owned by Henry Fleming, the sheriff. We (Jim and his partner, Lock) prospered in spite of competition, as whisky was still twenty-five cents a drink, and there was plenty of customers. I got tired of it after a time and sold out to my partner, to accept a position as deputy sheriff under Fleming. In those days the rough element was in a majority and it took constant watching to keep them in order. Every county did not have its sheriff and deputies as now (1902 when this was written), and Fleming had twelve attached counties to cover. His territory took in all the northwestern part of Texas to New Mexico and No Man's Land . . .'' (See: o.c. *Early Days in Texas, page* 128.)

Buffalo hides, bones, chips—were quite the industry in these days prior to Allison's move over to Lincoln county, New Mexico. He did not interest himself in the profits arising out of these trades as did Reynolds, Rath, Hamburg, Frye, Chapman and others. When Lee and Reynolds dissolved partnership, the former sold his place on Russell creek east of Mobeetie, as well as his share in the store to Van Horn. Allison often conversed with Charles Goodnight, Billy Dixon, Thomas Bugbee and Charlie Rath. He thought Goodnight too dictatorial for his good. It was Goodnight who convinced him of the necessity of joining the cattlemen's association for his own good. Once in, he liked it and continued in Lincoln county until he rebelled against the dictatorship of the chairman there. He did not feel that he could continue in an association that permitted its president to become so demanding.

January 17, 1881. The Third District Court at Mobeetie was in session. Allison was one of the twelve jurors. Henry Munson was on trial for murder. He was a shoe and boot maker by trade. The jury found him guilty and he was sentenced to be "hung by the neck until dead." Munson refused to believe that the jury could have the last word. He insisted on another hearing. In the August session under Judge Frank Willis he was freed of the murder charge and went back to his boot making. Next, the jury decided that John McCabe, who killed Grainger Dyer was "not guilty." Allison seems to have been well behaved and far different from the Las Animas days as a juryman. He did not call for drinks nor did he seek to bully the court. A warrant was served Clay Allison, but he seems to have avoided court proceedings, being represented by none other than Henry Hamburg, banker, merchant, and Mobeetie's leading citizen. To have been vouched for by one of the leading men of the Panhandle speaks well for the esteem in which Clay Allison was held. Hamburg had a high regard for Alison's ability both as a rancher and as a depositor in his bank. Foot bailiffs were paid $7.50 a term. The fact that Allison was paid this amount on April 9, 1881, is indication that he served in this capacity. Rinehart, the former sheriff of Colfax county in New Mexico, and the object of many of Allison's foibles, avoiding serving on either the petit or grand juries, either because of his experience with the officers from Dodge City who arrested him falsely or because he was done with whatever smacked of courts. He was in Mobeetie as a druggist. He was able to bring the officers who arrested him falsely to justice. He later moved to Tascosa to delve into real estate. That Allison was able to serve five days at a time on a jury without influencing the thinking of any of his fellow jurors and without inciting them to drink shows the success of Dora's encouragement. That he was a cattleman of substance is proven in the deferment, preference and consideration shown him by Dick Bussell, Goodnight, Bugbee, Mose Hays and others, who were particular about the company they kept. Allison also served on the jury from October 21 to 25, as stated above. It is interesting to note that both Parrsell and Elliott were friends of his but he did not let them bias his decision.

By other standards Allison outlived his time. Had he died stopping a bullet like Billy the Kid, Pat Garrett, Jim Courtright, or disappeared in mystery like Colonel Fountain, he might have been the hero of epic, screen and TV. But his death as the result of an accident put a wet blanket over all his other daring deeds. He received but passing mention from all writers of outlaw incidents. They seem to hold it against him that he was not the killer type like Doc Holiday, Hardin, Bass any more than he was a gun slinger as we understand the connotation. They jeer at the possibility that there may be a grain of truth in his remark that he never killed a man who didn't need killing. Bat Masterson's brother once said that Allison's reputation was strictly local; that he was beneath the consideration of the more notable gunfighters around Dodge. Bat differed from his brother. He had contracted to write his views for *Human Life Magazine,* went on a vacation and forgot all about Clay Allison. It is amusing to read some authors who make reference to Masterson's article on Clay Allison, with every indication that they have read it thoroughly. Here is what the Reference Department of the Library of Congress came up with:

"Although we have examined all the issues of *Human Life* (Boston, Human Life Publishing Co.) from October, 1906, to September, 1910, we have been unable to locate an article by 'Bat' Masterson on Clay Allison. We did find the series of articles by Masterson, entitled, 'Famous Gun Fighters of the Western Frontier,' the first article of which announced that Clay Allison and others were to be subjects of future articles. The first article appeared January, 1907, and four appeared thereafter in February, April, May and July, 1907. No other articles of the series appeared, and Clay Allison was not the subject of any of these . . ."

Z. Curtis, who once worked for Clay Allison as a cowboy (and still living at Springer, New Mexico) agreed that Allison was a man of his word. If Allison said he never killed a man who didn't need killing, that was enough for Curtis. And he ought to know. The Curtis family lived in the Cimarron country during the days of the Maxwell Land Grant War. Said his old friend in the *Fort County Globe,* March 8, 1881:

"Clay Allison, a man with a pretty well established reputation in New Mexico as a man of his word, in affairs of honor, seems to be thriving in his new home in Hemphill county, Texas. He bought a herd of cattle two years ago, paying therefore $3,200. At various times since he has sold beef to the value of $2,800 and is now on the eve of selling out for $9,000.''

The *Las Vegas Optic* also quoted this in its March 15 issue. The eventual history of the property is as follows:

Allison sold the homestead property to O. S. Wright; the range sections to W. W. Peet in 1883. Peet sold to the railroad townsite company of the Houston & Texas Railroad. The railroad people sold to William Lander, who in turn sold it back to W. W. Peet and Martha Peet in 1887, these property deeds being witnessed by Judge E. E. Polly and E. H. Duke of Hemphill county. Allison still maintained his interest in the Washita property, which his brothers continued to operate. For some reason, possibly because they tired of ranching and preferred farming or perhaps they were averse to the move to Lincoln county, followed as it was by another move to Pecos, Texas, they decided to return to Tennessee. With Clay's consent they sold to the S. R. E. Land and Cattle Company of Tarrant county (Texas) the range property—''six hundred and forty acres situated in Hemphill county and known as Sect. No. 18, Block No. 1, as surveyed for the H. G. A. Railroad Company ... and six hundred and forty acres of land situated in Hemphill county, known as Section No. 20, Block 1.... both sections above described being on the waters of the Gageby creek.... etc. witness our hand this 24th day of October, 1883.'' Thus the Allisons gave up their land in the Texas Panhandle.

While John and Munroe seem to have returned to Wayne county in Tennessee they did not remain there long, but seem to have come back to Colorado and other western states. As an old timer told the author: ''Allisons—I seem to recollect the name way back, but they be in these parts no more. Ain't herd t'em en quite a spell.''

During his Panhandle days Allison often visited the McNulty Camp on Adobe Wall creek. When McNulty decided on a foreman and manager for the Turkey Track (1881) he selected J. M. Coburn of South Texas. Two years later C. B. Willingham, sheriff of Tascosa, was hired as ranch boss and superintendent. Allison picked up many of his ideas about ranching from the Turkey Track outfit. Another friend of his was David Hargrave, range boss of the Half Circle U. John A. Chambers, Mose Hays, Henry Thompson, Jim Mabon, Gene Johnson, Red Gates, Sam Johnson, John Gerlach, John Bradborn, Indian Jim, Riley Garrison (colored cook). At times they all helped Allison during the round-up and branding season. The Turkey Track cowboys during the days Allison visited it, were J. M. Coburn, Willingham, Woods, Logan, Tom Coffee, Jess Winne, Cal Merchant, Jim Simpson, McSanford, Shell, Jim Caffery, John Caffery, Billy Dixon and Dick Bussell. This latter (1845-1935) was quite a buffalo hunter, often serving on the jury with Clay Allison, and was his best friend during the Panhandle days.

Just a few miles up the Gageby creek west of old man H. Anderson's place, the Allisons built a little log house near the creek as a ranch headquarters for their herd of horses and cattle. John A. Chambers saw it often and described it in his *Log of a Bashful Cowbay,* a three-volume manuscript of his days in the Panhandle. He died before he could have them published and no one has made any effort to further the effort. Chambers said this house had the customary dirt roof and dirt floor. John and Clay were married and their wives very hospitable and pretty. Munroe (which he also spelt Monroe) was single. Clay was crippled and used a cane to get down from his horse, a crooked handled walking stick which he hung to the horn of his saddle when he rode. **Munroe** always rode with his six-shooter buckled tight around his slender waist. Chambers said he became quite attached to the Allison boys despite their reputation. "Clay was always a dangerous cowboy to dispute with even out on the range without liquor and gin." (c.o. page 226, vol. 2.)

Chambers distinctly remembers the incident at Mobeetie. "It was at Mobeetie that Clay Allison went into his act of riding naked. He called himself Chief Mogull and did his riding in imitation of a savage Indian. All he wore was his six-shooter. He rode up and down the street of Mobeetie, shooting into the air, and giving the Indian and Rebel yells. No one dared dispute with him that day, unless they took a drop on him and wanted to kill him. Nobody wanted to do that because they felt that was the way he had to 'shoot off his gun' (i.e., let off steam), to relieve his funny feelings, and nobody disputed with him that high, lonesome day. . . ." (Ibid, Chambers o.c.)

The Allisons, Chambers thought, moved to Lincoln county, New Mexico, in the summer of 1884 because he remembers that a rich fellow from Fort Worth named Peter Smith, who manipulated for the S. R. E. cattle around Forth Worth, drove up the trail to the Gageby. Jube Thurmond was trail boss on the drive and with him were George Pruyear, Frank Cole, Frank Young and Thurmond's sons. Chambers says they were the ones who settled on Allison's place. It could be that they rented since courthouse records fail to reveal the Thurmonds as purchasers. Allison's neighbors were Mr. and Mrs. John Brown. Their son Rich Brown managed the place after John died. After Rich died his widow rented it. Rich Brown may have acquired some of the Allison land before his death. Clay would not have liked the idea of the land being broken up into small fields for planting alfalfa, wheat and a little cotton. When he moved to Lincoln county he thought he had the answer— the open range, cattle country, free of homesteaders.

Chapter Eight

THE PECOS COUNTRY

Between the Pecos and the Black rivers, on the sites of Loving and Malaga in southeastern New Mexico, you come upon the area where bold Comanche Indians relieved P. Chisum, brother of the more widely known John, of a herd of cattle in 1873, at the time Clay Allison was working to build up his own herd. The stolen cattle were driven south of Guadalupe Point, where many were butchered and the remainder kept for a beef herd. Despite Comanches, cowboys came to like this country. Here two trails led into La Valle de los Siete Rios, both from the south. One branched off from the old Chihuahua Trail at Del Rio up the Pecos to the Butterfield Trail at Horsehead Crossing; the other crossing the Pecos a little farther north at Pope's Crossing. Native New Mexicans from Bonito, Tularosa and Socorro sought to use the country as a feeding range for sheep. A few even attempted a settlement calling the place Siete Rios because of the seven little streams that fed the Pecos. Mescalero Apaches objecting strenuously forced them to move but the name Valley of the Seven Rivers stuck.

Pop and Marm Jones pioneered out of Virginia, coming by oxcart, and settling along the banks of the Hondo in 1867. This place is now known as the Gail Ranch. Tom Jones, said to be the first Anglo born in Lincoln county, first saw the light of day on this ranch. A roving spirit, somewhat like Clay Allison, Pop moved on to the Ruidosa on what is known as the Bonnell

Ranch. Both these places were sold to Frank and George Coe who figured so prominently in the Lincoln County war. After selling out on the Ruidosa the Jones family together with some prospective settlers moved to the site of Seven Rivers and located on the east bank. Discovering that the drinking water was better on the land off the opposite bank, they re-moved. Also it was so much easier to ship cattle from this side to Pecos City in Texas. The country was good for cattle.

Thus in the early 70's thirty men, most of them former Texas Rangers, all of them quick on the draw, minute men against Indians, rustlers and homesteaders, loaded their families and goods into covered wagons and founded the village of Seven Rivers northeast of the site of Carlsbad. Dan Beckett, Dick Turknett, Pete Corn, Lafe McDonald, George Wilcox, Levi Watson, Joe Woods, George Larrimore, Ed Peril, Charlie Gambel, Buster Gambel, Pop Jones, John Jones, Will Jones, Sorn Jones, John Fanning, Bill Nelson—frontiersman all, they opened the valley to ranching because of the shortened distance to the fast-growing outlet and market at Pecos City to the south. The town grew. Captain Sam Sampson opened the first store—a saloon and trading post—located near where Seven Rivers flowed into the Pecos. Gordon & Benton opened a store just below Sampson's, followed by a still larger mercantile company owned by Pierce & Semore. Fred Sheremyre did a nice business with his quaint boot shop. Marm Jones, not to be outdone, opened a restaurant. Dee Bardett had a drug store and was looked upon as the town physician, usually called to attend gunshot wounds. A blacksmith moved in, more saloons and the town became a perfect set-up for the visits of Bob Edwards, Billy the Kid, Dave Rudabaugh, Dave Mathers, Jim Greathouse and other less popularized outlaws who made the best of their new opportunities by converting the town into another Dodge, Tombstone, and a general hangout place for gunfighters. Tavern killings were not the exception. They were the rule. The first four men to occupy the new cemetery died with their boots on. Here the range war was at its peak. Sheepherders were shot and thrown into shallow graves, their toes sticking out.

Connected with the Pierce store was a saloon. Tom Fensing was the bartender. One night he got into an argument with John Northen, the gambler. Six-shooter law. The gambler died on the spot. Fensing, a bullet in his stomach, ran to Pop Jones' place, hid in the wood box behind the stove. When Pop came for some firewood the next morning he discovered the corpse. Les Dow succeeded Fensing as bartender until he killed Zac Light. Will Doughty took the mail by wagon from Benon (now Elk) to Seven Rivers. Jessie J. Roscoe was the stage driver. Once in a fight with Indians his left arm was shot off but he continued to drive to town where he had the arm amputated and when the wound healed resumed work.

There was a signal point south of Seven Rivers where Roscoe lit a fire for smoke signals. When the ranchers and cowboys saw the smoke they knew that the mail was in and called for it. Ash Upson, the school teacher and Justice of the Peace, was a native New Yorker. He migrated to Denver early in life and became associated with the *Rocky Mountain News* (a newspaper that still serves the public). It was through his influence that Minnie Jones, fifteen years of age, became the first postmistress of Seven Rivers. The postoffice was at the Reed Ranch.

The really big cattle drives got under way in 1881 when Clay Allison was just beginning to enjoy his new home on the Washita. There was talk in Mobeetie of the beehive activity at Seven Rivers; of how the cattle there seemed to thrive better than in most places; how it was the ideal spot for the white-faced Hereford now making its bid to push the longhorn out of existence; of the closer markets that saved valuable poundage on steers. Allison decided to range his cattle in the Seven Rivers county mostly by way of a test to see if it was everything the cowboys claimed. John and Munroe had already sold out in Colfax county and moved into the Gageby region of the Panhandle. While they seemed to be getting along fairly enough they thought they could better themselves elsewhere and pitched in with Clay on the move back to Lincoln county in New Mexico. Dora, who was at home wherever Clay was, felt that the change would be for the better. Thus: "For and in consideration of the sum of one thousand dollars to us in hand paid by the S. R. E. Land and Cattle Company of the County of Tarrant and the State of Texas, the receipt of which is hereby acknowledged, do by these presents bargain, sell, release and forever quit claim, unto the said heirs and assigns, all our right, title and interest in and unto that tract or parcel of land lying in the County of Hemphill and the State of Texas, described as follows: Six hundred and forty acres of land situated in Hemphill county and known as Section No. 18, Block No. 1, as surveyed for the H.G.A. Railroad Company, being the same tract of land applied for by J. W. Allison under provision of Sect. 5. . . . Approved April 12, 1883. . . . Also six hundred and forty acres of land situated in Hemphill county known as Sect. 20. Block .... Both sections above described being on the waters of the Gageby creek." The paper was signed on October 24, 1883, but not entered into the official records of the courthouse until 1887, when Tom McGee was sheriff. Those interested in seeing the originals of these transactions may find them at the Hemphill county courthouse in Canadian and at the Wheeler county courthouse in Wheeler.

All the ranchers of the Seven Rivers district welcomed Clay Allison, for they knew of his business acumen, his love of cattle and horses, and thought that he might be a help to the Justice of the Peace in establishing law and order. His word was his bond. Whatever else he may be accused of, no one denied that he was not a truthful man. Taciturn by nature except when he was "Chief Mogul," which was becoming a rarer occasion now, thanks to Dora's efforts, cowboys and cattlemen alike respected his judgment. Not that there were those who still hoped for the chance of out-drawing the mighty Clay Allison. These there would be to his dying day, but not one would have the chance. When Allison would be stopped it would not be by lead. Accidents always happen, they say. One certainly happened to him. When he arrived at Seven Rivers he was already a legend.

Chisum came to know the Pecos country through the efforts of Oliver Loving and Charles Goodnight. Following their trail he brought six hundred beeves to Fort Sumner and obtained a contract to deliver ten thousand more. By this time he was so impressed with the Pecos valley that he decided to make it his range. It has been said that Clay Allison worked for him during that short interim before moving into the Cimarron country. During the 70's it has been said that he had the largest holdings of cattle in the world. His ranch extended from Fort Sumner on the Pecos two hundred miles southward to the Texas line. He tolerated no settlers. At the time Allison was on trial for murder Chisum's herd numbered one hundred thousand head. Then Comanches, Apaches, Navajos, rustlers got busy. Other ranchers built up strong competition. This Chisum could tolerate but the inroads of rustlers annoyed him. That is why he welcomed the prospect of a Cattlemen's Association. Chisum died a few months after Allison located in the Seven Rivers country, but he lived long enough to unite the stockmen of Lincoln county against cattle thieves. The Chisum estate had a history all its own in the hands of J. J. Hagerman and later Cornell University. At present it is a modern irrigated farm. Allison often visited the Chisum ranch even after the death of the old trail blazer.

Here is an interesting editorial on Clay Allison, found in the *Las Vegas Optic* (May 12, 1886):

"Time was perhaps in the early and trying days of New Mexico when men carried their lives in their hands; juries rendered their verdicts before the cases were heard in court, and men settled their differences at the point of a six-shooter, and our headlines mentioned at the head of this column would have struck terror to the hearts of those who were the sworn enemies of Clay Allison, and even those who were not, would have feared that his presence was an indication that trouble was to follow; for that he was, and is, a brave, determined man, who will sell his life dearly under any circumstances that may come up, fighting at the drop of a hat, and to the bitter end, for a friend, and vindicating his rights at all hazards, none who then knew him, or know him now, can deny.

"Clay Allison has no doubt had as many tragic adventures as any man in the West, but he could not be the bad man at heart he is painted to be, and still number among his friends the character of men that he now does. The scenes and the tragedies of other days, in many of which he was the hero, perhaps more from necessity than from choice, are fading from his mind and he no longer cares to have them referred to.

"Five years ago, with $10,000 in his pocket, he passed through Las Vegas. The money was invested in a ranch and cattle on the dividing line between Texas and New Mexico, and he has since made this place his headquarters. He spent last summer in Sedalia, Missouri, paying an occasional visit to his ranch and seeing that his cattle were properly handled by the men in charge. (Evidently another try at playing the gentleman, since he had been to Sedalia a few seasons previously.) As an indication of the thrift that attended him, it may be stated that an Englishman recently offered him the neat sum of $73,000 for his ranch and cattle.

"Reporter—What is the occasion of your visit to our city, Mr. Allison?"

"Allison—I am here for a two-fold purpose; (a) I am driving across the country to the best market I can find, with 1,500 head of as fine steers as were ever branded. My herd will reach Springer in about twelve days and I will make my headquarters there until the steers are disposed of; (b) I came to have my picture and a sketch of my career appear in the Stock Grower of your city. As the price charged by this journal is not made public, and as I have a proverbial delicacy about matters so personal to my humble self, I will ask some of my friends to obtain the information for me. Besides a portrait of myself I have eight men and a dog—a shepherd dog that does not talk much but thinks a great deal, and it is my earnest desire that their portraits also appear in the same issue of the Stock Grower that mine does.

"Reporter—Mr. Allison, is it true that you have withdrawn from the Lincoln County Stock Association and are opposed to such organizations generally?

"Allison—Young man, I am. I gave notice to Mr. Anderson, President of the Lincoln County Stock Association of, my intention to withdraw from that body at least two months before he would consent to drop my name from their books. I am a free American citizen of the United States and while my brain after my death will not weigh as much as Tom Catron's (Catron was a prominent Santa Fe attorney, land owner, politician and socialite of the day, accused by some as the leader of the Santa Fe ring that touched off the Maxwell Land Grant War, the death of Parson Tolby. Even in death he makes himself known. You can't miss his grave as you ride from Santa Fe to Albuquerque. The mausoleum bearing the name CATRON almost leaps at you from the cemetery.) Yet, I claim to be the happy possessor of sufficient brains to manage my own private business affairs without intervention of any association of other cattle raisers, be such association local or territorial. Of course, if any of these fellows who delight in splurging around the country under broad-brimmed white hats and in having their names and pictures emblazoned so boldly and so frequently in print, want to make an assessment against me for this—to them a laudable purpose—well and good, I will go down into my jeans and plank my share of the amount desired. But I have set my foot down on its heel pretty lively and shall no longer submit to any systematic extortions of these cattle associations in the form of fees, dues, and the like. . . . ''

After some more questions the editor commented: "The friendly visit of Clay Allison to this office this morning was much more welcome than have been visits of his to other newspaper offices in the Territory within the memory of man."

Allison stayed some time in Springer, where he met with very little success in an already overcrowded market. Joseph Clouthier, the merchant, advised him to drive the cattle on to Cheyenne where he was sure that Clay would have no difficulty in selling them at a good profit. One of the cowboys with Allison on this trip was James Howard. While the rip-roaring days of "hurrahing" the town were fading into the past, fandangos, drinking bouts, current popular dances and general good times were still sought after, and usually found, by the cowboys. Allison and his men attended the Saturday night dances at Springer. So did Josefita Carson, named for her mother, Josefita Jaramillo Carson, wife of the famous fur trapper, guide and scout. Howard was so taken up with Josefita that he asked permission to write. Although Allison and the other boys gave him a friendly ribbing, he weathered the storm and the romance blossomed. When Howard married, Allison lost one of his best cowboys. The *Raton Comet* carried this notice in its January 21, 1887, issue:

"Josefita Carson, the youngest and only remaining single daughter of the famous hunter and Indian fighter, Kit Carson, was quietly married at Springer on Sunday (January 15, at St. Joseph's Church by Rev. Joseph Accorsini—Allison was present at the ceremony) to James Howard. Mr. Howard came to Springer from Seven Rivers last May with Clay Allison, and having met Miss Carson at a ball, became an admirer of the young lady, and on Sunday last, as before stated, took her to be his wife, Miss Carson resided at the residence of Thomas O. Boggs, whose admiration and friendship for Kit Carson is known all over this Western country. Kit Carson, after having served his country faithfully and honestly, died poor, and Mr. Boggs took care of Carson's children, six in number, and raised them all. Mr. Howard and his bride are at present stopping at Mr. Boggs."

Allison made his way up to Wyoming by way of Raton Pass, stopping at Raton and Trinidad long enough to shake hands with his many friends, according to the *Optic* reporter (June 6, 1886), who seemed to make it a point to follow Allison's progress northward. As Clouthier prophesied, the cattle did bring a profit at Cheyenne. It was at this time that an incident occurs which has more variations than a score of music. Most authors place the scene at Las Vegas, possibly because the reporter caught Allison on the rebound as he returned from Cheyenne and got the story from him, which he promptly printed in the *Optic*. Without bothering to investigate further, the fact that it appeared in the Las Vegas paper satisfied them that the incident took place there. Allison made his appearance in Las Vegas on July 3, 1886, exactly one year to the date of his death. The *Optic* published the account of his experience four days later:

"Clay Allison, who has just left this city for Lincoln county, is known as a holy terror when he is aroused, and although increasing years and different conditions have made him less vindictive, he still has a decided fondness for getting even with his enemeis, and is pretty likely to do so as a general rule. Clay was up in Cheyenne a few days ago with a bunch of steers, about fifteen hundred head in number, which he sold at a good profit, and as he was suffering from a toothache while there, he went to a dentist to get relief. The dentist who was 'on the make' sized up the man as a cowman with plenty of cash and determined to make some money out of him. Instead of applying a little creosote to Clay's aching tooth he got him in his dental chair and proceeded to bore a hole in one of the cowman's best teeth for the purpose of filling it, which it didn't in the least need. He was a clumsy quack and he inadvertently broke about half a tooth off. Clay got mad and left and went to another dentist, who repaired the damage at the expense of twenty-five dollars, and told the victim that he had been treated by an arrogant quack who evidently wanted to make money out of him. This fired the blood of Mr. Allison, who fairly thirsted for revenge, and he got it, too. He proceeded to the quack's office, seized a pair of forceps, threw him down on the floor, and, in spite of the yells of the victim, inserted the instrument in his mouth and drew out one of his best molars. Not content with this, he grabbed for another and caught one of the front teeth together with a large piece of the upper lip and was tugging away at it when the agonized shrieks and yells of the poor devil upon whose chest Allison was pressing his knee, drew a crowd and ended the matter. The story is said to be absolutely true and Allison admitted it.''

A highly respected cattleman, Allison had grandiose ideas for his little daughter Patsy, born before he left the Gageby country. He spoke of her often to his friends, and on the trail as he gazed into the campfire she was part of the dancing flames. The thought of her hurt him.

She was a cripple. No doctor he took her to seemed capable. When he stopped at the Grand Central Hotel, owned by a friend of his named David Gage, well known in Denver for his bigness of heart as well as his hotel, Allison told him that the object of his visit was to find a medical man who could help his daughter. Gage said he would inquire around. Once when he thought he had located a specialist, Gage notified Allison, who brought Patsy up from Seven Rivers for an examination. The specialist told Allison there was nothing he could do. Allison returned to the Grand Central with such a woebegone look that Gage was at a loss as to how to pacify him. Allison blamed himself for his daughter's condition, saying that he was cursed by God for having cut loose once in a while in the past. Patsy's affliction took much of the wildness out of him and mellowed his thinking. After her father's death, she was able to receive the medical attention she needed and grew up to be a fine looking, healthy young woman. It was not lack of consideration on Allison's part but the advance of medical science that was able to remedy the situation. Clay would have rejoiced at her happy and successful marriage.

Seven Rivers suffered a drought in 1886, growing steadily worse in 1887 and 1888. Cattle died of hunger, thirst, dust. The paradise of yesteryear became a fit topic for Dante's Inferno. The wars between sheep men and cattle men were renewed with increasing violence. Fences were here to stay. People began crowding the area so that a man felt he couldn't breathe. Capitalists from the East were drawing all kinds of plans for gullible settlers. Crowds were putting up huts in a place called Eddy which was to emerge as the modern Carlsbad. Up in the Panhandle new counties were being cut from the vast trackless plains—sliced off like a side of beef. Buffalo hunters gave up dreaming and returned to Dodge, Mobeetie, Camp Supply especially when the skin and bone trade fell off. Some stayed to work as cowboys on the

Turkey Track, Rocking Chair, Laureleaf, the Anvil and other once famous ranches along the Canadian. The iron horse moved in closer and closer to usher in a new era. Covered wagons, roving Indians, the drummer, trail boss, were marked for the past. There is no progress without death. Somebody goes when the new is accepted. All we know this age by is found in museums, books, the movies, TV and radio. Living those days again by visual education is never the same as having been a part of a glorious era. No matter how a five-year-old might react to a new toy at Christmas time, he would be glad to put it away in favor of an imitation six-shooter, chaps, cowboy shirt, jeans, a Roy Rogers or Gene Autry outfit, and no matter what games he plays he will always be ready for cowboys and Indians, stage hold-ups, posse chases. Why? Perhaps there will be something about the age in which Clay Allison lived that will never be lost and will always be sought like DeSoto looking for the Fountain of Youth, and it will pass on an and on from generation to generation, from young one with his toy pistol to grown-up with his TV set.

Men like Clay Allison, Bat Masterson, Wyatt Earp, were ready to hang up their six-shooters and accept the intrusion of progress, wondering about the wild ways and days of their youth. Allison built up his ranch systematically, with an eye to the rising industry of the packing house, the growth of the stock yards, the increased demand for beef, yet he hoped to hold on to things as they were by living along the last frontier. Guns many would continue to carry but only as a precaution against rattlers, coyotes, wolves and sometimes for game. The gunfighter seeking glory as a killer of the top man was to bow before the rise of the art of fisticuffs, measured out by weight like beeves at a stock show, on display before jeering or cheering crowds depending on whether the boxer was the favorite or unpopular. Society waved aside the man with the gun now classifying him a criminal and giving him a number and time in the Territorial pen at Santa Fe. The thing to do was to build your home in town and send your children to good schools. On Saturday nights cowboys did not gang up anymore to take pop shots at lights. Even this had a name now—rowdyism. Fortunately, the cowboy himself was to seek compensation for the loss of these privileges by stimulating competition between outfits out of which was to develop the rodeo as we know it today. Mobeetie ran such contests between the soldier and the cowboy. Pecos, Texas, staged such contests between cowboys for the benefit of the public. Canadian was the first town to recognize the commercial value of rodeo. The six-shooter, too, went the way of all things past. Cattlemen relied more and more on marshalls, posses, sheriffs, private detectives to hunt down the rustler and horsethief. Rustling still goes on in spite of planes, cars and broadcasts. And will go on as long as people continue to eat beef. The rustler has kept abreast of his times in his technique. For a while the rope replaced the six-shooter. When caught, the thief dangled from a tree, and not in imitation of monkies. Prowess with the gun was fast becoming a matter of ability with traveling Wild West shows which grew out of the craze to keep the West alive in the minds of Easterners, and to make money for Buffalo Bill, Pawnee Bill, and many others who brought the Wild West into show business. All this was a passing parade before Allison's eyes. Caught in the vortex of things that were and afraid of things as they are the only thing to do was to settle down to things as they would be. All too many ranchers lived in two homes. The town house where the family lived and the children attended school; the ranch house where the rancher, his foreman and some of the hired help lived. Usually the rancher stayed at the town house during the winter months and the family stayed at the ranch house during the summer months where the children were occupied with milking, gardening and other household chores. The boys cut wood for the old Majestic stove, for gas and electricity in the kitchen had not as yet turned the corner. This was known as "gentleman ranching."

The advance of the railhead meant more time on the range. The rancher usually followed the chuck wagon from section to section, building or mending fences, watching for signs of coyotes or other predatory animals. Because of the now widespread use of barbed wire, it meant cutting fence posts, fencing, dividing neighbors' stock, building gates and cattle guards, keeping your cattle from intruding on your neighbors' ranges, making sure that his did not cross to your range. While there wasn't a cattleman who wasn't delighted that buffalo roamed the range no longer, nevertheless, there was not one to be found who did not regret the freedom of the range that these extinct animals enjoyed. Of course, the hide market was higher than it ever was. So was the meat and bone industry. No reason to lament the money flowing in as it never did before. The cattleman had a place in the sun. Eastern girls dreamed of marrying a rich cattleman from Texas as a later generation was to set its cap for the rich Texas oilman. There was the tip of the hat to the cattleman as it should be, but with a fickle public how long would this last? Even Allison was astute enough to recognize that before long syndicates would cut the cattleman down to size. Packing houses would maintain their own ranges and the small rancher would go back to being small.

John and Munroe were aware of this, too. Farming in Tennessee would not bring the financial returns as ranching in Texas, but when interested parties lowered the boom they would be just where they started. One day they pulled stakes—sold out all—land, cattle, ranch house—lock, stock and barrel. They took the trail back to Waynesboro. Their further ventures are no concern of ours here. Clay stayed. No doubt the parting was sad, especially between Dora and her sister, John's wife. But they were to live many years to be able to see each other at frequent intervals. Clay never saw his brothers again.

The drought made everybody touchy. The banker tightened his grasp. Loans were not as liberal nor as frequent. Seven Rivers slowed up. People began to welcome buyers. Dr. H. Burdett, possibly from lack of business, took on the job of deputy sheriff. Old man Pierce, the leading merchant, sold out to W. F. Docking & Company. The town melted away. Today it is but a memory, its soul keeps company with the multitude of other ghost towns that make New Mexico unique among the Western states, that had their share. No matter what the count, New Mexico tops them. Sporadic forays revived scenes of the past. Up in the Panhandle many friends from the Mobeetie area abandoned the historic site to set up shop in the new railroad town of Canadian. Hamburg, Bussell, Montgomery, a whole litany of them, located in this new shipping center. Several old timers claimed that they saw Allison in Canadian in the spring of 1887, when the site was known as Hogtown over near the Anvil Ranch where J. Studer lived.

Alison's foreman during these Seven Rivers days was J. McCullough, his brother-in-law. He does not seem to have been Dora's brother but a McCullough from Waynesboro who married Clay's sister, Mary, and came out to the Southwest to try life as a rancher. Some have said that he was trail boss on the drive to Cheyenne. Alex Simpson, who was a boy at the time, remembered Clay Allison as stopping at Hogtown, but paid him no heed because he looked like any other cowboy to him, although he did hear his elders talking about "that mankiller Allison." He remembers him as tall, face bronzed by the sun, and quiet. The city of Canadian was not to start construction for several months yet and when it did, Hogtown, a couple of miles away, folded up.

Across the Territorial line to the south another town shaped out of the void. Near the eastern boundary of Reeves county, on the Pecos river, the Texas and Pacific railroad established a stop known as Pecos Station, which dignified itself with the name, Pecos City, and today accepts just the name Pecos. One of the ranchers here is said to have found the bible given by Mrs. Bonney to her son, Billy the Kid, hidden in a cave on the rangeland bought by Clay Allison. People who have seen the book have identified the name scratched on the title page as that of William Bonney. It is possible since Billy often "holed out" here before settlers and cowboys brought life to the quasi-desert. During its "teeth-cutting" age Pecos was as lawless as any other frontier town and here the term "Pecosin" originated. In cowboy lingo this means weighing down your victim with rocks after you shot him and dumping his body into the Pecos river. This idea was to catch on during the Roaring Twenties when bootleggers made a practice in New York of taking their victim for a "ride" from which there was no return. Throwing their victim into the East river after tying him down with rocks was already old stuff in this Pecos section of Texas. Rodeo is said to have originated here at Pecos as a sport thought up by competitive cowboy outfits, a distinction which the city of Canadian would dispute, although Canadian did not seem too active when the location for a cowboy museum went abegging. What Oklahoma City will do remains to be seen.

Many authors have Billy the Kid drinking at the bars in Pecos. Now, we are not out to discourage those who worship at the shrine of this outlaw. Why all the homage? If they wish to believe that The Kid drank in a city that did not exist, more power to them. Billy was shot by Pat Garrett on July 14, 1881. The town of Pecos was not established until about the time he was killed, and then it was just Pecos Station with Alvan Walter Calahan, the station agent, also serving as the postmaster. Perhaps a bar was put up in 1881 when the railroad came to the valley. But on Christmas Eve of 1880, Billy, along with Rudabaugh and Pickett, fell into the hands of the law and was imprisoned in Las Vegas, Santa Fe and Lincoln. Following his escape he clung to the Fort Sumner area, some say for romantic reasons. These few weeks of freedom may have brought him a time or two to Pecos. But would he be so bold? Knowing he was a wanted man? Drinking in a newly founded hamlet where he was not certain he had a friend? How do these things get started, anyway? No doubt Billy and Clay may have crossed paths before 1881, because Allison was a frequent visitor to the Chisum ranch even before moving to the Seven Rivers area. Allison was in no way mixed up in the Lincoln County War and his opinion of the Kid was not favorable. Had they faced each other at gunpoint it would have been interesting reading, indeed, especially since Allison seems to be favored as faster on the draw. Of course, lovers of Billy will dispute this, just like lovers of Wyatt Earp dispute that Allison could have made a mighty interesting episode of their encounter at Dodge, had he faced Earp without Winchesters decorating the background.

Toyah, on the San Martin Draw, was platted in 1881. In four years it had a population of sixty. But, small as it was, wild and wooly days were to make it as notorious as Pecos. Here Sheriff J. T. Morris met his death. How well he knew Clay Allison is hard to say, certainly not as well as his successor, L. S. Turbo, who often had dinner at the Allison place when Clay bought it from the McNallys.

The Toyah country and the Pecos country were the last that Clay Allison was to know. No doubt had he lived he might have moved again. No sooner settled at Seven Rivers than he was off again to the infant city south of him where Patsy, now aged five, would ready herself for school. Besides, Dora was expecting again.

People who knew Clay in Pecos described him as tall, slim and seemingly dark complexioned, due perhaps to long exposure in the sun. As the town was close to the ranch he bought on the river near the famous Y crossing, Clay decided to buy the J. J. McNally place on Fifth and Cypress, which would create the impression of quite a city. On the contrary, when Clay interested himself in a "city" home the population of Pecos City numbered one hundred and fifty. The land was part of the Hudson & Great Northern survey, and the New York & Texas Land Company.: It sold for two dollars an acre. McNally, a native of Chicago, built a small one-room home on the corner lot already mentioned. Close by lived Mark Mitchell. It was their daughter, eight at the time, who became the intimate friend of Patsy Allison, and their mothers were more like two sisters, so much were they in and out of each other's house. It was Mrs. Mark Mitchell who saw Dora through the dark days following Clay's accident. The friendship continued even after Dora as Mrs. Lee Johnson moved to other parts.

When Allison bought the McNally place he renovated it, adding on a few more rooms. Another friend to visit often was Jake Owens, known to readers of Western folklore for the part he played in the Lincoln County War. He is was who piled up the brush against the door of the McSween home in Lincoln. He had a small business in Pecos City and was once numbered among Allison's cowhands. Some scandal monger (and where won't you find them), full of inuendoes, tried to start the story rolling that Clay became jealous of Owens' attentions to Dora and was on his way to Curry to kill him the day he met with his fatal accident. As if Clay had anything to worry about regarding Dora's affections. But then there are people with minds like that. Always trying to shape a wedding ring into a triangle. The fact that Clay took time to load a wagon full of wood and drove a team of horses when the occasion would have called for his war horse and war whoop, helps to shrug off this version of his rendezvous with death. Arm chair authors and parlor authorities have come up with a thousand versions regarding this accident, but all are more or less agreed that the fall from the wagon was the immediate cause of death.

The wee little town of Pecos held a special election to incorporate as a city several months before Clay moved his family from his adobe house camp on the ranch, situated as it was near the Y crossing of the Pecos north of Pecos City. Many old timers agree that Clay Allison was the original pioneer to settle this particular area; others say that Tom Gray or some cowboys from the Hashknife outfit were the first settlers. Whoever was the first is of little importance; the fact remains that Clay Allison was the owner at the time of his death. W. D. and Woody Johnson, brothers, built a drift fence from the southwest corner of New Mexico west to the Pecos river in an effort to keep stock from drifting south to the river during severe storms. More often as not cattle roamed south against the fence, breaking through, much to the disgust of Allison's cowboys, whose job it was to mend the breaks as well as to cut out these cattle from the Allison brand in the spring. These Johnson brothers may have been related to Lee Johnson the lumber and cattle man of Pecos who married Dora some time after Clay's death. Also it may have been some dispute with one of these brothers that gave rise to the interesting legend of the fight in the grave with a Johnson in a disagreement over a water hole.

During the 80's when the drought of the early years was followed by repeated floods of the later years to bring "see-saw" prices in beef, the Johnson brothers bought out small ranchers who preferred greener pastures elsewhere or merely to get out of the uncertainty of ranching. Many had moved from the East, bringing their stock with them only to be disillusioned. They were relieved when the Johnsons asked to buy them out. The fact that the Lee Johnsons sold the ranch and the adobe camp house to the Johnson brothers is an indication that Allison's will left all to Dora. They sold not because it was unprofitable but because they moved to Fort Worth to expand their interests as well as to give Patsy the benefit of an education in a larger city. The Johnson brothers turned the place over to J. Barber, who in turn gave it to his son Bill. Sid Kyle bought it from Bill Barker. Buck Jackson bought it from Kyle. The Jackson family still retains possession. The deed to the house in Pecos reads as follows:

"J. J. McNally and wife to R. C. Allison:

"We, John J. McNally of the first part, in consideration of the sum of $75 in cash, paid by R. C. Allison, the receipt whereof is hereby acknowledged, have granted, bargain, sell, alien, convey and confirm unto the said R. C. Allison, party of the second part, his heirs and assigns forever, the following real estate to wit: Lot number eighteen in Block number sixty-six in the town of Pecos City in Reeves county, State of Texas—To have and to hold, and all singular, the above described and conveyed premises and property, with all the rights, privileges, hereditaments and appurtenances thereunto belonging or in any wise appertaining unto the said R. C. Allison, party of the second part, his heirs or assigns forever, and they the said parties of the first part, do hereby bind themselves unto the said party of the second part, his heirs and assigns, that they are well seized of all and singular, the said property and premises; that they have good right and lawful authority to make this sale and conveyance of the same; that the said property and premises are free and clear of all and every incumbrance and that unto the said party of the second part, his heirs and administrators will forever warrant and defend the same against all adverse lawful claim or claim whatsoever. In witness thereof we do hereunto affix our hands and seals using scrolls for seals, this 15th day of December, A. D. 1886...." (Deed Records—Reeves Co., Vol. 2, pp. 284-85.)

In order to make certain that the property definitely belonged to McNally, since in a new town property changes frequently and swiftly, Allison, always the shrewd business man, wrote to W. H. Bassett, a notary of the State of Illinois, and McNally's friend, asking him for a testimonial letter as to McNally's trustworthiness. Allison seemed satisfied with Bassett's testimony.

John McCullough rode in to the new railroad center at Pecos City to investigate the possibility of shipping cattle from that point. No one ever questioned neither his ability as a foreman for Clay Allison nor the intent with which he labored in the interests of a man who would create jobs if he had to in order to keep the family together. Tired from the long ride from the Seven Rivers country, where some of the Allison cattle still grazed, he stopped at a cantina for the touch and go drink that always made the cowboy wonder why he drank the stuff, and made him hanker for it if he didn't. A desperado named Jen Clayton happened to be in the saloon at the same time. Hearing that John was Allison's brother-in-law, the thought came to him that this was as good a time as any to make a name for himself as the slayer of Clay Allison. McCullough would relay the message. He walked up to the bar, pushed the foreman out of his way and called for a drink. The play was old stuff to McCullough.

"Where I come from that means a fight," jeered the gunman.

"Where I come from that's just bad manners," said McCullough quietly.

"Maybe you let your brother-in-law do your fighting for you. Hear it told he's quite a man with the gun. Now, that's mighty interesting. Just mighty interesting. You tell him for me that Jen Clayton doesn't think he's such a mighty man with a gun. Tell him Jen Clayton will be awaiting." Drawing his gun, he shouted:

"Get going."

Knowing that Clay often came to Pecos for supplies, and fearing he might be ambushed, McCullough told him of the incident and of the gunman anxious to test his metal. Allison saddled his horse, rode into Pecos and inquired for Clayton. The streets cleared as if by magic. All activity ceased in the cantina when some patrons recognized the tall, slim visitor standing in the doorway.

"Which one of you is Jen Clayton?" he asked, addressing the room generally.

There was no backing away. Clayton stood up from the card table.

"I am." Neither defiant nor humble, just matter of fact.

"Hear you want to fight me, Allison is the name. Clay Allison."

"Talk," said Clayton. "Just whisky talk. Drunk, I guess."

"Well, if whisky does that, drink."

He had the bartender fill a glass.

"Drink."

Clayton drank. Another and another.

"Well," asked Allison, "are you ready?"

"I have no fight with you. Leave me alone," pleaded the thoroughly shaken gunfighter.

"If you ever talk that way again, I will take a bullwhip to your hide and lash you into strings."

Clayton was cured for keeps. He settled down to some usefulness in the community, maintaining respect and admiration for Allison until the end of his days.

Over on the San Martin draw the other little village of Toyah (Indian for much water) was making a bid for the Pecos trade. Round-up crews camped here, rode into the town to "hurrah" it in regular Western fashion.

Allison's cowboys, getting into the swing of things, shot out the lights, windows, drank up what the cantina had to offer and set the little spot of sixty on its ears, much to the disgust of a cowboy from another outfit, who selected one of Allison's men as the target of his abuse. As a result of these insults both parties concerned agreed to meet at one o'clock on the following afternoon to fight a duel with pistols. Why Allison's man consented to such a contest can only be explained by his pride or his spunk, since he had a crippled right hand which he always kept covered with a glove. As the time approached Allison noticed the cowboy showing increasing tension, nervousness and worry. Asked if anything bothered him he explained the arrangement to Allison, adding that as a gentleman he would keep his part of the deal despite the fact that his right hand was useless and he could draw but poorly with his left. Both boys had arranged to ride for the crest of the hill near the draw. When at the top they were to blaze away at each other. Allison thought it a one-sided affair and thought it would be equalled if he took over for his cowboy. As the boy from the other outfit rode to the top of the hill he noted that the other rider was not the one he agreed to fight with. He rode closer to see who it was. One look at Allison's determined face, he wheeled his horse and never stopped until he was back in his own camp. Later when he found out about the crippled hand he regretted the whole affair and was grateful that he did not draw before riding closer to get a good look at his opponent. He said that when he saw Allison he recognized the famous fast-on-the-draw rancher and decided that discretion was the better part of valor. He made tracks but fast. The boys in his outfit agreed with him.

Innately Allison was a sensitive man and placed high evaluation on the opinions of friends. Psychologists would say that his bravado with the six-shooter was a sublimation, or even a behavior pattern, a matter of asserting himself because of a complex. Any remark disparaging to good character irked, irritated and hurt. Anyone who knew Clay Allison was agreed that even under the influence of liquor he was as steady on the draw as when completely sober. The fact that no one was ever injured by him when he shot at them in drunken glee testified to this. They are also agreed that he was a handsome figure of a man and the remarkably unflattering etching found in Otero's first volume of *My Life on the Frontier* would have scared even Dora. In the etching Allison is portrayed as a veritable Fagin out of Dickens, or Shylock out of the *Merchant of Venice*. While the engraver sought to picture him a desperado, he only succeeded in giving us a filthy ragpicker with side arms.

Word came to Allison, possibly through his brother-in-law, who was his foreman, that two cowboys of his outfit were rather cryptic in their remarks about him. Some have it that it was actually McCullough himself. This brother-in-law seems to have settled in Texas and established himself as a fairly successful rancher. One of his sons died in Texas in 1956. A grandson is named Clay for Allison. This does not sound as if Clay and his brother-in-law did not get along. Writers must pin the incident on someone, so they make the brother-in-law the scape-goat. Actually no one knows for certain who Allison got word of the criticism against him from. All we know is that it was very uncomplimentary and it circulated freely in the area around the Y crossing. McDonald and his brother-in-law Laramore (seemed to be a standard arrangement in those days to work with in-laws) were in Pecos loading their freight wagons for the Seven Rivers run. Clay happened by and in conversation with his two friends remarked that he was going to work the range toward the Crossing, and while there take care of the two cowboys for what he termed vicious lies against his character. The freighters knew him well enough to understand that he would be drinking along the way, for he was sensitive about hurting anyone who worked for him. The liquor was not a booster but rather forgetfulness in an effort to get something painful over with as fast as possible. Humoring him as they loaded their wagons, they all set out together. At nightfall they bedded for the night on the open plain. Meantime Clay rode home and came back later driving the family buggy. He had a late supper with the freighters. He was in an ugly mood, having worked self-pity to the pitch of a sadly abused person. He would have to kill those two cowboys. Anxious to avert a catastrophe, Laramore invited Allison to stay at the camp that night, hoping by idle talk to divert his mind from the fixation that the two abusers were a menace to society and had to be eliminated. After several hours Laramore and McDonald worked him into a better frame of mind, and agreeing that perhaps the boys meant nothing by their talk, Clay promised the freighters that he would not kill the cowboys, provided they promised never to speak to him nor in any way mention his name when he was about. He would not fire them. McDonald and Laramore vouched for the fact that drunk or sober Allison kept his word. If these were the terms he laid down for sparing the lives of the two hands, these were the terms he would go by.

The freighters also counted these two intended victims as friends. So pleased were they that Allison had a change of heart that McDonald saddled one of the horses for an all-night ride to spread the good news to the men. These, on their side, knowing Allison's reputation with a gun, had decided to lie in ambush. They had no intentions of being caught unprepared. Even an ambush, they admitted, would be rather risky, for Allison had a way of tracing a line of fire. He was uncanny when it came to guns and shooting. Glad to learn that Allison changed his mind about gunsmoke, they accepted the terms. Meantime, Allison stayed in camp to await the success or failure of the freighter's mission of mercy. Allison insisted that Laramore sleep in his buggy while he made his bed on the ground. When McDonald returned, he asked him to sleep in the buggy because of his hard ride. As they had to move on, it was agreed that the buggy would be tied behind Laramore's freight wagon, McDonald stretching out in it for a more restful repose. Allison's team of horses were tied to the back of the other freight wagon, and Clay took his place in the driver's seat. The four-horse team headed for the Y crossing. The road, cut by ruts over the prairie, still had its quota of bunched sacatone grass, salt grass clusters, large pebbles, thick layers of dust. Hoping to increase the speed of travel, Allison cracked the whip, causing one of the horses to lunge forward, bringing the left front wheel hard against a cluster of salt grass, upsetting Allison, who was unprepared for the severe bump. He pitched forward, striking his head against the wheel with such impact that his skull was fractured. The fall proved fatal. McDonald awoke with a start. It was too late to render any assistance. Again he saddled a horse, rode to Pecos, where he called upon Mrs. Mitchell to break the news to Dora.

The day was Sunday, July 3, 1887.

Mrs. Mitchell told her as gently as she could, hoping that the sad news would not cause another calamity. Dora, too, realized that she would have to take a hold on herself for the sake of the child she was carrying. The Mitchell girl, then eight years old, was present when her mother visited Mrs. Allison. After all these years, herself an invalid and acquainted with intense suffering, she still remembers quite vividly the grief stricken face as Dora gripped her mother's arms, repeating over and over: "Oh, no. No. No. No."

The body was brought to the Newell Hotel. At three afternoon the whole town assembled for the last rites. Fortunately the preacher had not left for other parts, as he had not as yet established residence in Pecos. Services conducted, the funeral procession wended its way to the cemetery just below the site of the packing house. Six graves were filled when the body of Clay Allison was taken there. It was raining that Sunday afternoon when the mortal remains of Clay Allison found rest in the soil near the Pecos river. In his own way he helped to build the nation as much as Earp, Carson, Masterson, and others, pathfinders of new frontiers, good and bad.

He rested but his legend lives on.

The *Ford County Globe* for July 26, 1887, commented:

"Clay knew no fear. To incur his enmity was equivalent to a death sentence. He contended that he never killed a man willingly, but out of necessity. He was an expert with his revolvers and never failed to come out best in a deadly encounter."

When Dora's second daughter was born she was named Clay in honor of her father. Dora married a second time and moved to Fort Worth, where she died. In Tennessee, Colorado, Texas and New Mexico there are relatives who have keepsakes and are proud of their relationship. Many dedicated their lives to refuting writers who insisted that Allison was a killer and a gunslinger. Whatever he was or wasn't no one can gainsay that he has become a legend. And in this is his glory: As long as books on the Southwest will be read and written, he will never die.

NOTE

In placing this bibliography before the public we are not seeking to impress but merely answering the need for interested parties. Following the publication of former books the author always received letters asking where a student or another author would be able to obtain such and such material. Let this rather serve as an aid rather than an indication of the vast research on the part of the author.

Appendix A

BIBLIOGRAPHY
PRIMARY SOURCES

(a) COLLECTIONS—PUBLIC AND PRIVATE

The M. M. Chase Papers........Some in possession of the author; others in possession of Mrs. Troy Smith of Raton, N. M.
Ths Mrs. Mary Lail Collection..Cimarron, N. M.
The Mrs. J. Abreu Collection...Springer, N. M.
The Davis Papers..............Albuquerque, N. M.
The Fordyce Papers............Museum Library, Santa Fe, N.M.
The Freeman Collection........Topeka, Kansas
The Mills Collection...........Las Vegas, N. M.
The Mrs. V. Webster Papers...Albuquerque, N. M.
The Maxwell Land Grant Papers.Raton, N. M.
The F. Alpers Papers..........Cimarron, N. M.
The Bishop FitzSimon Papers...Amarillo, Texas
The Ritch Papers..............Huntington Library, San Marino, California

The Panhandle Papers.........Panhandle Museum, Canyon, Tex.
Confederate Files ....Historical Society of Tennessee
Nashville, Tenn.
County Files ....Nashville, Tenn.
Colfax County Papers.........Raton, N. M.
Southwestern Collection........Room 328, New York Public Library
Southwestern Shelf............Texas Tech. Library, Lubbock, Texas
Southwestern Collection........Colorado Springs Public Library, Colorado Springs, Colo.
Southwestern Collection........Barker Library, University of Texas, Austin, Texas
The Raton Range Collection....Raton, N. M.
The Reeves County Collection...Pecos, Texas
The New Mexico Collection....Bancroft Library
University of California
Berkeley, California
War Department Records......Archives Building, Washington, D. C.
General Reference &
 Bibliography Division........Library of Congress, Washington, D. C.
Geneology Collection..........Public Library, Amarillo, Texas
The Bush Collection...........Public Library, Amarillo, Texas
The J. A. Chambers Papers.....Frank Chambers, Canadian, Tex.

(b) RECORDS AND DOCUMENTS

Wheeler County Courthouse Records....Vol. 1, Wheeler, Texas
Wheeler County District Court Book....Vol. 1, Wheeler, Texas
Wheeler County Book of Certificates....Vol. 1, Wheeler, Texas
Treasurer's Office—Register of Warrants ....Vol. 1, Wheeler, Texas
Treasurer's Office—Register of Warrants ....Vol. 2, Wheeler, Texas
Wheeler County Record of Marks and Brands ....Vol. 2, Wheeler, Texas
Wheeler County Justice's Civil Docket...Vol. 1, Wheeler, Texas
Hemphill County Civil Docket.........Vol. 1, Canadian, Texas
Minute Book of Reeves County.........Vol. 1, Pecos, Texas
Deed Book of Reeves County..........Vol. 2, Pecos, Texas
Deed Book of Colfax County..........Book B, Ratron, N. M.
Wills and Bonds, Gibson County, Tenn...Book D, 1846-1860
Nashville, Tenn.
Gibson County, Tenn., Marriage Book...1824-1860, Nashville, Tenn.
Wayne County, Tenn., Marriage Book...1857-1898, Nashville, Tenn.

Wayne County Circuit Court, Execution Docket, 1837-1840.............Nashville, Tenn.
Wayne County—Wills and Inventories..Vol. O, 1848-1857,
　　　　　　　　　　　　　　　　　　　Nashville, Tenn.
The Allisons in the Civil War..........Tennessee Historical Papers, Nashville, Tenn.
Tennessee Folklore Bulletin............Nashville Public Library
　　　　　　　　　　　　　　　　　　　1935-37)

(c) WAR OF THE REBELLION RECORDS

Series 1, Vol. XLV, Part II............Washington, D. C., 1894
Series 1, Vol. XLVII, Part II..........Washington, D. C., 1895
Series 1, Vol. XLVII, Part II..........Washington, D. C., 1895
Confederate Military History (12 Vols.).Confederate Publishing
　　　　　　　　　　　　　　　　　　　Co., Atlanta, Ga., 1899
United Daughters of the Confederacy
　Magazine ....All issues from 1951-56
American Geneological Biographical
　Index (14 Vols.)..................Middleton, Conn., 1952
Dictionary of American Biography......New York, MCMXLIII

Appendix B

BIBLIOGRAPHY

SECONDARY SOURCES

Nordyke, Lewis—
　Great Roundup
　　Wm. Morrow & Co., N. Y. 1955
Hyer, William—
　The Land of Beginning Again
　　Tupper & Love, Inc., Atlanta, Ga., 1952
Adams, Andy—
　The Log of a Cowboy
　　Riverside Press, Cambridge, Mass., 1931
Brown, Dee; Schmitt, Martin F.—
　Trail Driving Days
　　Charles Scribner's Sons, N. Y., 1952
Arnold, Oren—
　Thunder in the Southwest
　　University of Oklahoma Press, Norman, Okla., 1952
Nelson, Oliver; Debo, Angie—
　The Cowman's Southwest
　　Arthur Clark Co., Glendale, Calif., 1953

Webb, Walter Prescott—
   The Texas Rangers
      Houghton Mifflin Co., N. Y., 1935
Waters, William—
   Western Badmen
      American Publications, Covington, Kentucky, 1954
Horan, James D.; Sann, Paul—
   Pictorial History of the Wild West
      Crown Publishers, Inc., N. Y., 1955
Casey, Robert J.—
   The Texas Border
      Bobbs Merrill Co., Inc., N. Y., 1950
Vestal, Stanley—
   Queen of the Cowtowns—Dodge City
      Harper & Bros., N. Y., 1952
Custer, Elizabeth B.—
   Following the Guidon
      Harper Brothers, N. Y., 1890
Wright, Robert M.—
   Dodge City, The Cowboy Capital of the Great Southwest
   (No date—no publisher's name)
Lake, Stewart—
   Wyatt Earp, Frontier Marshall
      Houghton Mifflin Co., Boston, 1931
Penfield, Thomas—
   Western Sheriffs and Marshalls
      Grosset & Dunlap, N. Y., 1955
Hendricks, George—
   The Badman of the West
      The Naylor Co., San Antonio, Texas, 1950
Custer, Elizabeth B.—
   Tenting On the Plains, or General Custer in Kansas and Texas
      N. Y., 18—
Rister, Carl Coke—
   Southern Plainsmen
      University of Oklahoma Press, Norman, Okla., 1938
Keim, De. B. Randolph—
   Sheridan's Troopers
      David McKay Co., Philadelphia, Pa., 1889
Clarke, J. S., Publishing Co.—
   Tennessee, the Volunteer State
      4 Vols., 1923
Foster, Austin P.—
   The Counties of Tennessee
      Nashville, Tenn., 1923
Morrison, Leonard Allison—
   History of Alison or Allison Family—1135-1893
      Boston, 1893

Raine, Wm. M.—
    Guns of the Frontier
        Houghton Mifflin Co., N. Y., 1940
Nix, Evert Dumas—
    Oklahombres
        N. Y., 1929
Gard, Wayne—
    Frontier Justice
        Norman, Oklahoma, 1949
Dalton, Emmett—
    When the Dalton's Rode
        Doubleday, Doran & Co., N. Y., 1931
Horan, James D.—
    Desperate Women
        G. P. Putnam's Sons, N. Y., 1952
Hunter & Rose—
    Album of Gunfighters
        Bandera, Texas, 1951
Johnson, Gen. J. E., C.S.A.—
    Narrative of Military Operations
        N. Y., 1874
Reed, Major D. W.—
    The Battle of Shiloh
        Washington, D. C., 1903
Rice, De Long—
    The Story of Shiloh
        Nashville, Tenn., 1919
Horn, Stanley F.—
    The Army of Tennessee
        Bobbe, Merrill Co., N. Y., 1941
Morton, John Watson—
    The Artillery of Nathan Bedford Forrest's Cavalry
        Nashville, Tenn., 1909
Fagan, W. L.—
    Southern War Songs
        M. T. Richardson Co., N. Y., 1890
Cleaveland, Agnes Morley—
    Satan's Paradise
        Houghton Mifflin Co., Boston, Mass., 1952
Lambert, Fred—
    Bygone Days of the Old West
        Kansas City, Mo., 1948
Knight, Oliver—
    Fort Worth
        Norman, Okla., 1953
Griffen, Guy—
    Six-Shooter's Who's Who
        Bancroft Library, Berkeley, Calif.

Otero, Miguel A.—
   My Life On the Frontier
      Press of the Pioneers, N. Y., 1935
Clark, O. S.—
   Clay Allison of the Washita
      Frontier Press of Texas, Houston, 1954
Cunningham, Eugene—
   Triggernometry
      Caldwell, Idaho, 1952
Coole, John W.—
   Hands Up or Thirty-Five Years of Detective Life in the Mountains and On the Plains
      Denver, Colo., 1897
Gordon, General Thomas, and Pryon, J. P.—
   The Campaigns of Lt. Gen. N. B. Forrest and of Forrest's Cavalry
      Blelock & Co., New Orleans, La., 1868
Dale, Edward Everett, and Wardell, Morris L.—
   History of Oklahoma
      Prentice Hall, N. Y., 1948
American Guide Series—
   Oklahoma; Arizona; New Mexico; Tennessee; Colorado; Texas
Foreman, Grant—
   A History of Oklahoma
      University of Oklahoma Press, Norman, Okla., 1942
Foreman, Grant—
   Down the Texas Road
      University of Oklahoma Press, Norman, Okla., 1936
McIntyre, Jim—
   Early Days in Texas
      McIntyre Publishing Co., Kansas City, Mo., 1902
Harwood, Thomas, D.D.—
   History of New Mexico Missions
      2 Vols., Albuquerque, N. M., 1910
Nevins, Allan—
   The Emergence of Modern America
      Macmillan Co., N. Y., 1927
Howles, Charles C.—
   This Place Called Kansas
      University of Oklahoma Press, Norman, Oklahoma, 1952
Siringo, Charles A.—
   A Texas Cowboy
      Wm. Slone Associates, N. Y., 1950
Haley, J. Evetts—
   Charles Goodnight
      University of Oklahoma Press, Norman, Oklahoma, 1949
Haley, J. Evetts—
   Jeff Milton, A Good Man With a Gun
      University of Oklahoma Press, Norman, Oklahoma, 1948

Appendix C

BIBLIOGRAPHY
NEWSPAPERS

Ford County Globe............Dodge City, Kan., Mar. 15, 1881
Ford County Globe............Dodge City., Kan., Mar. 2, 1880
Ford County Gazette..........Dodge City, Kansas, 1886-87
Hays City Sentinel............Hays, Kansas, 1887-88
Hays City Star................Hays, Kansas, 1879-86
The Cowboy...................Dodge City, Kansas, 1884-86
   (This paper contains some interesting data on Mysterious Dave Mather and Dave Rudabaugh—two notorious outlaws who came to violent ends in Las Vegas, N. M., and Parral, Mexico.)
Livestock Journal of New
   Mexico ....Raton, N. M., May 14, 1886
Livestock Journal of New
   Mexico ....Raton, N. M., July 22, 1887
Topeka Times ....Topeka, Kansas, 1878
Las Vegas Optic..............Las Vegas, N. M., June 7, 1886
Ford County Globe............Dodge City, Kan., July 26, 1887
Raton Comet..................Raton, N. M., January 21, 1887
Las Vegas Optic..............Las Vegas, N. M., May 12, 1886
Trinidad News ....Trinidad, Colorado, July 20, 1888
Santa Fe New Mexican........Santa Fe, N. M., All issues from 1870 to 1886
Cimarron News and Press......Cimarron, N. M., Jan. 10, 1907
Weekly New Mexican.........Santa Fe, N. M., Aug. 28, 1877

Appendix D

BIBLIOGRAPHY
MAGAZINE ARTICLES

My Chronicle of the Old West
   H. H. Husell—Cattleman's Magazine, August, 1951
Grub for the Trail
   Wayne Gard—*Ibid.*, December, 1952
Old Fort Hays
   James Harvey Beach—Kansas Historical Review, Vol. XI, pp. 571-581

Able To Kill
    Alwyn W. Knight and Wm. B. Hartley—True Magazine, June, 1948
Seven Rivers, New Mexico
    Fordyce Papers—Santa Fe, New Mexico
Clay Allison
    M. G. Fulton—Southwest Historical Review, Dallas, Texas, Vol. XV, No. 2
The Old Y Crossing
    Bob Beverly—Cattleman's Magazine, Feb., 1952
Roads North
    H. E. Stocking—*Ibid.,* January, 1952
The Clifton House (Interview)
    Fordyce Papers—Alvin Stockton, Stockton Ranch, Jan., 1937
Northern New Mexico in 1870 (Interview)
    Fordyce Papers—Alvin Stockton, Stockton Ranch, Jan., 1937
Off the Beaten New Mexico Path
    George FitzPatrick
Series of Articles on Clay Allison and other Notorious Outlaws appearing in the Albuquerque newspapers and collected by Mr. and Mrs. Henry Meyerhoff of Penticton, British Columbia, Can. These articles were written at various times during 1933 and 1934.
Capture of the Allison Gang
    F. A. Hyatt—Colorado Magazine, Nov., 1935
New Mexico Magazine
    Various Issues, Santa Fe, N. M.

www.ingramcontent.com/pod-product-compliance
Lightning Source LLC
Chambersburg PA
CBHW030131240426
43672CB00005B/104